A Guidebook for Teaching

COMPOSITION

A Guidebook for Teaching
COMPOSITION

GENE STANFORD

Associate Professor of Education and
Director of Teacher Education Programs,
Utica College of Syracuse University

MARIE SMITH

Teacher of English
Horton Watkins High School
St. Louis, Missouri

Allyn and Bacon, Inc.   Boston   London   Sydney   Toronto

This book is part of A GUIDEBOOK FOR TEACHING Series

Library of Congress Cataloging in Publication Data

Stanford, Gene.
  A guidebook for teaching composition.

  (A Guidebook for teaching series)
  Bibliography: p.
  1. English language—Study and teaching (Secondary)
2. English language—Composition and exercises.
I. Smith, Marie N., 1920–   joint author.   II. Title.
III. Series.
LB1631.S683   428'.007'12   77-2356

ISBN 0-205-05872-8

Printing number and year (last digits):
10 9 8 7 6 5   85 84 83 82 81 80

Contents

Preface

This is not, we hope, just another book about teaching expository writing. From its inception, we have tried to make this a book that will serve a unique purpose: providing the classroom teacher with so many specific ideas and resources for teaching students to write that he or she could never use them all. There are already too many books that outline in a general way the "best" way to teach composition, that urge the teacher to adopt one approach or another. But most of these, although they contain many excellent, thought-provoking ideas, do not go very far beyond describing a general theory of teaching writing and suggesting a few exercises to implement it.

By contrast, we have attempted to produce a comprehensive handbook with an emphasis on practicality. We began by resolving to cover all forms of writing that most classroom teachers teach, from expository paragraphs to more "creative" forms such as poetry and fiction. Since so many different types of writing needed to be addressed, and since some teachers give one kind (expository or creative) more of their energy than the other, we decided to limit this book to expository writing, so that we could include the wealth of practical material teachers have been looking for, and deal with creative writing in a separate book.

This volume, then, deals with how to organize a composition program, how to mark student papers, how to teach expository paragraphs, essays, and research papers, and how to teach skills of revision. In its companion volume, *A Guidebook for Teaching Creative Writing*, we have dealt with giving students experiences to stimulate them to write, teaching them to create images and people and events, and writing about literature. Taken together, the two books cover the entire range of high school writing activities. For convenience, the teacher can choose whichever book deals with the kind of writing he or she stresses.

For each type of writing that it deals with, *A Guidebook for Teaching Composition* provides instructional objectives, notes for brief presentations by the teacher to explain new concepts to the class, classroom activities, discussion questions, small group activities, projects, individual assignments, annotated lists of useful books and audio-visual materials, and even sample evaluation items. Perhaps the most valuable feature of the book is the section of Reproduction Pages, which can be used to make masters for spirit duplication or transparencies for the overhead projector—saving the teacher hours of preparation time.

Although the book often suggests a sequence of activities that might be useful in teaching a particular skill, the teacher can choose those materials and strategies that he or she wants to use, without being locked into prescribed lesson plans. In general, for each topic the book provides:

1. An introduction to the concepts that the section or chapter deals with
2. A list of objectives that the methods and materials in the chapter help the

student achieve, saving teachers the tedium of writing behavioral objectives for lesson plans

3. Teaching strategies, including total class activities, explanations by the teacher, independent projects, small group tasks, and worksheets

4. Sample evaluation devices, for determining whether the student has achieved the objectives of the unit

5. Annotated lists of materials, including books, films, filmstrips, cassettes, and slide-tape programs.

Rather than promote a single approach to teaching writing, our goal has been to suggest activities and materials that teachers with a wide variety of teaching styles and philosophies will find useful. Thus, for example, although we describe numerous activities that put students to work in small groups, we have usually included explanations of how the same activities can be used with students working on their own. The reader is encouraged to understand the rationale for each of the approaches and to choose those which are most consistent with his or her own goals and students' needs.

However, we do have our own set of biases—our own viewpoint, if you will—based on our own philosophy of education developed from a number of years of teaching writing in many different settings. This viewpoint is likely to be evident throughout the book. We believe, for example, that students learn more when they are actively involved in the process than when they are sitting passively. In addition, we believe that learning is enhanced when students are interacting with other persons and that students can learn from one another as well as from the teacher. We believe, also, that developing a skill such as writing is generally most successful when the skill is broken down into small steps or subskills, and approached sequentially rather than randomly. And finally, because writing almost always involves self-disclosure, we are convinced it must take place in a climate that is free from threat.

Most of the activities and approaches included in this book were developed for and used successfully with our own classes. We feel confident, therefore, that many other teachers will find them practical and useful. But we have no way of knowing whether *A Guidebook for Teaching Composition* has been helpful without feedback from those people who use it. We invite you to write us your comments about the book, using the Feedback Form that appears at the end of the book (p. 373). It can be torn out and mailed with a minimum of inconvenience. We promise you a personal reply, and will sincerely appreciate your suggestions. They will help us decide what kinds of changes to make when we revise *A Guidebook for Teaching Composition* and what kinds of activities to include in future books in the *Guidebook for Teaching* Series. (A guide to teaching language and a guide to teaching literature are both presently in development.)

Although most of the material in this book is derived from our own experience, we acknowledge the contributions made by a number of other persons. Paul Janeczko, Jerome Megna, Roger C. Schustereit, and Robert Evans gave us permission to include teaching materials that they developed. Our students John Richardson and Joe Finkelstein contributed samples of their writing. The National Council of Teachers of English, and Holt, Rinehart and Winston made it possible for us to use excerpts from material that they had published previously. Finally, our special thanks go to Deborah Perry, who helped prepare the resource lists.

Gene Stanford

Marie Smith

1

Designing the Composition Program

On the walls of caves, on buffalo hides, on tablets of clay and monuments of stone, our ancestors struggled with pictures, then symbols representing objects, and finally symbols representing sounds, to create a form of communication more permanent than the wind that carried their voices. The needs for writing were much the same two thousand years ago as they are today. Archaeologists have found the laws of Hammurabi, the mystical poetry trying to explain the universe of Lao Tzu, the laundry list of a man named Theophanes, and letters from a little schoolboy named Theon to his father. Civilized people everywhere keep records of daily activities, set down philosophical insights, and communicate with friends and family at a distance.

Writing is as essential now, and anyone who cannot write is deprived of participation in many important activities of our culture. But there is a wide range of kinds of writing in our society, and the methods of teaching writing must vary according to the purposes of the person who is learning to write.

The most basic need for writing is in everyday business transactions and personal communications. Grocery lists, job applications, notes to the repairman, records for taxes or business, and telephone messages all require, minimally, legible handwriting, decipherable spelling, and understandable syntax. In addition, for those concerned about a reputation as an educated person, these communications require the use of standard English. For most students, the basic writing skills gained in the first six years of schooling are sufficient for these simple writing tasks. However, for students who arrive in high school without the rudiments of spelling, punctuation and syntax, remedial tutoring may be necessary. And even advanced students may need help in preparing for the more complex writing tasks demanded in our computerized society. The state of Oregon, for example, has recently instituted a plan that requires all students who graduate from high school to possess certain minimal "survival skills." While some may argue that teaching students to fill out income tax forms is not an appropriate goal for the English teacher, if no one else in the school is teaching this survival skill, the English teacher may have to accept the responsibility.

Informal interpersonal communication is the second type of writing that most people in our society engage in—some very rarely and others for hours every day. Love letters, thank you notes, letters to mother asking for money, letters to friends, sympathy notes, and persuasive letters all require skills different from those used in practical communication. Use of standard English is not essential, but skills in style, description and characterization can be useful for such writing, as is a sense of appropriateness for the audience and the occasion. Many of the skills of good essay writing can transfer easily to letter writing, but they are not likely to do so unless the teacher points out the possibility. And special instruction in more effective interpersonal communication can probably be justified for all students.

In addition, many people use writing as a way of exploring ideas and of understanding themselves and others better. At one time or another in their lives, they may use writing in a diary or journal, poetry, or even letters to friends to explore their own thoughts and philosophical ideas or their relationships to things, people or events. Recognizing that putting a feeling on paper often makes it easier to cope with, some use writing to help handle such emotions as anger, fear, loss, and hurt.

A final use of writing is the sharing, exploration, and evaluation of ideas. In high school and college, students use writing to demonstrate their understanding of other people's ideas. Journalists, both student and professional, and other nonfiction writers provide the major means of disseminating thoughts and information.

A writing program needs to take into consideration all these possible uses of writing as well as the needs of the individual students. Everyone in our culture needs to be able to use writing for the first and second purposes—for nuts-and-bolts business writing and friendly communication. However, only part of the population uses writing to express feelings or to share ideas. It is therefore probably not productive to expect every student to do extensive reflective writing or to develop finesse in the use of the essay.

However, as adult education and re-education become increasingly possible and popular, it is not possible to decide that a student is not "college prep" and therefore does not need to write essays. It is probably appropriate to require all students to demonstrate competence in utilitarian writing and letter writing, but to accept minimal competence with the essay and reflective writing from most students, and to allow students to choose how much proficiency they will develop in these latter modes.

APPROACHES TO TEACHING WRITING

There are a number of possible ways to go about teaching writing—all have some use, but all also have limitations. The major approaches which most teachers find useful are 1) imitation, 2) following rules and patterns, 3) trial and error with criticism, 4) extensive writing, and 5) instruction in grammar.

Imitation is one of the most basic human methods of learning, and, deliberately or not, almost all writers have employed imitation to some extent in their learning to write. Early research in the teaching of composition indicated that exposure to good literature could have as powerful an effect on improvement in writing as actual writing practice could have. Certainly, a student who has never read a good essay is unlikely to write one. Thus, many teachers find it useful to expose composition students to many examples of good writing in hopes that some of the techniques will rub off. Other teachers are more deliberate in their use of imitation. They give students a passage by a good writer and ask them to produce a piece of writing on a different topic in the same form and style as the model.

Imitation is usually fairly effective in teaching style and patterns of organization. Most people's minds work in such a way that they are better able to produce what the teacher wants if they have a model to show them what is expected. Of course, the limit to learning by imitation is that as long as one is imitating, one is not a creative artist. This is not a problem for most high school English teachers, who are rarely faced with students who can be termed "artists"—and it is certainly simple enough to devise individualized assignments for students who find imitation confining.

For students who are so deficient in writing skills that even imitation is not possible, dictation can be an effective teaching method. This approach is rarely used in modern American schools, but is described in detail in *How the French Boy Learns to Write* by Rollo Walter Brown. (See the resources list at the end of this chapter.) Students who are quite deficient in basic writing skills can practice spelling and punctuation, as well as "get the feel" of fluent composition by writing dictations.

A second method of teaching writing, *following rules and patterns*, is particularly effective when combined with the use of models as described above. In this approach, teachers precede writing assignments with direct instruction in how to write. For example, the teacher may explain that a paragraph is a general statement (topic sentence) followed by specific statements that explain or support the general statement. The teacher may give the students several examples, having them locate the general statement and the specific statements, and then assign them to write a paragraph in this form. The teacher may discover that students do not understand the difference between a general statement and a specific statement and thus will have to go back and give more explanations and examples, perhaps having them identify which is general and which is specific in a number of pairs of sentences. This approach assumes that there are certain principles and formulas that good writers generally follow and that students can benefit from learning them before starting to write.

However, if taken to extremes this approach can have harmful effects. Janet Emig, in her analysis of the writing processes of twelfth graders (see *The Composing Processes of Twelfth Graders* in the resource list at the end of this chapter), points out that most of the principles and formulas taught in English classes, such as the five-paragraph theme and the need for every paragraph to have a topic sentence, are not practiced by the best professional writers. The five-paragraph theme, she points out, exists nowhere in literature except in the American high school classroom. This rather artificial pattern of writing (an introduction, a thesis statement with three divisions, and a conclusion which recapitulates the thesis statement and its divisions) can be useful for producing a coherent piece of writing in a limited time, as when writing an essay test, but it is hardly conducive to creative thought and imaginative exploration of ideas. As Emig reminds us, it is not the way good writers compose, and to bill it as such to students is dishonest. Many of the formulas drilled into generation after generation of students are non-existent in articles in better magazines and books. It is often useful for the writing teacher to try grading a few articles in *Harper's*, *Saturday Review*, the *New Yorker* or other high quality magazines according to the formulas and rules taught to students. John Ciardi and his colleagues are not likely to fare too well.

Certainly, basic patterns such as the topic sentence followed by specification can be helpful in improving the writing of average students and for giving students conscious control over the writing process. But too much emphasis on such artificial patterns as "the paragraph developed by cause and effect" as distinguished from "the paragraph developed by reasons" may create unnecessary confusion in some students and be unnecessarily restricting to creativity. At the very least the teacher must not imply that writing by formula is the approach used by good professional writers, but should tell students honestly that this is one way to write over which it is relatively easy to develop conscious control.

A third method of teaching writing is simply to ask students to write and then to *criticize the results.* While trial and error is extremely frustrating and unnecessarily punitive for most students, highly creative and advanced students who feel cramped and constricted by models and formulas and who are highly motivated to write well may thrive on this method. For students who object to formulas or models, the teacher may find an effective alternative to be an individual contract, with students free to write in any style they like and the teacher critiquing the work.

For average students, though, it is generally helpful to give some preliminary instruction before making the assignment, and then to let the students know after they have completed the assignment how well they put the principles into practice. Most students will feel less frustration about having their work criticized if they have been taught *how* to approach an assignment before having to start writing.

Almost all students, though, can benefit from receiving feedback from the teacher in the form of criticism (used in its positive sense). Suggestions for marking and evaluating student writing are given in the second part of this chapter.

Still another approach to teaching writing is what might be termed *extensive writing* or *free writing.* Daniel Fader and Elton McNeil in their *Hooked on Books* and Ken Macrorie in *Writing to Be Read* and his other books advocate that teachers do less teaching of *how* to write and simply encourage students to write as much as possible. They see the teaching of principles and the criticizing of students' work as inhibitors of students' impulses to express themselves. Their approach focuses instead on freeing students to write about the things that matter to them, in a manner that each student chooses, without the fear of a poor grade for not meeting the teacher's expectations. The emphasis is on *quantity* and *student choice:* students improve their skills by extensive practice, and since they write about things that really matter, the results are more likely to be good because they are "real."

The approach often utilizes journals, in which students write regularly (sometimes at home each day, sometimes in class one day a week) and which are not graded—often not even read—by the teacher. For many teachers, the journal can produce very exciting results:

> In my experience student response to the journal has been almost universally positive, making it the closest thing yet to a sure-fire teaching device. The so-called nonwriters like to write in journals, while "writers" go beserk writing in them. Teachers enjoy reading journals. In short, all of the problems traditionally associated with writing seem to be almost magically solved when people try the journal.[1]

For others, the journal is less a panacea. For one thing, it does not take into account the two most basic ways humans learn: by precept and by example; it depends only on practice. To assume that regular, profuse writing in a journal will make one a better writer is like assuming that practicing the piano is sufficient to graduate from playing "Leap Frog Leap" to *Moonlight Sonata.* Most of us also need lessons to show us *how* to play better and a sympathetic teacher to point out our mistakes.

Nevertheless, when used in conjunction with other methods, the journal and other "free" writing activities can be valuable. They tend to counteract the restricting influence of teaching principles and patterns. Students are encouraged to deal with ideas and issues that

---

1. Stephen N. Judy, *Explorations in the Teaching of Secondary English* (New York: Dodd Mead & Company, 1974), p. 87.

have significance for them. If the journal is not graded, they are more likely to feel free to express themselves honestly. Having been liberated to explore ideas that really matter, students may find themselves thinking about things they want to communicate to others. These ideas can then be expanded in more structured writing assignments.

Instruction in grammar is the final approach to teaching writing that we will examine. Once considered absolutely essential in the preparation of a good writer, a technical knowledge of grammar is no longer viewed by most teachers as adding much to the student's ability to write. Knowing the names of the parts of speech or being able to diagram a sentence, for example, does virtually nothing to improve writing skill, as countless research studies have confirmed.[2] Even excessive concern for teaching mechanics, such as usage, punctuation, and spelling—which some teachers often confuse with grammar—has little effect on students' compositions. An ability to proofread, spot errors and correct them, is useful in preparing a composition for the audience—particularly for publication—but this skill is editing, not composing. And proficiency in the former is not necessary for proficiency in the latter.

If there is a possible exception to the principle that instruction in grammar does not improve writing ability, it is in the case of transformational/generative grammar. Two studies published by the National Council of Teachers of English[3] conclude that students' fluency improves and the complexity of their sentences increases when they are taught transformational grammar. However, a later NCTE publication[4] claims that such results can be achieved through practice exercises without formal instruction in grammar. And, of course, "syntactic maturity" is only one aspect of good writing. Other skills most certainly have to be developed as well. Therefore, concerning the value of grammar instruction, we agree with most leaders in the profession, that, as Theodore Hipple states, "perhaps most pernicious of all the reasons for the failures in the secondary school efforts to produce abler writers, is the insistence of many teachers that inordinate amounts of time spent on the study of formal grammar will produce, as if by magic, students who write well."[5]

ORGANIZING FOR INSTRUCTION IN COMPOSITION

Having surveyed the five most frequently utilized approaches to the teaching of composition and assessed their strengths and weaknesses, what can we say about choosing the right approach and implementing it in the classroom?

First of all, it is essential to know your purpose in teaching writing to a particular class at a particular time. What is their present level of writing skill? What are their future writing needs likely to be? What does your school's or your state's curriculum guide require you to teach? What composition skills do you judge to be most important for these students to master? What do the students want to learn about writing? Are these students who talk and write freely about their own ideas and feelings, but who could use help in organizing and developing their ideas? Or are they students who are so concerned about meeting standards

2. J. Stephen Sherwin, *Four Problems in the Teaching of English: A Critique of Research* (Scranton, Pa.: Intext, 1969).

3. Donald Bateman and Frank Zidonis, *The Effect of a Study of Transformational Grammar on the Writing of Ninth and Tenth Graders* (Urbana, Ill.: National Council of Teachers of English, 1966) and John C. Mellon, *Transformational Sentence-Combining* (Urbana, Ill.: National Council of Teachers of English, 1969).

4. Frank O'Hare, *Sentence Combining* (Urbana, Ill.: National Council of Teachers of English, 1973).

5. Theodore W. Hipple, *Teaching English in Secondary Schools* (New York: Macmillan Company, 1973), p. 149.

of correctness that they are afraid to turn loose and say what they really mean? Are the majority of the class gifted students who may have talents for creative writing they want to develop? Or are they relatively nonverbal students who are unlikely to attend college, and who want and need to master more practical forms of communication? Are almost all bound for college and thus sure to be faced with research papers and writing about literature? Are they seventh graders for whom a complete, well developed paragraph is an appropriate goal, or are they high school seniors who have been writing multiparagraph essays for several years? None of these are simple questions to answer, and no response will always apply to every student in the class. But before embarking on a composition program, it is important to think carefully about what students in the class *really* need to learn about writing. Only then can you begin planning how to teach them.

In a year-long English course, composition is only one of many skills that need attention. After deciding what composition skills students need to master, you should work out a sequential plan for teaching these skills, beginning with the more basic and moving toward the more advanced. In most of the following chapters—particularly Chapters 2 and 3—we have organized the suggested learning experiences in a rough sequence of this type.

Once you've outlined the sequence of skills or skill-building activities you plan to follow, you face the decision of whether to teach all of these skills in a single composition unit of, say, four to ten weeks duration, or to intersperse them with other activities such as reading, language study, and oral communication. The single unit on composition has its attractive features: 1) students can perceive the orderly progression of skill development, 2) assignments come soon enough after each other that students don't forget what they've learned from one before beginning the next, 3) you don't have to "juggle" many different kinds of materials and activities, but can concentrate on the development of one set of skills, and 4) students are more likely to realize that improvements are taking place in their writing ability.

But there are serious drawbacks to a single unit on composition. First, the work load for students (writing papers) and for you (responding to papers) is likely to be very heavy. Second, students—and you—are likely to tire of working on one set of skills for such a long time, and boredom and resistance are almost inevitable. On the other hand, spacing the composition work assures that you won't be flooded with hundreds of papers to respond to, and provides the variety that can help prevent boredom. And so it would seem that interspersing the composition activities with other aspects of the course is the best approach.

But one must be on guard against several potential problems. If you have not thought through carefully the sequence of activities before the term begins, you are likely to lose sight of the skills you are building, and instead of an orderly progression you're likely to end up giving students a random, unrelated, disjointed set of experiences. You must also guard against letting too much time elapse between composition activities, and you may often need to review briefly what skills students have previously studied before introducing new material.

With elective programs gaining popularity, the planning of a composition program has become a serious problem in many schools. Faced with the prospect of a student changing teachers every nine weeks (or more or less often) over three or four years, the teacher concerned about the serious business of developing skill in composition is tempted to throw in the towel, decide that composition isn't important after all, and settle back and enjoy teaching "Sports in Literature" or "Literature of the Occult." Real creativity is required to plan an effective composition program that is consistent with the freedom of choice and flexibility so important to elective programs.

Many schools with elective programs require some sort of basic composition course of all students before freeing them to select from other electives. The rationale is that in this one nine to twenty week course, the student will learn basic principles that will be reinforced in other courses by writing assignments related to the course content. In some cases the plan works well; in others, not so well.

Another approach is to design an individualized composition program that a student completes totally outside of the regular elective program. Students work in a Writing Lab one or two days per week on assignments tailored to their particular needs. The Writing Lab is supervised by teachers who are specialists in composition and do not teach in the regular elective program.

Still another approach is for the English faculty to agree on a sequence of skill-building assignments to cover the entire range of composition skills that they consider minimally essential. All students must complete the sequence over the span of two or three years, regardless of what electives they choose. The specific topic for each assignment is suggested by the teacher of the elective, but the type of writing assignment (paragraph developed with examples, persuasive essay of at least five paragraphs, etc.) depends on where the student stands in terms of the sequence. Thus, in "Sports in Literature," the teacher may make a writing assignment—say, a composition on the role of women in athletics—for which one student would submit a single paragraph and another student a research paper.

MARKING STUDENTS' COMPOSITIONS

In the preceding sections we have been concerned about the decisions the teacher must make *before* students write. But even after you settle on a writing program, make the assignment, and finally collect the papers, the problems have not ended. For now you are faced with the question of how to respond to what the students write.

This dilemma is examined somewhat humorously in an "educational drama" by Roger C. Schustereit, which summarizes many of the current issues related to marking of compositions:

THE BIG C—A MELODRAMA[6]

CHARACTERS:

Cynthia, *a student*
Harold, *a student*
James Landry, *English coordinator, must have horn rimmed glasses*
Louise Hathaway, *a new teacher, must have innocent look*
Clifford Plater, Alice Stein, and Richard McGowen, *all seasoned veteran teachers with looks to match*

   SCENE I: *The hall just before lunch.* Mr. Landry *is on the way to* Louise Hathaway's *classroom when he overhears a conversation between two students,* Harold *and* Cynthia, *in front of their lockers.*

---

6. Roger C. Schustereit, "The Big C—A Melodrama." (Unpublished manuscript) Used with permission of the author. The bibliography from Mr. Schustereit's article has been incorporated into the resource list at the end of this chapter.

Cynthia: How's it going, Harold?

Harold: Hi, Cyn. I guess O.K.

Cynthia: Did you get your paper back from Mrs. Hathaway yet?

Harold: Yah. (Harold *hands the paper to* Cynthia)

Cynthia: (*after a quick glance, handing Harold his paper*) Wow, it looks like she bled all over it.

Harold: (*amused, as he walks toward the lunchroom*) Yah, ya' just got the scenic tour of the red C.

   (Mr. Landry, *stifling a grin, enters* Louise Hathaway's *room.* Louise *is seated at her desk laborously considering a pile of compositions, red pencil in hand.*)

Landry: Hi, Louise. Ready for lunch?

Louise: (*slightly startled*) No, Jim. I've got too much grading to do. I turned two sections back, but I still have three to go.

Landry: Yah, I heard Harold talking about his paper in the hall.

Louise: That Harold. He makes so many grammatical mistakes. I just don't know.

Landry: (*amused, yet condescending*) Yes, he was commenting on the predominant color of his paper.

Louise: (*defensively*) Well, I try to give them feedback. I know a teacher needs to comment on written work; I try to say what I feel's appropriate.[7]

Landry: (*gently*) O.K., but filling a page with corrections in red may do more harm than good.[8]

Louise: (*sarcastically*) Well, what am I supposed to do? Use green ink?

Landry: No, you're supposed to quit grading and come on down to the office for lunch.

   (*The two leave together*)

   SCENE II: *The English Office during lunch.* Mr. Landry *and* Louise *enter. They find* Clifford Plater, Alice Stein *and* Richard McGowen *seated and, in various stages, eating lunch.*

Cliff: (*with good humor*) Alas, the perpetrator of the composition unit arrives.

Landry: Very funny, Cliff.

Cliff: (*walking to coffee pot*) Ah yes, group, he has a supply of Murine for the eyes and liniment to keep the fingers nimble.

Alice: (*very serious*) Come on. Grading isn't all that painful.

Cliff: (*mock surprise*) Oh, really?

Louise: Jim and I were just getting into that subject, but his hungry stomach cut off the discussion.

Alice: (*emphatically*) No, really. Composition correction has changed from some kind of pursuit in red ink by a bleary-eyed monster.[9]

Cliff: (*resuming his seat*) Wow, I didn't know we had a resident poet.

Alice: Ah, come on. You can cramp your fingers and ruin your eyes all you want to marking every comma splice and misspelling, but that kind of correction is no better than moderate evaluation by the teacher when it comes to really improving the quality of writing.[10]

Louise: Well, what do *you* propose?

---

7. E. B. Page, "Teacher Comments and Student Performance: A Seventy-four Classroom Experiment in School Motivation," *The Journal of Educational Psychology,* 49, No. 4 (August, 1958), 173–81.

8. Ray C. Maize, "A Theme a Day," *NEA Journal,* 42, No. 6 (September, 1953), 335–36. (Hereafter referred to as Maize)

9. Joseph Mersand, "What Has Happened to Written Composition?" *English Journal,* 50, No. 4 (April, 1961), 231–37.

10. Lois V. Arnold, "Writer's Cramp and Eyestrain—Are They Paying Off?" *English Journal,* 53, No. 1 (January, 1964), 10–15.

Alice: Let the kids do their own correcting.

Cliff: Oh, sure. I've tried something like that, but I still wonder if it's not just a way for us to get out of the work.

Landry: I read an article in *English Journal* about a study that showed that students' correcting their own papers wasn't really any better or worse than when the teachers did it.

Cliff: (*interrupting*) See what I mean?

Landry: But, the teacher method required eight times as many after school hours as the peer method did.[11]

Louise: Is that for real?

Alice: (*rising to throw a paper sack away*) Sure it is. I don't read or grade a single paper outside of class.

Cliff: How do you manage that—give study periods?

Alice: (*grinning*) We have a resident cynic too. (*pause*) The kids do most of the correcting. I divide them into groups, and they do most of the tedious work. Then, they select the best papers, and we take a look at them as a class.

Louise: How do you do that?

Alice: (*resuming seat*) I use the opaque projector or have my student aide ditto them.[12]

Louise: Do the students do a good job?

Alice: Other than being a bit too critical at times, after they get a general idea about evaluation they do a pretty darn good job.[13]

McGowen: (*upon completion of that last sandwich*) But what about the student who never has a paper selected as best?

Alice: Well, it usually works out. But I like to think that while a student thinks about and criticizes somebody else's paper, his paper and its weaknesses are on his mind.[14]

McGowen: I had this prof in Oregon who did something like that. We met as a class only once a week. We got our assignment and then wrote the paper. Then we met in groups of three or four and went over each other's papers. But what really helped was when the groups got together with the prof for fifteen minutes or so with all the comments of all the students summarized.

Landry: How did your professor get ready for the conferences?

McGowen: After the groups got together, we turned in the papers. He really looked more at the criticisms than the papers themselves. He claimed it really cut down on his grading time.[15]

Cliff: What did he do with all that free time away from class and grading?

McGowen: Played golf, he said.

Cliff: Now that sounds like a good idea. (*pause*) You know, I like student involvement and all, but I still like to do the grading.

Louise: I *do* know what you mean.

Cliff: When I start a composition unit, I have the students determine norms for mechanics, and then I do the rest of the evaluation.

McGowen: I don't follow you, Cliff.

Cliff: Well, they decide on certain criteria for spelling, run-ons, and so on. If a paper meets the criteria, I grade it. If it doesn't, I put "not acceptable" at the top, and they try again.

11. Robert V. Denby, "NCTE/ERIC Report-Composition Evaluation," *English Journal*, 57, No. 8 (November, 1968), 1215–21.

12. Maize, pp. 335–36.

13. Loren V. Grisson, "Student Leadership in Evaluating Compositions," *English Journal*, 48, No. 6 (September, 1959), 338–39.

14. Ken Macrorie, *Uptaught* (New York: Hayden Book Co., Inc., 1970), 95.

15. Charlton Laird, "Freshman English During the Flood," *College English*, 18, No. 3 (December, 1956), 131–38.

Alice: But you're still marking their errors.

Cliff: No, I don't mark specific mistakes. I just put "N/A" at the top.

Louise: Isn't that a bit rough?

Cliff: Well, we have writing lab sessions in class to work on common problems where they work in groups, and I set up rotating student-teacher conferences to work on individual papers.[16]

Alice: But you're still spending a lot of time cramping your fingers.

Cliff: (*with mock sarcasm*) "Into each life a little rain must fall!"

Alice: (*dully*) Ho. Ho. Ho.

Cliff: What we need to do is get Jim to hit up the school board for a computer to do the grading.

Landry: Thanks a bunch, Cliff.

Alice: Seriously, there is a computer they use for grading themes. It even puts out personalized feedback.[17]

Cliff: Just go have a little rap with friendly ol' HAL.

McGowen: God, I wonder how much that would cost?

Landry: Too much.

Cliff: Well, we could hire lay readers.

Landry: I proposed that last year.

Louise: Wait a minute. What are lay readers?

Cliff: Housewives—qualified, of course—who grade papers on a part-time basis. They supposedly do a good job though.[18]

Louise: Why did the board say no?

Laughter

Landry: Well, other than money, they said they were afraid part-timers would be too distant from students' individual needs and problems.[19]

Louise: Well, why not hire a regular teacher to do nothing else?[20]

Landry: Money again.

Cliff: Yah, and who would want that job? You'd spend all your salary on Murine and liniment.

McGowen: Well, I don't need the liniment, but sometimes I need throat lozenges to go along with the Murine.

Alice: Throat lozenges?

McGowen: Yah, I use a tape recorder for corrections.

Louise: Are you kidding?

McGowen: No, I can give clearer, fuller corrections with a tape than I can with a red pencil.[21]

Louise: (*interested*) How do you do it?

16. Sister Miriam Bernadette, "Evaluation of Writing: A Three-Part Program," *English Journal*, 54, No. 1 (January, 1965), 23–27.

17. Arthur Daigon, "Computer Grading of English Composition," *English Journal*, 55, No. 1 (January, 1966), 46–52.

18. Paul M. Ford, "Lay Readers in High School Composition Programs: Some Statistics," *English Journal*, 50, No. 8 (November, 1961), 522–28.

19. Paul H. Kreuger, "Some Questions on the Lay Reader Program," *English Journal*, 50, No. 8 (November, 1961), 529–33.

20. Marcia Mahnke, "Aide-to-Order for the Composition Teacher," *English Journal*, 53, No. 1 (January, 1964), 40–41.

21. Nachman Cohen, "Correcting Compositions without a Pencil," *English Journal*, 39, No. 10 (December, 1950), 579–80.

McGowen: Well, the kids number each line of their papers so I can refer to their specific weaknesses. It lets me talk personally with each student.

Louise: Is it faster?

McGowen: When I first started using tapes, I got carried away. But after a while you get the hang of it, and it gets better.[22]

Bell Rings

Cliff: Well, an end to another episode of the English Faculty's sandwich and potato chip symposium.

SCENE III: *The hall two weeks later, just before lunch.* Mr. Landry *rounds the corner and overhears another conversation between* Harold *and* Cynthia.

Cynthia: Hey, Harold, I heard Mrs. Hathaway was doing something different on grading your themes.

Harold: Yah, she's telling us where we messed up on those cassettes we had to buy.

Cynthia: Hey, that's the way McGowen does it. How do you like it?

Harold: (*amused*) It's O.K., I guess. Now I get to hear the red C in her own voice!

As Schustereit's "melodrama" illustrates, views on what constitutes good marking of papers vary considerably. But one point is clear: evaluating students' compositions for the purpose of grading is quite a different process from marking students' compositions to help them improve their writing. If a teacher is interested only in evaluation, there is no need to put any marks on the paper at all except for a letter or number at the top or bottom. Simply grading is a real temptation to the overworked teacher, but it does nothing to teach the student about writing—and most teachers realize they are hired to teach, not just grade.

Therefore, we must search for an effective way to respond to students' writing so that it helps them improve their skills. Specifically we need a method that does not require an inordinate amount of the teacher's time.

To be most helpful, the teacher's response to a composition should provide the student with feedback—that is, accurate information about his or her performance. Good feedback is focused, specific, and constructive. Instead of providing focused feedback, however, many teachers—such as Louise Hathaway in "The Big C"—flood students with more information than they can possibly assimilate by marking every conceivable error. These teachers confuse commenting on a composition with proofreading, although the two processes are quite different. Proofreading is correcting the mechanical errors in a piece of writing. This is a very useful skill, and is needed for almost any piece of writing that is going to be judged by its reader. A proofreader does a great service for his or her friends by correcting their errors in letters of application or school reports, or even friendly letters. However, the proofreader rarely teaches the writer how to improve writing skill. Example I (see page 13) is a student's paper that has been proofread rather than responded to. The student receiving this paper back from the teacher is likely to be so overwhelmed with all the corrections as to not even bother to read them all, let alone figure out what is the matter with each "error." Were this piece of writing headed for publication, such editing/proofreading would probably be welcomed, but we assume it is not being published. Therefore, the teacher is hardly justified in such heavy editing, which will probably only discourage the student.

---

22. Lee Frank Lowe, "Theme Correcting via Tape Recorder," *English Journal*, 52, No. 3 (March, 1963), 212–14.

Since good feedback is focused, the teacher should limit comments to one or two types of errors and should provide explanations and suggestions for correcting them. Two things are about as many as we can expect the average student to learn from feedback on an assignment such as this. Thus, in Example II (page 14), we will see how the teacher focuses the feedback on two of the students' major recurring errors, and explains them in enough detail that the student can understand why they are errors.

Also, it is even more likely that a student will remember a suggestion made by the teacher if he or she is required to practice the skill immediately. The "assignment sheet" on page 15 has been used by one of the authors to give students individualized practice related to the errors made in their own compositions. The error is marked on the composition with the number corresponding to the assignment on this sheet. The sheet is attached to the composition, and the teacher fills in the blanks indicating what practice exercises the student should complete. In some cases, as for error #2, the teacher gives the student specific instructions for practice exercises tailored to a particular problem not covered in the text. Thus, the student cannot simply look at the comments on a paper and disregard them, but must understand the nature of the problem and practice writing sentences that are error free.

Good feedback is also specific. In order to improve their writing, students must know exactly what the teacher likes or dislikes about the paper. Instead of saying "good organization" at the end of the paper, it is more effective to note "good transition" and "effective topic sentence" at the points where they occur.

Feedback should also be constructive and should include both positive and negative elements. Students need to be told when they are doing well. In the atmosphere of our schools, most students do not trust their own judgment—or it never occurs to them to make any judgment of their own work. Thus, the teacher's response is extremely important. A student who has spent hours constructing a creative introduction to an essay and is given no recognition for it by the teacher, may assume that it was not any good after all or conclude that it was certainly not worth the trouble it took. Learning theorists tell us that behavior that is rewarded will persist. And naturally, we want the good things students do in their writing to persist. Hence, we have to be careful to praise the things that students are doing right as well as point out the things they are doing wrong. And when we feel we must point out errors, comments should be phrased as suggestions for improvement, not punishment. Note in Example III (page 16) how the teacher praises or recognizes several aspects of what is in many ways a lackluster essay, and points out problems as gently as possible. Note too how the teacher includes a personal reaction or two to let the student know that the content is being responded to as well as the form.

To summarize: compositions should not simply be graded. They should be marked to help students improve their writing skills. The teacher's comments should focus on a reasonable number of errors, rather than attempting to proofread and correct every single error. Instead of revising the paper for the student, the teacher should point out ways the paper could be improved and have the student make the changes. Furthermore, good features of the composition should be praised, even if they are not particularly outstanding, and the teacher should react in a personal way to ideas in the composition.

Of course, this kind of thorough commenting on students' papers is quite time-consuming, and most teachers do not have time to make such extensive comments on as many papers as students need to write. Therefore, the teacher may need to discover approaches to marking papers that save time yet give students the help they need. Several of these were mentioned briefly in the short play that introduced this section. One of those

EXAMPLE I RESPONDING BY PROOFREADING

CARS I WOULD NOT WANT TO OWN

There are Over a quarter of a million automobiles sold in the United States each year. Many types are available; foreign cars and American cars, convertables and sedans, big cars and little cars. This variety is the result of the wide range of tastes of the driving population. There is three kinds of cars which doesn't suit my taste at all, and which I would never own. One type is impractical, another is little and ugly, and a third is poorly made.

An example of an impractical car is the Excalibur SS, perhaps. It bears a strong resemblance you have never seen one of these cars. to the Dusenberg of years ago or to an old MG, early 1951 or 1952. One of the things I don't like about it are that it only comes in a convertable model. That's fine in the summer or on a sunny day, but when it rains or when winter comes, it's rather impractical. Winter is perhaps the roughest though, Mainly because the car is not even equipped with a heater. And the softtop has plastic side windows and a plastic rear window that leaks and yellows in the sun and becomes brittle with age. This car is fitted with a 327 cubic inch engine from the Corvette Stingray. The car does not weigh more than 2000 pounds, compared to the Corvette, which weighs approximately 3200 pounds this year. With over 350 horsepower and so little weight, the Excalibur is very dangerous, you can't come near controlling it on acceleration around curves or on a panic stop. Combining these shortcomings with a $10,000 price tag, you have a very impractical car.

Another

A car that I wouldn't want is one of those ugly little foreign "bugs" you see everywhere. The Volkswagen is a good example. This simply isn't my idea of a car with good looks. In addition, it's to small for safety. If you were hit in the side by a large car or by a truck, you'd be finished. You also can't ride for great distances in comfort, because the engine is to noisy and the interior is cramped. Another shortcoming is that Volkswagen's are to common. I don't want a car that every mother's son has, and if you look around any large parking lot in this city, you are bound to see at least ten Volkswagen's. Besides being so common, this car is to underpowered for freeway driving. It's almost impossible to pass a car on the expressway at sixty miles per hour, if there is a stiff crosswind blowing, you would think you were on a roller coaster. This is both unpleasant and unsafe.

The third type of car that I wouldn't like to own is one that is cheaply made. Ford Mustangs fall into this class. My family owned one once, and before we got rid of it the muffler fell off at least five times. By the time we sold it six months later, there was rattles in every corner. Meanwhile, the paint had started peeling off, to say nothing of the first layer of chrome on the bumpers. To top it off, whenever the driver made a hard left turn, the door on the passenger's side would fly open. My uncle owns a Cougar, and it doesn't have these problems.

Add Conclusion summarizing

EXAMPLE II FOCUSED FEEDBACK

Ann— you're having trouble with several grammar rules: 1) "to" is a preposition meaning towards; "too" means excessively and is an adverb. Find 4 placed in your third paragraph where you used the wrong one of these words. 2) a verb agrees with (matches) the subject, even when it does not follow it. Note the sentences I have marked.

CARS I WOULD NOT WANT TO OWN

There are over a quarter of a million automobiles sold in the United States each year. Many types are available; foreign cars and American cars, convertables and sedans, big cars and little cars. This variety is the result of the wide range of tastes of the driving population. There is three kinds of cars which doesn't suit my taste at all, and which I would never own. One type is impractical, another is little and ugly, and a third is poorly made.

An example of an impractical car is the Excalibur SS, perhaps you have never seen one of these cars. It bears a strong resemblance to the Dusenberg of years ago or to an old MG, early 1951 or 1952. One of the things I don't like about it are that it only comes in a convertable model. That's fine in the summer or on a sunny day, but when it rains or when winter comes, its rather impractical. Winter is perhaps the roughest though. Mainly because the car is not even equipped with a heater. And the softtop has plastic side windows and a plastic rear window that leaks and yellows in the sun and becomes briddle with age. This car is fitted with a 327 cubic inch engine from the Corvette Stingray. The car does not weigh more than 2000 pounds, compared to the Corvette, which weighs approximately 3200 pounds this year. With over 350 horsepower and so little weight, the Excalibur is very dangerous, you can't come near controlling it on accelleration around curves or on a panic stop. Combining these shortcommings with a $10,000 price tag, you have a very impractical car.

A car that I wouldn't want is one of those ugly little foreign "bugs" you see everywhere. The Volkswagen is a good example. this simply isn't my idea of a car with good looks. In addition, its to small for safety. If you were hit in the side by a large car or by a truck, you'd be finished. You also can't ride for great distances in comfort, because the engine is to noisy and the interior is cramped. Another shortcoming is that Volkswagen's are to common. I don't want a car that every mothers son has, and if you look around any large parking lot in this city, you are bound to see at least ten Volkswagen's. Besides being so common, this car is to underpowered for freeway driving. Its almost impossible to pass a car on the expressway at sixty miles per hour, if there is a stiff crosswind blowing, you would think you were on a roller coaster. This is both unpleasant and unsafe.

The third type of car that I wouldn't like to own is one that is cheaply made. Ford Mustangs fall into this class my family owned one once, and before we got rid of it the muffler fell off at least five times. By the time we sold it six months later, there rattles in every corner. Meanwhile, the paint had started peeling off, to say nothing of the first layer of chrome on the the door on the passenger's side would fly open. My uncle owns a Cougar, and it doesn't have these problems.

Group_____ Period _____

ERROR NO.   ASSIGNMENT

1.   Study carefully the explanation on pages *128 – 132* in
      your grammar textbook, paying particular attention to rule
      number *6g* on page *128*. Determine how this applies
      to the error you made in your composition. On a separate sheet
      of paper work exercise *14*, page *130* and turn it
      in with the revision of your composition.

2.   Study carefully the explanation on pages *226* in
Write ten sentences, each   your grammar textbook, paying particular attention to rule
containing two complete   number_____on page_____. Determine how this applies
thoughts, the second of   to the error you made in your composition. On a separate sheet
which begins with   of paper work exercise_____, page_____and turn it
he, she, or it.   in with the revision of your composition.

3.   Study carefully the explanation on pages *454* in
Example: My mother   your grammar textbook, paying particular attention to rule
is a good cook; she   number *21K* on page_____. Determine how this applies
makes good cake.   to the error you made in your composition. On a separate sheet
                         of paper work exercise_____, page_____and turn it
                         in with the revision of your composition.

4.   Study carefully the explanation on pages *146* in
      your grammar textbook, paying particular attention to rule
      number *7C* on page *146*. Determine how this applies
      to the error you made in your composition. On a separate sheet
      of paper work exercise *15*, page *148–149* and turn it
      in with the revision of your composition.

5.   Study carefully the explanation on pages_____in
      your grammar textbook, paying particular attention to rule
      number_____on page_____. Determine how this applies
      to the error you made in your composition. On a separate sheet
      of paper work exercise_____, page_____and turn it
      in with the revision of your composition.

6.   Study carefully the explanation on pages_____in
      your grammar textbook, paying particular attention to rule
      number_____on page_____. Determine how this applies
      to the error you made in your composition. On a separate sheet
      of paper work exercise_____, page_____and turn it
      in with the revision of your composition.

7.   Study carefully the explanation on pages_____in
      your grammar textbook, paying particular attention to rule
      number_____on page_____. Determine how this applies
      to the error you made in your composition. On a separate sheet
      of paper work exercise_____, page_____and turn it
      in with the revision of your composition.

8.   Study carefully the explanation on pages_____in
      your grammar textbook, paying particular attention to rule
      number_____on page_____. Determine how this applies
      to the error you made in your composition. On a separate sheet
      of paper work exercise_____, page_____and turn it
      in with the revision of your composition.

EXAMPLE III POSITIVE REINFORCEMENT

First page

CARS I WOULD NOT WANT TO OWN

There are over a quarter of a million automobiles sold in the United States each year. Many types are available; foreign cars and American cars, convertables and sedans, big cars and little cars. This variety is the result of the wide range of tastes of the driving population. There is three kinds of cars which doesn't suit my taste at all, and which I would never own. One type is impractical, another is little and ugly, and a third is poorly made.

An example of an impractical car is .the Excalibur SS, perhaps you have never seen one of these cars. It bears a strong resemblance to the Dusenberg of years ago or to an old MG, early 1951 or 1952. One of the things I don't like about it are that it only comes in a convertable model. That's fine in the summer or on a sunny day, but when it rains or when winter comes, its rather impractical. Winter is perhaps the roughest though. Mainly because the car is not even equipped with a heater. And the softtop has plastic side windows and a plastic rear window that leaks and yellows in the sun and becomes briddle with age. This car is fitted with a 327 cubic inch engine from the Corvette Stingray. The car does not weigh more than 2000 pounds, compared to the Corvette, which weighs approximately 3200 pounds this year. With over 350 horsepower and so little weight, the Excalibur is very dangerous, you can't come near controlling it on accelleration around curves or on a panic stop. Combining these shortcommings with a $10,000 price tag, you have a very impractical car.

A car that I wouldn't want is one of those ugly little foreign "bugs" you see everywhere. The Volkswagen is a good example. this simply isn't my idea of a car with good looks. In addition, its to small for safety. If you were hit in the side by a large car or by a truck, you'd be finished. You also can't ride for great distances in comfort, because the engine is to noisy and the interior is cramped. Another shortcomming is that Volkswagen's are to common. I don't want a car that every mothers son has, and if you look around any large parking lot in this city, you are bound to see at least ten Volkswagen's. Besides being so common, this car is to underpowered for freeway driving. Its almost impossible to pass a car on the expressway at sixty miles per hour, if there is a stiff crosswind blowing. Its almost like you were on a roller coaster. This is both unpleasant and unsafe.

The third type of car that I wouldn't like to own is one that is cheaply made. Ford Mustangs fall into this class my family owned one once, and before we got rid of it the muffler fell off at least five times. By the time we sold it six months later, there was rattles in every corner. Meanwhile, the paint had started peeling off, to say nothing of the first layer of chrome on the bumpers. To top it off, whenever the driver made a hard left turn, the door on the passenger's side would fly open. My uncle owns a Cougar, and it doesn't have these problems.

suggestions, having students correct each other's themes, bears examination in greater detail here.

If organized properly, having students mark each other's papers has benefits far beyond merely saving the teacher time. One approach, which also improves students' skill in working together, is to divide the class into small groups of three or four students and tell them that they are to help each other improve their papers. Explain that each student will be given not only the grade for his or her own paper, but also the average grade for the papers in the group. With advanced students, little more in the way of instructions is required. For most students, though, it is helpful to focus their attention on only one or two specific aspects of writing. For example, after you have taught students how to write paragraphs with a clear topic sentence, let the group help each other review their paragraphs, making sure that each paper has a good topic sentence. Thus, students don't get bogged down or totally confused over what to look for in suggesting improvements. With slightly more capable students, you might require each small group to designate one member to check spelling, one to check punctuation, one to check organization, and one to check content, etc.

Students who are particularly skillful in one aspect of writing could be designated as tutors, and could either be directly assigned to help those students with problems or could be listed as available when needed. For example, Doreen may be an excellent speller, but she may write very dull papers. She could be appointed tutor for spelling, but could be encouraged to seek help from someone else in how to make her writing more interesting. If students are used as tutors, it is wise to spend time discussing ways of being helpful. Classes could brainstorm and the teacher could list on the board behaviors that students find valuable in someone who is assisting them. They will probably list such things as clear explanations, friendliness, and encouraging the person to do things themselves. Then they could list behaviors that are not helpful, such as ridiculing others or implying that a person is hopeless and can never learn.

The possibilities and advantages of student tutors, if the approach is well organized and the students are instructed properly, cannot be overemphasized. The tutor as well as the tutee can learn a tremendous amount about the subject matter, and also about human relations. Most students naturally develop their own informal tutoring networks. Unfortunately, some teachers see students helping students as cheating, because the teacher views his or her primary role as evaluating rather than teaching. It is important to encourage students' natural concern and willingness to help each other. To counteract any tendency of students to do the work for others rather than help them learn, you may need to discuss with students the ways that they can be most helpful to each other: for example, writing papers for others actually hurts them in the long run because they do not learn from it, but it is helpful to sit down with friends and give them suggestions—reminding them of the rules they learned in class, giving them tips about ways to think up topic sentences or support for topic sentences, etc. Point out that simply correcting a friend's errors is generally not the most helpful thing to do, but that explaining how to avoid those errors can be very helpful.

A carefully organized plan for involving students in the grading and marking of papers has been suggested by Jerome Megna.[23] In our view his S.E.G. program (Sensitivity, Exposure, Grading), gives too much emphasis to grading and not enough to making suggestions that will help writers improve their skills. Nevertheless, the structure he suggests can be utilized with whatever emphasis the teacher desires.

---

23. Jerome F. Megna, "The S.E.G. Method of Teaching Composition." (Unpublished manuscript) Used with permission of the author.

In the first phase of the program, "Sensitivity," the teacher's role is to make the students sensitive to one another. They must be made willing to express their personal feelings and willing to accept the feelings of the others. Techniques for the achievement of this goal will vary, depending upon class size, existing conditions of class intimacy, and general level of maturity. I have found it helpful to have the class form a huge circle and to ask each student in rotation to tell the rest of the class about himself or herself. Although I encourage everyone to ask questions of the individual who is speaking, the person must always be made to feel comfortable declining to answer.

At first, the teacher may have to be the "asker of questions," but as the others begin to feel more at ease, they will gradually assume the role. The teacher should tell about him or herself too when his or her turn comes up in rotation. It is important that no one feel embarrassed or threatened by what is said. This phase of the program may last as long as three or four complete sessions.

The second phase, "Exposure," can usually be completed in four sessions, but this, too, may vary from class to class. This phase entails exposing the students to the process of how themes are corrected and evaluated. Here, the teacher has the opportunity of "thinking out loud" while correcting individual themes. The entire class is asked to write in pencil or type a paragraph or two on any subject of their choosing. After making transparencies of fifteen or twenty of the compositions, the teacher begins the evaluation process on an overhead projector, keeping in mind to preserve the anonymity of each writing. A magic marker is useful for corrections and marginalia. Students are asked to memorize correction symbols and are encouraged to comment on the evaluation process as they are watching it.

The purpose of this phase is to establish criteria in grading. As the sessions progress and more students express themselves on the grading process, the class as a whole will begin to evolve its own philosophy of evaluation through establishing guidelines for the writing of themes. This phase is both dialectic and democratic. The students are told that they will eventually assume the responsibility of applying these criteria to one another's themes. When all the students understand and agree to the method of evaluation, the second phase of the program is completed.

"Grading" is the final and most complex phase of the program. Before initiating this phase, the students must be grouped in clusters of no more than six but no fewer than four Students are usually willing to group themselves, but sometimes a teacher's intervention may be necessary. After the grouping has been done, it is useful to have each group spend an entire session with one another in order to come to know each other better. Although no special goals need to be set at the beginning of this session, if there is still strong reserve among members of the group, the teacher may wish to provide an agenda for each group in order that they might achieve greater rapport.

Toward the end of this session, each group elects a secretary who is responsible for facilitating the procedure for the grading sessions. After the election of secretaries, the teacher assigns to the entire class their first theme. It is suggested that the first theme be from three to four-hundred words in length, typewritten (if possible), and stapled in the upper left-hand corner. The front page of each theme should be the title page and this should contain only the following information: (1) the last four digits of the social security number of the student (or some other identifying number); (2) the title and date of the theme; and (3) the chronological number of the theme which the student is writing.

The grading session begins by having the secretaries of each group collect the themes in their respective groups. After they check to see that the themes are nameless and numbered, they give their batch to the secretary of a designated group. If there are four groups, the first theme grading session can be arranged as follows:

> Group 1 will give their themes to Group 2
> Group 2 will give their themes to Group 3
> Group 3 will give their themes to Group 4
> Group 4 will give their themes to Group 1

In order not to penalize any group by having their papers rigorously graded by the same group consecutively, the numerical pattern should be shifted during the following session.

> Group 1 will give their themes to Group 3
> Group 2 will give their themes to Group 4
> Group 3 will give their themes to Group 2
> Group 4 will give their themes to Group 1

During the third grading session, Group 1 will give their papers to Group 4, etc. The teacher should record the shifting patterns of exchange so that no group receives the same people's papers for two consecutive sessions.

Besides theme collection and distribution, the secretary of each group has three specific responsibilities: (1) to make sure each person in the group has the opportunity to read, comment upon and grade each theme; (2) to inscribe in Roman numerals in the upper left hand corner of each title page the "rank" the group has collectively assigned to it; and (3) to staple "q-sheets" to the top middle portion of the title page of each theme.

The Roman numeral "rank" is based upon the group's decision as to which theme is best, second best, and so forth. It may be decided by a secret vote or by the grades which the group has assigned to each theme. The criteria for the "best" are creativity, originality, interest, and anything else that the group collectively decides an outstanding theme should possess. Mechanical flawlessness is not necessarily a hallmark of the "best" theme. The "best" themes of each group should be reproduced and distributed to the entire class for discussion before the next theme grading session.

"Q-sheets" are quarter sheets of paper. Before beginning to grade the themes, each person in a group should have as many q-sheets as there are themes for the group to grade. Each q-sheet should contain the following information: (1) the last four digits of the social security number of the theme which was graded; (2) the personal comments which the grader wishes to make; (3) a grade; and (4) the full signature of the grader. Graders may assign grades with a plus or a minus, but "split" grades should be discouraged. The grades may range from A to F and some groups may decide that any theme which has more than a certain number of mechanical errors merits the grade of F despite its content.

Mechanical errors should be corrected on the theme itself, using the symbols memorized in phase two of the program. These mistakes are usually in spelling, diction, punctuation, grammar, organization and logic. If a grader is unsure of the mechanical correctness of a theme, he or she is encouraged to ask fellow members of the group or the teacher for assistance. More personal, subjective comments should be written on the q-sheets. These may include what he or she considered the level of interest of the theme, the continuity of ideas, the transitions between paragraphs, etc. After grading a theme and writing a q-sheet for it, the grader should pass the theme along to the next person in the group but hold on to the q-sheet. In this way graders are not prejudiced by the marks assigned to the theme by previous graders. By and large, students view the assigning of grades very seriously and come to realize the complexity of the evaluation process.

When all the students of one group have read and graded the themes assigned to them, they assist the secretary in stapling all the q-sheets to the top middle portion of each of the respective title pages. It is at this point that the secretary attempts to elicit from the group members which theme they consider best, second best, etc. The secretary then inscribes this "rank" in Roman numerals in the upper left hand corner of the title page. When the "best" from each group is reproduced, distributed, and discussed, the teacher should prod the class into refining its criteria for future evaluation. The distribution of the "best" themes also provides an incentive for the individual student to write an especially good theme.

When themes are returned to the authors, they reread their papers with the corrections, comments, and grades, and self-evaluate their own papers at the end of the theme. The grades they received on the q-sheets may not always correlate. It may even happen that the writer of the theme feels that the comments are unfair or irrelevant. He or she is encouraged to discuss with the individual graders why they assigned the grades they did. Beneath the author's own reactions to the comments and evaluation of the respective merit of the corrections, the student then assigns him or herself a grade. Usually this grade corresponds to the mean or median grade assigned by the group who corrected the theme, but this is left up to the individual student. At the very end of the session, the teacher collects the themes. By reading the comments and grades of the group who evaluated each paper, their corrections and marginalia on the theme, and the reaction, defense (if any), and self-evaluation of the student who wrote the theme, the teacher can diagnose the difficulties of the writer in a fraction of the time it would otherwise have taken.

By the third session, the elaborate procedures of the S.E.G. method are carried out effortlessly by the students. Significant improvement in writing techniques and style will be apparent to anyone who reads themes from the first grading session and from the fourth or fifth session. Because of the high level of participation, students, given their choice, prefer the active, self-evaluation S.E.G. method to more traditional methods of learning composition.

RESOURCES ON DESIGNING A COMPOSITION PROGRAM

Below is a selected list of books and other materials useful in planning a composition program. Addresses of publishers can be found in the alphabetical list on pages 151–153. Prices, where given, are only approximate, since changes occur frequently.

Explorations in the Teaching of Secondary English by Stephen N. Judy. A general language arts methods text. Includes discussions of numerous aspects of teaching composition. Paperbound. Dodd, Mead and Co.

Teaching Composition in the Senior High School by Samuel J. Rogal. Designed for intern and in-service teachers in order to help them structure the composition program. Discusses the program's purpose, organization, format, requirements, scope, flexibility, limitations, and restrictions. Also provides instruction in teaching formal aspects of composition—the teacher's responsibilities, legitimate writing assignments, the importance of good student-teacher relations. Paperbound. $1.75. Littlefield, Adams and Co.

Writing for the Fun of It by Robert C. Hawley and Isabel L. Hawley. Discussion of the overall writing program—teaching writing, motivating, organizing, practicing the learning and rules of mechanics, coordinating literature with writing. Numerous suggestions for activities, and instruction related to evaluation. Clear and direct. Very helpful resource. Paperbound. Education Research Associates.

On Righting Writing edited by Ouida H. Clapp. A practical collection of teaching ideas. The 1975 report on Classroom Practices in Teaching English. Paperbound. $1.95. National Council of Teachers of English.

Teaching Written English Today by W. K. Jones and A. J. Francis. Discusses learning to write, steps in finding ideas, advanced writing, and style. A foreword to teachers along with a section on criticism and evaluation—sample student papers, and teacher's comments. Paperbound. J. Weston Walch, Publisher.

The Composing Process of Twelfth Graders by Janet Emig. Report of a research study in which twelfth graders gave autobiographies of their writing experience and composed orally in the presence of an investigator. Findings confirm that school-sponsored composing is "extensive" (reportorial, cognitive) and self-sponsored writing is more reflective (affective, spontaneous, investigative). The author suggests new ways of teaching composition, based on her findings. Discusses prewriting, planning, oral composition, and student behavioral patterns while engaged in compositional process. Well-substantiated research. Excellent. Paperbound. $3.75. National Council of Teachers of English.

Teaching High School Composition edited by Gary Tate and Edward P. J. Corbett. A collection of writing on composition, including a special section on evaluation. Oxford University Press.

They Really Taught Us How to Write edited by Patricia Geuder, Linda Harvey, Dennis Loyd, and Jack Wages. Recognized as outstanding writing instructors, a number of high school teachers describe a variety of methods for teaching composition. Examination of pre-writing activities, the writing process itself, and evaluation practices, along with a look at various types of writing—journalistic, creative, analytical, and expository. Excellent ideas and suggestions. Paperbound. $4.75. National Council of Teachers of English.

Teaching English in Secondary Schools by Theodore W. Hipple. Deals with a variety of aspects of teaching English, including "Classroom Approaches to Written Composition," "Selected Issues in the Teaching of Composition," and "Composition Evaluation." A good general resource for teachers. Hardcover. The Macmillan Co.

Uptaught by Ken Macrorie. A book that presents more emphasis on simply letting students write freely than on giving feedback, but peer evaluation through discussion of writing is used. The author considers computerized grading to be an imposition on students' creativity. Paperbound. $3.95. Hayden Book Co., Inc.

Reflections on Writing edited by Stephen N. Judy. A special issue of *English Journal*. Contains numerous articles on teaching writing, including "How to Get Kids to Write," "How to Completely Individualize a Writing Program," and "Evaluating Creative Writing." Helpful ideas, tips and suggested teaching techniques. Informative and instructive. *English Journal*, April, 1975, Vol. 64, No. 4, pp. 60–72. National Council of Teachers of English.

How the French Boy Learns to Write by Rollo Walter Brown. This classic report on teaching composition in French schools has been used as a model in American schools. Includes complete course outlines concerning composition, grammar, literature, and classroom practices as well as a rationale for learning a foreign language in order to improve skills in one's native language. Paperbound. $2.75. National Council of Teachers of English.

Emphasis: Composition edited by Richard Knudson. A special issue of *The English Record*. Fourteen articles including "A Sequence of Writing Tasks for a Twenty-Week Composition Elective for Juniors and Seniors." Interesting and informative articles. Paperbound. *The English Record*, Winter, 1974, pp. 33–110. New York State English Council.

"The Theme-A-Week Assumption: A Report of an Experiment" by Frank Heys. Deflates the theory that more writing produces better writing. *English Journal*, May, 1962, pp. 320–22. National Council of Teachers of English.

Teaching/Writing edited by Ben F. Nelms. A special issue of *English Education*. Articles include "Freeing Teachers to Write," "Five Half-Truths about the Teaching of Composition," and "Teaching Writing" by English teachers with a special interest in composition. *English Education*, Vol. 6, No. 2, Dec. 1974/Jan. 1975. National Council of Teachers of English.

Research in Written Composition by Richard Braddock, Richard Lloyd-Jones, and Lowell Schoer. Summarizes existing information about composition. Detailed review and summary of several excellent studies. Bibliography included. Paperbound. $2.95. National Council of Teachers of English.

Writing Aids through the Grades: One Hundred Eighty-six Developmental Writing Activities by Ruth Kearney Carlson. Presents numerous activities designed to promote and encourage composition. Outstanding suggestions for involving even the most

reluctant writer in composition and communication. Paperbound. Teachers College Press.

Teaching English Today by Dwight L. Burton, Kenneth L. Donnelson, Bryant Fillon, and Beverly Haley. A general language arts methods text. Includes sections on teaching written composition, teacher accountability, evaluation of student performance, and evaluating as a monologue or a dialogue. Helps teachers to set standards, plan for effective instruction, and evaluate in a fair and consistent manner. Hardcover. $5.95. Houghton Mifflin.

RESOURCES ON MARKING AND EVALUATING COMPOSITIONS

Below is a selected list of books and articles on marking and grading papers. Addresses of publishers can be found in the alphabetical list on pages 151–153. Prices where given, are only approximate, since changes occur frequently.

Suggestions for Evaluating Senior High School Writing by the Association of English Teachers of Western Pennsylvania. Illustrates effective methods of evaluating student work with numerous examples, models and explanations. Answers pertinent questions: how do teachers develop fair and consistent evaluative standards, what is the ideal relationship between content and mechanics, how extensive should the teacher's comments be? Presents a lucid rationale and examples of student papers that have been effectively evaluated, along with definite and trenchant instructions and remarks to the teacher. Paperbound. $2.45. National Council of Teachers of English.

Suggestions for Evaluating Junior High School Writing edited by Lois M. Grose, Dorothy Miller, and Erwin R. Steinberg. Discusses procedures, principles, and methods for evaluating junior high school papers. Presents three sets of graded themes for grades seven, eight, and nine. Clear and direct. Provides helpful instructive remarks and information directed to both the student and the teacher. A handy, useful guide for teachers. Paperbound. $2.15. National Council of Teachers of English.

A Guide for Evaluating Student Composition: A Collection of Readings edited by Sister M. Judine. Seven separate articles examine the evaluator and cover standards, marking, guiding, and praising the student. Specific discussion of evaluating the theme,

expository writing, and junior and senior high school papers. Includes articles on types of grading, essay and composition rating scales. Excellent collection. Paperbound. $3.25. National Council of Teachers of English.

"Freshman English During the Flood" by Charlton Laird. Previews the Oregon Plan for composition feedback based on peer evaluation and student-teacher conferences. *College English*, Vol. 18, No. 3, December, 1956, pp. 131–38. National Council of Teachers of English.

"Objective Correlation and the Grading of English Composition" by J. T. Leahy. Humorous article on how to "grade" English compositions. *College English*, Vol. 25, No. 1, October, 1963, pp. 35–38. National Council of Teachers of English.

"Myth and Method" by Carolyn Logan. States that teachers should make their comments on themes positive so students won't be inhibited in writing. *English Journal*, Vol. 59, No. 4, April, 1970, pp. 548–50. National Council of Teachers of English.

"Theme Correcting via Tape Recorder" by Lee Frank Lowe. Although it's not time saving, using the tape recorder for theme feedback allows more personal and lengthy comments. *English Journal*, Vol. 52, No. 3, March, 1963, pp. 212–14 National Council of Teachers of English.

"Aide-to-Order for the Composition Teacher"

by Marcia Mahnke. Using teachers as lay readers on a full time basis. *English Journal*, Vol. 53, No. 1, January, 1964, pp. 40–41. National Council of Teachers of English.

"What Has Happened to Written Composition?" by Joseph Mersand. Maintains that "Composition correction has changed from a pursuit in red ink by a bleary-eyed teacher-detective to a constructive evaluation which is shared in by the student-writer and the class." *English Journal*, Vol. 50, No. 4, April, 1961, pp. 231–37. National Council of Teachers of English.

"Teacher Comments and Student Performance: A Seventy-Four Classroom Experiment in School Motivation" by E. B. Page. Study shows that written comments have a positive effect on "effort, or attention, or attitude, or whatever it is that causes learning to improve." *The Journal of Educational Psychology*, Vol. 49, No. 4, August, 1958, pp. 173–81.

"What Criteria Do You Use in Grading Compositions?" by Paul F. Schumann. Calls for increased objectivity in grading compositions by developing and using explicit criteria for evaluation. *English Journal*, Vol. 57, No. 8, November, 1968, pp. 1163–65. National Council of Teachers of English.

"Writers Cramp and Eyestrain—Are they Paying Off?" by Lois V. Arnold. Study shows that intensive evaluation is no more effective in improving the quality of writing than moderate evaluation. *English Journal*, Vol. 53, No. 1, January, 1964, pp. 10–15. National Council of Teachers of English.

"Correcting Compositions Without a Pencil" by Nachman Cohen. Before tape recorders, they used Edison Recording Disks for composition feedback. *English Journal*, Vol. 39, No. 10, December, 1950, pp. 579–80. National Council of Teachers of English.

"Computer Grading of English Composition" by Arthur Daigon. Mechanization in the classroom via machine–graded compositions. The machine's grades correlate significantly with the grade assigned by humans. *English Journal*, Vol. 55, No. 1, January, 1966, pp. 46–52. National Council of Teachers of English.

"An AV Aid to Teaching Writing" by Virginia Fitzpatrick. Using tape recording for teacher comments. *English Journal*, Vol. 57, No. 3, March, 1968, pp. 372–74. National Council of Teachers of English.

"Lay Readers in High School Composition Program: Some Statistics" by Paul M. Ford. Positive statistics on a lay reader program. Based on theory that students need to write more to improve compositions, and lay readers made this possible. *English Journal*, Vol. 50, No. 8, November, 1961, pp. 522–28. National Council of Teachers of English.

"Student Leadership in Evaluating Compositions" by Loren Grissom. Advocates that students become involved in theme correction before turning them in to the teacher. *English Journal*, Vol. 48, No. 6, September, 1959, pp. 338–39. National Council of Teachers of English.

"Students Like Corrections" by Katherine Keene. Points out the value of marking errors and mentions giving themes two grades—one for mechanics, one for interest value. *English Journal*, Vol. 45, No. 4, April, 1956, pp. 212–15. National Council of Teachers of English.

"Redpencilitis: Cause and Cure" by Joe W. Andrews. Presents the teacher's red pencil as an economical meeting ground for composition feedback. *English Journal*, Vol. 42, No. 1, January, 1953, pp. 20–24. National Council of Teachers of English.

"Can We Evaluate Compositions?" by T. A. Koclanes. Urges that when teachers correct themes, they look for writing improvement, not just give a grade. *English Journal*, Vol. 50, No. 4, April, 1961, pp. 252ff. National Council of Teachers of English.

"Some Questions on the Lay Reader Program" by Paul H. Krueger. Negative opinion on lay readers due to their lack of knowledge of students. *English Journal*, Vol. 50, No. 8, November, 1961, pp. 529–33. National Council of Teachers of English.

A Scale for Evaluation of High School Student Essays. Brief outline of standards for evaluating essays giving specific consideration to key areas—content, organization, style, and mechanics. Presents several sample essays with critical comments. A useful reference. Paperbound. $1.25. National Council of Teachers of English.

Measure for Measure edited by Allen Berger and Blanche Hope Smith. Forty-three articles dealing with measurement, testing, and evaluation, including a section on grading compositions. An excellent presentation of a variety of classroom teachers' ideas and experiences related to evaluation and grading. Paperbound. $1.95. National Council of Teachers of English.

Emphasis: Use and Misuse of Standardized Testing edited by Richard L. Knudson. This special issue of *The English Record* contains eleven articles dealing with evaluation and testing. "The Limitations of Standardized Tests as They Apply to Measuring Growth in English Curriculum Areas," "Grades and Growth in a Writing Program," and "A Proposal for a Test in English for Students in Grades 11 and 12." A helpful resource for teachers. Paperbound. *The English Record*, Vol. 26, No. 2, Spring, 1975. New York State English Council.

"Evaluation of Writing: A Three-Part Program" by Sister Miriam Bernadette. Suggests criteria for mechanics set by students, lab writing, and student-teacher conferences for feedback. *English Journal*, Vol. 54, No. 1, January, 1965, pp. 23–27. National Council of Teachers of English.

"Evaluating a Theme: Twenty-five High School and College Teachers Analyze and Grade a High School Theme" edited by A. K. Steven. The same student essay is evaluated, graded, and commented upon by twenty-five different English teachers. The diversity of opinion is interesting, the comments are enlightening, and the grading is often surprising. Thought provoking. *Newsletter of the Michigan Council of Teachers of English*, Vol. 5, No. 6, Spring, 1958, pp. 1–16. National Council of Teachers of English.

"NCTE/ERIC Report - Composition Evaluation" by Robert V. Denby. Reports that peer group evaluation of composition is not significantly more helpful to students than teacher evaluation, but it is much less time consuming for the teacher. *English Journal*, Vol. 57, No. 8, November, 1968, pp. 1215–21. National Council of Teachers of English.

Wad-Ja-Get? by Howard Kirschenbaum, Sidney B. Simon, and Rodney W. Napier. An excellent discussion of grading fallacies and alternative grading systems, plus a consideration of grading creative writing. Paperbound. Hart Publishing Co., Inc.

Assessing Compositions: A Discussion Pamphlet by A Subcommittee of the London Association for the Teaching of English. Presents thirty student compositions along with in-depth teacher's comments and grades. Very helpful reference. Clear and easy-to-understand evaluative framework. Paperbound. London Association for the Teaching of English.

2

Teaching Students to Write Paragraphs

In the usual progress of learning, the baby learns to say words, the small child learns to speak short sentences, and the early schoolchild learns to write in sentences. The student writer then reaches the point of learning to communicate by paragraphs, and it is here that the die will be cast: he or she becomes an effective writer or does not, depending on whether he or she learns to write by paragraphs.

In order for students to master paragraph writing, they must first understand what a paragraph is and how it functions in writing. They must see that a paragraph is the basic formal unit by which writers convey their ideas. It is in the paragraph that the writer's generalizations are finally expressed on the detailed level and are finally made specific and complete for the benefit of the reader.

Students must understand that a paragraph consists of a single limited statement formulated with care and developed in detail. To say it in another way, it is a general statement illuminated or elaborated by specific statements. It is the building block of larger writings such as essays, reports, news stories, novels and short stories. The paragraph, in short, is where writing happens.

But a good paragraph doesn't just happen. Good writers know what they are doing and make deliberate choices, rather than putting down sentences as they come to mind with no conscious reason. Making the proper choices as one constructs a paragraph is a skill that can be taught rather than left to chance. The lessons and activities in this chapter teach students how to make the right choices in composing paragraphs. They are presented here in logical sequence, beginning with more rudimentary skills and proceeding to more sophisticated ones. In general, we suggest that you schedule the activities in the order in which they are presented. However, as some are likely to be too difficult for younger or less able students, not all may be suitable for any particular class.

OBJECTIVES

As a result of the learning experiences in this chapter, students should be able to:

1. Construct a topic sentence that is limited enough to be developed in one paragraph.
2. Construct a topic sentence that summarizes a given set of details.
3. Choose an appropriate means for developing a topic sentence with specific statements.
4. Eliminate any specific details that do not support, explain, or illustrate the topic sentence.
5. Arrange the specific details in the best order.
6. Improve the coherence of their paragraphs.
7. Write paragraphs that are well developed, logically organized, unified, and coherent.

LEARNING EXPERIENCES

TOPIC I: TOPIC SENTENCES

1. *Teacher Presentation.* Explain to students that a topic sentence is so called because it is a sentence about a topic. It is *one* statement about *one* topic, *one* subject. And it is a sufficiently limited statement that can be completely developed in detail in one paragraph. The function of the paragraph is to do just that—to develop the topic sentence in complete detail. Students need to know that the topic sentence determines what can go into a paragraph, and that no statement can go into the paragraph that is not related to the topic sentence. Following is a list of topic sentences which you might find useful in discussing the nature of the topic sentence with your students or which you can use for some of the suggested activities or for assignments as you desire. The list also appears on Reproduction Page 1, which can be used to make a spirit master for duplicating the list to distribute to students or to make a transparency for use with an overhead projector.

Sample Topic Sentences

We never got along well after that.

Household plants add much to the charm of any house.

A cat's diet should not be varied from day to day.

A brisk walk after dinner can have a number of beneficial effects.

Some girls wear so much make-up that it detracts from their charm instead of enhancing it.

Putting too much effort into getting high grades can prevent one from profiting fully from an education.

I would rather take an examination than write a paper as a means of being graded.

Physical education classes are a source of embarrassment to many students.

The average student—the one who makes mostly C's—is spared many problems in school.

The room had been thoroughly ransacked.

Her locker looked like the nest of a pack-rat.

The mailman on our route had good cause to fear dogs.

Many students truly enjoy going to school.

There are many satisfactions to be gained from making bread.

Students in the 1970's seem more apathetic toward social issues than they were in '60's.

The bee is, indeed, a busy insect.

Green beans are easy to grow.

Only humankind does not order its days by the sun.

Lawn mowing need not be a boring task.

Breakfast is my favorite meal.

A good banana split is a work of art.

It was my fault more than his that we did not remain friends.

A boy can learn much from owning a dog.

I was never able to learn in her class.

It was a day made for kites.

I began to think the hour would never end.

She seemed to delight in making me feel foolish.

Their names suited their personalities.

Many students feel that they should strive to use fancy language when they write.

For the invalid, particularly, food should be made visually attractive as well as nutritious.

Even the experienced pilot needs to return to flying school periodically.

Wood furniture will soon be priced out of the market for all but the rich.

It is easier to learn from a teacher one likes.

Some lessons are harder to learn than others.

The students resented having to go outside to smoke.

I never could believe the principal was my pal, even though my spelling teacher said he was.

Of course, short hair does have its advantages.

Fences are not always barriers between people.

Schoolrooms are usually drab and uninteresting looking places, at least in high school.

One cannot stay well informed just by reading one newspaper.

All too often people will treat their best friends as they would not treat their worst enemies.

Good manners have never been near the top of my list of most significant human values.

It turned out to be a terrible day for me.

She seemed to enjoy being miserable.

His term paper was a real work of art.

There, perched on my window sill, was an insect which looked like nothing so much as a miniature tyrannosaurus rex.

In many ways he was different from the rest of the fellows in our crowd.

Most of us would have a hard time tracing the origin of our personal beliefs.

I somehow felt especially at ease in her class.

Most of us find it easier to tolerate faults in ourselves than in others.

2. *Activity.* Since a topic sentence is a *general* statement supported, explained, or illustrated by *specific* statements, it is essential that students understand fully the concept of general vs. specific. After explaining the concept, give the class several pairs of words, one of which is more general than the other: car/Ford, language/ French, etc. Have students decide which word is more specific than the other. Then read or write on the board pairs of phrases, one of which is more specific than the other: getting dressed/putting on my socks, my grandfather/elderly persons I have admired, the view from my bedroom window/an apple tree in my neighbor's yard, etc. If students need still more practice, give them a list of pairs of sentences, one of which is more general than the other: My mother spent an hour doing the grocery shopping/It took her ten minutes to decide between ground beef and ground chuck, etc.

3. *Activity.* Reproduce the following list of topic sentences (which also appears on Reproduction Page 2) and distribute it to students. Some of the topic sentences are sufficiently specific to be developed in detail in one paragraph. Others are too broad and general, and would require an entire essay or even a book. Some make two or more statements in one sentence and are therefore poor topic sentences. Working with the class as a whole, discuss and evaluate the topic sentences on the list. Identify the poor topic sentences and choose the good ones. Answers are shown below in parentheses.

Both dogs and cats have some habits which make them difficult to keep as pets in a small apartment. (Bad—two subjects)

Dachshunds make fine watch dogs. (OK)

Drinking eight glasses of water a day promotes good health. (OK)

The earth's oceans may already be irreversibly polluted. (Bad—too broad)

There are many reasons why scientists consider it a mathematical certainty that human life similar to our species exists somewhere in the universe. (Bad—too broad)

Cockroaches are equipped to survive us all. (OK)

Politics have fallen into disrepute in our society. (Bad—too broad)

It is not difficult to paint a house. (OK)

World War II did not result in the social dislocations in Germany that were so disastrous after World War I. (Bad—too broad)

Revisionist historians are giving us a much different view of the American Revolution than the one most of us gain in elementary school. (Bad—too broad)

A satisfactory definition of the term "pollution" must reach into many areas of our lives and environment. (Bad—too broad)

Weather, we are told, has significant effects on emotional balance and social behavior. (Bad—too broad)

The science of weather prediction has existed as long as there have been herdsmen and food gatherers. (Bad—too broad)

Psychological maturity is demonstrated by a giving, sharing, producing orientation to life. (Bad—too broad)

Stonehenge can be described as a huge calendar. (OK)

The rehabilitation of America's major cities will require a massive infusion of tax money. (OK)

Three of the players on our school's 1955 football team went on to illustrious careers as professional players, and two of these individuals later became successful politicians. (Bad—two subjects)

Our float trip ended in an adventure we had not foreseen and which we were ill equipped to handle. (OK)

The secret of a successful camping trip lies in the preparations made before leaving home. (OK)

Parenthood is not as easy a task as many young people would argue. (OK)

Adolescence is not so much a time as a function. (Bad—too broad)

Students often complain about a class being boring without realizing that they themselves may share the responsibility for a class's failure to come alive. (OK)

Youngsters' patterns of behavior are established well before they enter school. (Bad—too broad)

Many famous men have come from disturbed and unhappy families. (Bad—too broad)

A walk over a western prairie at dawn reveals a richness of life forms and activities that rivals an awakening city. (OK)

The river, like a person, shows itself in ever-changing activities and moods. (OK)

4. *Activity.* Divide the class into small groups (about three or four students to a group). Perhaps the best way to do this is to divide the number of students in the class by either three or four. The answer you get is the highest that students should "number off" to. Have students number off, and then have all the 1's get together, all the 2's get together, all the 3's, etc. This procedure assigns students randomly so you don't have the same students working together all the time. Explain to the class that you will give all the groups the same subject and that in five minutes (or longer if you wish) you want each group to come up with as many specific details about it as they can. Less able students may profit from your doing one subject with the total class as an example. Here are some subjects to assign:

> a crisp fall day
> a friendship's ending
> an overcrowded school
> a warmly hospitable family
> an autumn walk in the woods
> cafeteria after lunch

As the groups are working, circulate among them to make sure they are arriving at details, not general statements. When groups have finished listing all the details they can think of, have them write a statement about the subject which will include as many of their details as possible. Then have them eliminate any details which do not fit with the general statement. When all groups have finished, let them read their general statements (topic sentences) and revised lists of details to the total class. At the end of the lesson, assign students to choose one general statement and list of related details and to turn them into a paragraph.

5. *Activity.* Assign each student to prepare a list of details about the view out of his or her bedroom window. As each student reads the list of details to the class, have the other students try to make a statement about each view based on the details read. These could be written on the board, and the student who brought the descriptive details could choose the sentence which best summarizes his or her list. Other subjects suitable for this activity: my little brother (or sister), my favorite person, my new car, my favorite after-school activity, etc. *Caution:* be sure the students understand they are to bring to class a list of details, not statements which could themselves be topic sentences. Here's an example (using "my little brother" as the subject):

Details about little brother: *eight years old, very loud voice, can't tie his shoes very well, always wants his way, fights with little sister, hates vegetables, swipes my records to play, always wants cowboy shows on TV, etc.*
Possible topic sentence: *Every annoying trait an eight-year-old can have, my little brother has in spades.*

6. *Activity.* Divide the class into groups of three to five students each, using the procedure suggested in Activity #4 above. Have each group make a list of details relating to some event, situation, feeling, or controversy which they know is familiar to the other members of the class. After they've made their lists, have them exchange them with another group and see if they can guess what the other students were thinking of and if they can construct a suitable topic sentence to include all the details on the list. For example, one group might list the following details: the team was over-confident; we fumbled a lot; the opponents intercepted three of our passes; the final score was embarrassing; we had many penalties. Another group might guess that the details all relate to "a game when everything went wrong" and might construct the following topic sentence: The football game was a disaster for us. Another example: the dogs howl at night; there are lights on at all hours of the night; car doors slamming wake me up; when the wind blows our way, the odor is bad; our property value has gone down. Topic sentence: It is not always pleasant living next door to a dog kennel.

7. *Activity.* Have the class interview one member (a volunteer) about how he or she spends spare time (or what the person likes on TV, or what kind of music he or she prefers, or what the person thinks a perfect friend is, etc.). Make a list of the details the interviewee reveals. Put it on the board for all the class to see.

   Then ask each student to write a topic sentence which makes a statement about how the interviewee spends spare time (or whatever). The statement should include as many of the details as possible, and should be suitable for development in one paragraph. For example, if the list of how George spends his leisure time is as follows: "listens to records, reads, daydreams, rides exercise bicycle, plays guitar, writes letters," the topic sentence might be "George doesn't need companionship to help him spend his free time." After several students have read their topic sentences, have the class interview a different person and repeat the exercise

TOPIC II: DEVELOPING A TOPIC SENTENCE INTO A COMPLETE, UNIFIED PARAGRAPH

1. *Teacher Presentation.* Remind students that the topic sentence determines what the development of a paragraph will be, since only detailed statements which support, prove, and specify the topic sentence can be included. All other details must be eliminated (perhaps to go into another paragraph with a different topic sentence). A very common way of developing a topic sentence is simply to break it into its logical parts such as ways, reasons, causes, results, components, steps, facts, etc. Here are some examples to use in clarifying this kind of development for your students. The important thing to remember is that it is the topic sentence that determines what goes into the paragraph because it is its parts which make up the development.

Topic Sentence	Parts
It was my fault we were not friends.	*things I did that were my fault*
There are three ways to knead bread.	*the three ways*
Grass is greener on the other side of the fence.	*reasons why*
The apple is unusually nutritious.	*how it contributes to nutrition*
We learned important lessons on our vacation.	*important lessons we learned*
There are many fascinating people in my class.	*examples of fascinating people*

2. *Activity.* Have the class, with you supervising, take the following list of topic sentences and name what the developmental parts would be if they were writing a paragraph about the topic sentence.

   I simply can't stand frogs.

   There are many historical sites near Philadelphia.

   America is the location of some of the world's largest lakes.

   Seniors are more mature than freshmen in many ways.

   My loyalty to her caused me a number of problems.

   Many breeds of tropical fish are suitable for a community tank.

   His fear of dogs is deeply rooted in past experiences.

   His unexpected appearance at the party was not a result of his loyalty to her.

   Their pranks almost destroyed the class.

   The coach knew how to pull the team together as a unit.

   We taught one another important lessons of camping.

   There are many ways to trim a Christmas tree.

   It's easy to carve a ham (wash a car, repot an African violet).

   She wished she had never given that speech.

   His flower garden was a showplace.

   Don't encourage students to come up with the actual details (content) of the paragraph. Simply have them specify what type of content the topic sentence calls for. For example, for the first topic sentence in the list, a correct response might be, "The reasons why the writer doesn't like frogs."

3. *Activity.* Choose three topic sentences from the list in Activity #2 above. Remind students of the identification of the developmental parts that the class agreed upon, and ask the students to suggest the actual detailed sentences that could make up the paragraph. Students could work as a class, under your supervision, or could divide into small groups, devise their lists of sentences and then come back together to share. Of course, in this activity students will have to use their imaginations and make up details they feel are suitable.

   EXAMPLE:

   <u>Topic sentence:</u> *"His fear of dogs is deeply rooted in past experiences."*

   <u>Detailed statements:</u> *"When he was three years old, he was attacked by a large Alaskan Husky. A wolf that looked like a dog lunged at his stroller when he was between one and two. A dead dog fell into his baby carriage. The neighbor's dog ate his pet cat when he was seven."*

4. *Activity.* Ask students to choose three different topic sentences from the list in Activity #2 above. Have them devise a list of developing sentences (as they did for Activity #3), except this time have them include both statements that belong in the paragraph and a few statements that do *not*. In other words, they are to deliberately violate the principle of unity by putting in statements that don't belong. Then have students, working in pairs or small groups, exchange their lists of sentences to see if they can identify and eliminate sentences that violate unity or that do not really pertain to the topic sentence.

5. *Teacher Presentation.* Tell students that there are a number of other ways to develop a topic sentence into a paragraph besides breaking the topic sentence into its logical parts. But the interesting fact is that it is the topic sentence, again, that determines the most suitable means of development. Depending on what method will most effectively specify the topic sentence, the writer may choose from these means of development: explanation, factual data, description, narrative, examples. Numerous other methods of development could also be considered, but these are the most useful.

6. *Activity.* Reproduce the paragraphs below using Reproduction Page 3 to make a master for the spirit duplicator. Give a copy to each student to read and to attempt to discern which of the main methods of developing a paragraph (explanation, facts, description, narrative, or examples) is used. (Answers: A - facts, B - narrative, C - examples, D - facts, E - description, F - examples, G - description, H - narrative, I - explanation, J - explanation.)

A. *It had never been a large high school as compared to many city high schools, and now it was shrinking. At its peak, the student body had never numbered more than 1500, and by 1975, when the World War II "baby boom" had pretty well expended itself, the entering freshman class was 200 students smaller than the freshman class of just five years before. In September 1974, the faculty numbered 113, and already there were signs of professional staff reduction. Three retiring teachers were not replaced, and the foreign language department, for one, lost one teacher who was not replaced. Both part-time assistant coaches went elsewhere. It was obviously a shrinking faculty. Specialists such as counselors, reading experts and teachers trained for working with learning disabilities numbered considerably fewer in 1975 than in 1970, and hardly a department did not suffer the loss of non-professional aides and clerks. The number of principals went from four to three in 1975, and the staff of librarians was reduced from four to two. The facilities did not change; the school looked as large as ever, but the truth was that in many important ways the school was becoming smaller.*

B. *By the time Winston was three years old, he had already used up three of his nine lives. When he was almost a year old, in June, he was hit by a car and badly shaken up. We found him lying on the back doorstep, eyes closed and obviously in a state of shock. He was breathing shallowly, but cried out strongly when we picked him up to carry him into the house. He must have been badly bruised, for he hardly moved for several days and cried whenever anyone inadvertently touched him carelessly. In time he did recover, a sadder and wiser cat who never went near the street again. His next near miss was a virus infection in the following October. Antibiotics got him well by Christmas, in time for him to be shot in the leg and stomach by a young man trying out his new Christmas present, a 22 rifle. This was Winston's worst trauma, and it took all of Dr. Benedict's devotion and skill to pull him through. He had wire stitches in his stomach and wore a splint for weeks, clumping around the house sounding like Old Pew, the peg-legged sailor in* Treasure Island. *In three months or so he was as good as new and he seems to be looking forward to his six remaining lives.*

C. *Some television commercials demonstrate such questionable values with regard to human behavior that one wonders just what lessons children are learning as they sit transfixed before the screen. Perhaps, from one famous commercial, they are learning that it is perfectly all right to over-eat and over-drink because a foaming tablet in a glass of water will take care of all harmful consequences. Or they may be watching a version of the oft-taught lesson that in order to be happy one must be loved by everyone and the way to be universally lovable is to use the best smelling mouthwashes, deodorants, and tooth pastes. For an even more telling example of pernicious teaching, the boys may be gleaning wisdom from a series of commercials which teach them that the way to manhood is through good masculine violence and group camaraderie with plenty of full-bodied beer thrown in. With TV broadcasting such lessons for many hours a day, one wonders if parental teaching stands much of a chance.*

D. *Off campus activities have become much more of an integral part of our high school. As recently as 1971, there were no activities away from the high school that were approved for the students. All students were expected to be in class or in one of the approved building areas from 8:15 a.m. to 2:45 p.m. No exceptions to this rule were allowed. In 1972, however, the school established a special program on an experimental basis. Fifty students, this first year, were permitted to attend school for a minimum of three hours and work at a job in the community for at least three more hours daily. A teacher was hired to meet with these students as a class at the high school and supervise their job experiences by maintaining a close contact with their employers. This program was so successful in meeting the needs of some students that by 1975, three hundred youngsters were enrolled in the work-study schedule and two additional teachers had been hired to work with students and their employers. There is now an almost equal number of students working as volunteers and trainees at various community support agencies for a portion of each day. This program is called Community Involvement, and it is available only to seniors as an enrichment experience. It seems a far cry from the school which was confined to one building and offered only six classes a day.*

E. *The noises of the storm surrounded us. The rolls of thunder never ceased, sometimes deep and roaring and sometimes dimly growling as if from a great distance. Periodically, sharp and dramatic crashes of thunder shook the house, warning of nearby lightning and sending the dog whining under the sofa for safety. The gutters soon overflowed and great streams of water splashed noisily down the front windows, while in the rear of the house an avalanche of water from the roof spurted from a downspout obstructed by leaves and splattered with great force on the patio stones. We were surrounded by rivers, it seemed, and through it all the heavy spray driven by wind sounded like bullets pelting against the roof and walls. The house creaked and quivered, feeling the strength of the gale, but it was a strong, well-constructed house, and inside it we felt, if not a sense of quiet, at least an absence of fear.*

F. *Some books read in childhood are truly unforgettable. Some of the characters, the places, the adventures experienced with so much excitement when one is quite young stay in one's mind as long as memory lasts. Such a character is Long John Silver in Robert Louis Stevenson's* Treasure Island. *Who, once acquainted with this wily old pirate, could ever forget him as he stomps along the decks of his ship, as quick on his crutch as other men with two good legs? As for Heidi, the little girl who lived in the Swiss Alps, who, having once roamed those upland meadows with her, could ever forget her as she drove her goats to pasture or milked them at the end of the day? She remains forever a child in memory. Childhood's memories of "The Song of Roland" and the friendship between Roland and Oliver are untarnished by any later historical knowledge, and the Knights of the Round Table still ride, in a golden haze of vague romantic memories, King Arthur at their head, with Lancelot, ever faithful, at his right hand. Who would give up these perfect childhood memories?*

G. *Whenever I looked at him, I thought of Uriah Heep, the groveling, obsequious, sly character in* David Copperfield. *This was unfair of me, because I knew nothing about him to justify the comparison, but there was something about the way he used his eyes, small and set deep in folds of flesh, that made me distrust his every word and deed. He darted little looks at me, and at others, as well, when he thought we were not watching him, and when caught in the act, winked and smiled and rubbed his hands for all the world like old Uriah. He never looked anyone full in the face, never held his gaze locked with one's own, but looked sidelong, or raised his eyes furtively from seeming to peer at something else beyond or beside the one he really wished to observe. Even after a year's experience of him, I would have been hard put to say what color his eyes were, lurking under the scraggly, sandy brows. I thought perhaps they had no color of their own, but like him, would take on whatever shade seem to fit the moment's need.*

H. *Roger and Steve sallied forth to try out the white water of the upper St. Francis River for all the world like experienced canoers who knew what they were doing. Both were powerful swimmers and intelligent, athletic young men whose bodies were well trained and adequate for any reasonable challenge. Both had been canoeing for a year or two and had encountered no challenge to shake their confidence. They decided that they would challenge the St. Francis, one of Missouri's heftier stretches of white water, and find out what real canoeing is all about. They would, of course, take every sensible precaution. Nothing could possibly go wrong, they thought. Four days later, when they brought home their dented and misshapen canoe, they knew what could go wrong.*

I. *Transplanting seedlings need not be a traumatic experience for either the seedling or the beginning gardener. Small plants, like small children, are remarkably hardy and resilient, and capable of withstanding all sorts of shocks to their systems. A very few simple procedures will help your plants come through transplanting successfully. You should transplant your seedlings only when it is cloudy or overcast or after the sun has set. Too much heat is hard for them to take when they are already undergoing strain. Strain is considerably reduced, also, if you take up each plant in a trowel-full of its own soil and set it down in a hole big enough to receive a cup or so of water and all the soil you have kept pressed around the plant's roots. When you have pressed the plant firmly into place and given it another watering, your job is done. You need not fret if the plant looks a little spindly and droopy; next morning, after a quiet night's rest in its new spot, your plant will look healthier and sturdier than ever.*

J. *Sometimes the student who talks and argues endlessly in class discussions learns less than the student who sits quietly, saying little or even nothing, but listening to the contributions of others. The talkative student may simply feel a need to defend his or her viewpoints against all other views, regardless of whether he or she has previously done much study in arriving at these beliefs. Or the student may feel that speaking with seeming authority will cause everyone to regard him or her as intelligent and well informed. Such a person may have an unconscious need to seem superior to others, a need that expresses itself in verbal contentiousness and a refusal to respect the views of others. Whatever the reasons for this talkativeness, it is apparent that the person cannot be thinking all the time he or she is talking, and it may be that the more thoughtful, silent student is actually engaging in a more productive activity. Since he or she is not continually producing output during the discussion, the more quiet student may well be receiving valuable input or at least be gaining insight into various viewpoints, while the constant talker and arguer will remain merely defensive of his or her own.*

7. *Activity.* Remind students of all the usual means of developing a topic sentence into a paragraph, including the one discussed in Teacher Presentation #1 (analysis) as well as the five introduced in Teacher Presentation #5. Have students, working as a total class or in groups, study the following list of topic sentences and agree on the best means of development for each one. The list also appears

on Reproduction Page 4, which can be duplicated and distributed to students or projected for the total class to see. Answers are given in parentheses.

A number of students in the audience could have taught that particular lesson as well as the teacher. (examples)

American cars are often named after animals or birds. (examples)

Every football lineman has his particular duties. (explanation)

Even in warm weather, mountain climbers have been known to die of a too sudden drop in body temperature. (facts)

There are three separate political groups in the United States. (analysis)

From the beginning, that vacation was more work than play. (narrative)

The halls were uniformly drab and dingy. (description)

The beagle has become a favorite of dog fanciers and outsells all other dogs in the United States. (facts)

Students in our school seem to fall into two categories. (analysis)

There are still many government figures whose names are not tainted by scandal or hint of corruption. (examples)

By the end of the season, the team had set five local records and three state records in various styles of swimming. (facts)

One should never wax a car without giving it a thorough washing first. (explanation)

One night the haunted house had visitors who were not ghosts. (narrative)

The bleachers were a kaleidoscope of shifting colors. (description)

The Gateway Arch in St. Louis, Missouri, is an architectural and technical marvel. (facts)

On a few occasions a President's wife has seemed to gain more respect and admiration than the President himself. (examples)

Many a famous beauty has found that her physical attributes have won her more misery than joy. (examples)

His records for passes completed and yards gained on ground exceeded those of all but two former players at his school. (facts)

Class discussion is an effective way for students to share knowledge and experience and, thus, to learn from one another. (explanation)

Great athletes, unfortunately, have not always proved to be great gentlemen. (examples)

Most of the space in a vegetable garden can be planted at least twice during the growing season. (explanation)

Long John Silver resides in the memory of all who have read Treasure Island. (description)

I remember very well the day a tornado struck our school. (narrative)

Tourism is Hawaii's most profitable business. (facts)

Their Christmas tree looked as if it had been trimmed by an interior decorator rather than the family themselves. (description)

My first blind date was an exercise in embarrassment and helplessness. (narrative)

Lights play an important part in any theatrical production. (explanation)

The dance was a great financial success in spite of high expenses. (facts)

It is a mistake to exclude students from curriculum planning. (explanation)

8. *Activity.* Divide the class at random into pairs or groups of three and assign each a topic sentence from the list in Activity #7 above. Have them come up with as many specifying statements as possible to develop the topic sentence in the manner designated. Have the students share their lists with the class.

9. *Evaluation.* As a means of checking how well students have mastered the skills taught by the preceding learning experiences (or as an additional practice exercise), assign the same topic sentence to each student. (See Teacher Presentation #1 for suggestions, or prepare one which is better suited to your class.) Have students, working individually, determine the best means of development, make a list of developing parts and statements and, finally, write a completely detailed paragraph. It would be helpful to collect the paragraphs and lists and reproduce them by spirit duplicator or overhead projector. Or, if necessary, read them aloud and let the class critique the lists and paragraphs and choose those which they feel were done most satisfactorily. Unless the trust level in the class is high, do not identify the writer of each paragraph. (If no means of reproducing are available, you might circulate the papers in class with students evaluating the papers on a point scale as in a diving match. Of course, if you have some students whose ability is markedly below the general level of the class, this approach would pose a problem and you might prefer not to circulate the papers.)

10. *Teacher Presentation.* Tell students: In life you, the writer, are often faced not with a list of specifying details or a topic sentence, but with a complex and often confusing situation, thing, event, or person to write about. It is *your* task to reduce this experience with all its random parts and details to writing. *You* will have to unify these details in one topic sentence and *you* must decide what means of developing best suits *your* purpose. Your task is to find a common element or theme in all (or most) of the details before you and to express this theme or element in a statement which becomes your topic sentence. You will then eliminate the details which can't be included under your topic sentence, choose the means of development which you see best suits your purpose and proceed with the writing of your paragraph.

Review with students the steps in the process:

1. Jot down all the ideas and details on the subject you can.
   EXAMPLE: messy hair, dirty shirt, untied shoes, cut-offs, sharp eyes, etc.
2. Identify common element.
   EXAMPLE: sloppy appearance (eliminate "sharp eyes")
3. State topic sentence.
   EXAMPLE: My friend Charlie always seems to look sloppy.
4. Decide on method of development.
   EXAMPLE: description
5. List specific details that you plan to use.
   EXAMPLE: all from above list except "sharp eyes"
6. Write paragraph.

If you need to provide students with other examples of how to turn a bewildering mass of details into a paragraph, utilize the following:

<u>Details:</u> *horns, streamers, whistles, snake dances, perspiring delegates, harried sergeants-at-arms, democratic caucus in a corner, demonstration under the stage, etc.*

<u>Topic Sentence:</u> *The convention floor was a noisy, seething mass of nonsense and serious political business.*

<u>Method of Development:</u> *Analysis.*

11. *Activity.* Have students work together as a class under your supervision on following the six-step process suggested in the Teacher Presentation above. Have them consider a place, person, situation, object, event, etc., and come up with a list of details. Then have them try to devise (as a group), a topic sentence which includes most of the details. They then should decide on a method of development, and settle on a final list of details that develop the topic sentence. You might even wish to have them write the complete paragraph as a group.

12. *Activity.* The list of random details below also appears on Reproduction Page 5. Duplicate it to distribute to students (if you prefer them to work individually or in small groups), or use the opaque projector or overhead projector or chalk board (if you prefer them to work as a total class). Tell students to find a unifying principle or theme in the list of details and to state a topic sentence covering as many of the given details as possible. Have them draw lines through details which do not fit their topic sentence and determine which method of development is most appropriate for their topic sentence. Possible answers are underscored; do not include these when reproducing details.

   A. *frequent dusty detours*
      signs and arrows re-directing traffic
      a red schoolhouse on a hill
      heavy equipment at work
      great piles of gravel
      garbage in a ditch
      cement mixers
      clouds of dust hovering over earth-moving machines
      birds flying overhead
      cows grazing peacefully in nearby fields
      workmen in colorful hard hats
      huge steam shovels gulping broken cement
      school children waiting for a bus

      Unifying Theme: dirty, busy road construction
      Eliminate: schoolhouse, garbage, birds, cows, and children
      Topic Sentence: We spent at least half of our tour driving through the dirt and
                      excitement of major road construction
      Method of Development: description

   B. *bleachers full of colorfully dressed spectators*
      dust rising from parking fields nearby
      the plunk of hard-hit balls on the clay
      applause after a long volley
      chefs busy at work in the clubhouse kitchen
      ball chasers scurrying out of the way
      swaying shade trees on the golf course
      spontaneous groan from crowd at missed lob
      tournament brought in $93,471.32
      crisp calls of line judges
      brilliance of white tennis costumes in the sun
      rising tension at each crucial point
      borders of scarlet geraniums edging the spectators' area

      Unifying Theme: vividness and excitement of tennis match
      Eliminate: dust, chefs, breeze, tournament take
      Topic Sentence: Excitement quivered in the brilliant summer air as the match pro-
                      gressed. Or: The tennis match was a scene of color and rising
                      excitement.

Method of Development: description

C. he was so harsh with his son that he left home
    his eating habits became irregular
    he carried on a continuous argument with his daughter over her dress
    he read the morning paper
    one day he told his boss that he disapproved of his methods of management
    he began drinking early in the day
    he quit attending church
    he read only best sellers
    he picked arguments with his long-suffering wife
    he refused to see his doctor or his psychiatrist
    he voted in all elections, as usual
    he was cruel to the dog, and even kicked him in the ribs one day
    he withdrew from lodge activities
    he had always enjoyed fishing
    he was a Yale graduate

Unifying Theme: disintegration of a man
Eliminate: morning paper, best sellers, voting, fishing, Yale
*Topic Sentence: As time went by, we watched him turn into someone very different
           from the George we had known.*
Method of Development: narrative

D. the Flurry rally was scheduled for 2:00 p.m., March 3, 1923
    4,000 people gathered at the site
    seventy-nine people were arrested
    there was a fire at 93rd Street
    fourteen people were hospitalized
    traffic was stalled for a six block area around the scene
    the speaker was to have been J. Singleton Flurry
    all but four of those arrested were released
    two persons were kept in the hospital overnight
    I don't like J. Singleton Flurry
    if the demonstrators had stayed out of the way, maybe the police could have done a
        better job
    the demonstrators opposing Flurry marched in the streets
    people should not flock to the scene of a riot
    the speaker's stand was demolished
    fire hoses finally dispersed the last of the crowd

Unifying Theme: report of a rally, demonstration and riot
*Eliminate: fire at 93rd Street, I don't like. . . . if the demonstrators. . . . people
           should not flock. . . .*
*Topic Sentence: The rally honoring J. Singleton Flurry ended with arrests and
           injuries after a demonstration by his opponents turned into a riot.*
Method of Development: Facts

E. it will not rise adequately without kneading
    the dough will be lumpy
    the final product will be heavy and dense
    bread is the staff of life
    yeast needs to be worked into every particle of the dough
    kneading works air into the dough, guaranteeing lightness
    kneading provides even texture
    kneading spreads yeast evenly, so when it ferments, it will cause tiny bubbles of
       carbon dioxide throughout the dough
    kneading is fun
    carbon dioxide bubbles stretch gluten in flour, thus leavening the bread

Unifying Theme: purpose and importance of kneading in making bread
Eliminate: staff of life, kneading is fun

Topic Sentence: Kneading is a very important part of bread making.
Method of Development: Explanation

F. *Gauguin did some of his most sensational work when he was wasting away with disease*
Toulouse-Lautrec was badly crippled as a result of a riding accident in his youth
Virginia Woolf suffered from precarious mental health and spent time in mental hospitals
Beethoven suffered from progressive deafness which finally became complete
Julius Caesar was an epileptic
John Milton lost his eyesight years before he wrote Paradise Lost
Franklin D. Roosevelt lost the use of his legs as a result of an attack of polio
Van Gogh continued to paint even when he was committed to an asylum
Sylvia Plath had periodic depressions which finally drove her to suicide
Marilyn Monroe had a tragic life

Unifying Theme: artists, writers, musical composers with mental or physical illnesses
Eliminate: Caesar, Roosevelt, Monroe
Topic Sentence: Many of the world's most renowned artists, authors and composers accomplished their great works in spite of the ravages of mental or physical illness.
Method of Development: Examples

13. *Activity.* Assign the class one place, person, event, or situation to consider. Tell them to make a list of the elements they identify, to look for a unifying theme or principle, to state a topic sentence and to eliminate all irrelevant details, to choose the means of development which is most suitable, and to write a paragraph. This is probably best done with students working individually, especially if they've done most of the preceding activities as a total group. Then have students share their paragraphs by reading them aloud in class, so they can compare to see how similarly or differently they perceived the same assigned subject.

TOPIC III: PUTTING DEVELOPMENTAL DETAILS IN THE BEST ORDER

1. *Teacher Presentation.*   Remind students that the developmental details of a paragraph consist of such things as statements of fact, reasons why, examples, causes, effects, steps in a sequence, component parts, explanatory statements, logical arguments, descriptive details, and events that form a narrative. Call to their attention that since only one statement can be written or read at a time, a writer must choose the order in which statements will come in the paragraph, and the choice should be based on some reason. In choosing an order for developmental details, many writers are guided by the following principles:

> *Climactic Order:* small to large, trivial to significant, inconspicuous to conspicuous, lacking in value to very valuable, fairly persuasive to absolutely clinching, etc.
>
> *Sequential:* chronological, steps in a process, numbers in a series, logical structure built argument by argument as in causation.
>
> *Spatial:* from place to place in order, from one element to those surrounding it, from near to far, from left to right.
>
> *Contrast:* either all aspects of one thing and then all of the other, or a point-by-point alternation.

2. *Activity.* Working with the class as a whole, give students the topic sentences and

accompanying details provided below. (Use Reproduction Page 6 to either duplicate and distribute the lists or to project them with overhead or opaque.) Have
the class read the topic sentence and decide what type of order might be the best
for the developmental details under each. Then have them number the details in
order. There may well be some legitimate disagreement, and this is to be expected. The important thing is that students learn to consciously order details.
Answers appear at the end of the list and are underscored.

A. *Topic Sentence:* *The lawn was a disgraceful mess.*
   Details: *weeds among flowers*
   pile of dead branches to one side
   an old automobile chassis beside the porch
   instead of grass there were weeds and bare, worn places
   bushes unpruned
   cement on front walk broken and crumbling
   fence sagging on left side of yard
   fence broken entirely on right side
   Best order is probably spatially as writer moves up walk to house.

B. *Topic Sentence:* *The conference went on all day.*
   Details: *opening speech at 9:00*
   lunch at 12:00
   pre-conference breakfast at 7:30
   workshops at 2:00 and 4:00
   cocktail hour
   seminar at 10:30
   Chronological order is probably best.

C. *Topic Sentence:* *He persuaded her to stay in the class.*
   Details: *he felt she would learn a lot*
   he told her it would get more interesting
   he thought she would enjoy the new people coming in
   he would flunk her if she dropped out
   Climactic order.

D. *Topic Sentence:* *She decided not to try for early graduation.*
   Details: *would have to go to summer school*
   none of her friends were graduating early
   her father opposed her graduating early
   she felt she was not yet ready for college
   there were still some courses at the high school she wanted to take
   Climactic order.

3. *Activity.* Using Reproduction Page 7, reproduce the paragraphs provided below
   either by duplicating or projecting with overhead or opaque. Have students
   (either as an entire class or working in two's and three's) read the paragraphs and
   determine what weaknesses they contain in the order of the details. Have students decide on a better order for the details and number them accordingly.
   When all have finished, have the groups or individuals compare what they have
   done and see if they agree.

A. *When you are baking a cake, it is important to double-check the ingredients as you
   put each one in. Being wrong with just one tablespoon of salt can mean an inedible
   cake rather than one of which you may be proud. Your first task is to read the recipe
   thoroughly and make sure you have all the ingredients on hand. The orderly habit of
   putting everything away after you have used it is also a good one to cultivate. Mix the
   ingredients in the order and in the manner instructed by your recipe. Be sure to turn
   your oven to the proper setting at the very beginning, so that by the time your batter
   is prepared, the oven is properly preheated. It is wise, also, to prepare your pan at the*

beginning, to avoid having to stop and do so at the last minute. If you follow your recipe carefully, there is no reason you cannot succeed every time you bake a cake.

B. *The history of the school was a chronicle of constant expansion and construction. An entire new wing of classrooms was added when the school was only five years old. The original building was finished in 1958 and had only nineteen classrooms. Completed in 1963, the new wing added six more classrooms as well as additional library space. The original library seated only fifty-eight students. The gymnasium was doubled in size by construction undertaken in 1971, making it possible for the girls to have their own facilities, and in 1972, the pool, which had been part of the construction plan of 1968, was completed after two years of work. The original library and gymnasium had been planned and built to allow for ease of enlargement. Plans for their expansion had been presented even prior to the 1968 addition, but unfortunately the district voted against such an improvement at that time. The school board was pleased that the district approved the new gymnasium and pool as well as the new wing.*

C. *Some students felt that there had been any number of occasions when the administration might have closed down the smoking lounge before the event which finally caused them to take action. For instance, there was a week early in the school year when freshmen who had come from the two different junior high schools began expressing animosity for one another, and several fist fights broke out when the faculty supervisor was not watching. Even worse, perhaps, was the time in January when a group of so-called "jocks" harrassed a group of chorus students and a real free-for-all broke out before order was restored. Fortunately, or so the student smokers felt, the girl who was paralyzed after being shoved down a flight of stairs outside the lounge was withdrawn from school by her parents, and the administration failed to connect her injury with the smoking lounge. Trash was scattered all over the area by student groups expressing displeasure with various actions by the principal, and the student committee charged with emptying ashtrays and policing the lounge quietly withdrew from business early in the year. Another example of student misuse of the lounge could be seen in the graffiti of all degrees of obscentiy which quickly defaced the walls.*

D. *Mrs. Burnell's yard showed the hours she spent each week caring for it. The flower border which stretched across the entire lot at the head of the house was a triumph of the industrious gardener. Not a weed could be seen among the rows and clumps of yellow daisies and dahlias, multicolored zinnia and cosmos, and flaming poppies. Just as vivid were the clumps of scarlet salvia by the sidewalk leading to the front door. On either side of the white cement walk, near the doorstep, were neatly clipped beds of English ivy. The picket fence which ran entirely around the property also supported occasional tendrils of ivy, as well as one scarlet climber rose to the right of the front gate. Other roses appeared occasionally down the left side of the yard, which itself looked like a lovingly protected putting green, with hardly a blade of grass standing out from its fellows. No crabgrass was tolerated here, and no dandelion ever profaned the perfect expanse of velvet green.*

E. *When I was eight years old, my family moved to a house very different from any home I had known before. When I was two, we lived in an old farmhouse with a large yard and huge elm trees shading the area where I played. That had been a wonderful place for a child to play. I had a fine play place later, also, when I was seven and we had a suburban bungalow with an enclosed yard and garden. It was from this bungalow that my father moved us—my mother, brother and me—to a townhouse in downtown Buffalo. Here there were no lawns, only sidewalks and streets and asphalt parking areas. I missed having a place to play. Even when we had lived in Chicago, during my first years at school, we were near a park, so that I didn't mind not having a yard. But in Buffalo we were far from any park, and my brother and I were not allowed to go far from home by ourselves. My mother solved our problem, finally, by converting the unused room on the third floor of our house into a play room, and here my brother and I spent many happy hours during the three years we stayed in Buffalo.*

4. *Activity.* Assign students at random to pairs or trios and provide them with a subject or a list of subjects from which to choose. Ask them to:
   1. list developmental details about each subject,
   2. arrive at a topic sentence, and then
   3. list the usable details *in order,* eliminating any details that don't pertain to the topic sentence.

   Then you may wish to have students, working individually from this point, write a paragraph based on the one ordered list of developmental details prepared by their group. The paragraphs could be read aloud and compared.

5. *Activity.* Have each student make a list of details that describe his or her bedroom and then find a unifying theme or principle and state this in a topic sentence. Each student should then place the list of usable details in order (identifying the ordering principle) and write a paragraph to be shared with the class or with one other student.

6. *Activity.* Have each student write a paragraph telling how to wash a car or perform some other common operation. Require students to follow the usual steps in writing the paragraph:
   1. make a list of details
   2. compose a topic sentence
   3. list the usable details in a logical order (in this case students will probably use sequential or chronological order)
   4. write the paragraph

7. *Activity.* Have each student write a paragraph giving examples of people who have had a great influence on him or her. Suggest that students follow these steps:
   1. make a list of people who have been influential
   2. arrive at a topic sentence that includes most of the people named
   3. decide on an appropriate order (i.e.: climactic or chronological)
   4. list the usable examples in the proper order, eliminating those that are not included in the topic sentence
   5. write the paragraph

8. *Activity.* Have students write a paragraph using one of the sentences below as their topic sentence:

   Basketball is more exciting than football for the spectators.

   The duties of the guards differ from those of the tackles.

   British rock groups have a musical style that is noticeably different from that of American groups.

   Cats make better pets than dogs.

   Require them to choose a means of organizing the details that makes the contrast clearly apparent.

9. *Activity.* Have students list, in writing, the steps one must go through to write a completely detailed and orderly paragraph about a place, person, thing, event, or situation. Have them meet in small groups to discuss how their lists differ and to reach an agreement on one list of steps.

10. *Evaluation.* Have students choose one topic sentence from the list in Teacher Presentation #1 on pages 26–27 and write a properly developed paragraph with details in a consciously chosen order. Have them exchange papers and evaluate the extent to which the principles learned so far were applied in writing the paragraph; or have them submit papers to you for grading.

TOPIC IV: MAKING THE PARAGRAPH FLOW SMOOTHLY

1. *Teacher Presentation.* Once students have learned to formulate a topic sentence and list developmental details in some sort of logical order, the paragraphs they write will be much improved, but often they will lack the essential ingredient of coherence. That is, the student writer will produce something that sounds more like a grocery list than a paragraph. Thus it is important to show students how to tie their sentences together and fill in the awkward gaps that sometimes occur between one statement and the next so that their paragraphs won't read like stilted, boring lists.

   Perhaps the most common means of achieving coherence—and luckily, the easiest to learn—is the use of logical connections and linking constructions. These are simply words or phrases which emphasize the logic of what is expressed while tying sentences and parts of sentences more closely together. The following list of various types of connecting expressions can be written on the board or projected for students to copy, or it can be reproduced and distributed to them. A good writer will make conscious use of this list when checking and revising his or her work.

   - CONNECTORS INDICATING TIME: soon, next, then, later, finally, first, second
   - CONNECTORS INDICATING CONTRAST: but, on the other hand, however, nevertheless, otherwise, yet
   - CONNECTORS INDICATING A SEQUENCE: in addition, also, furthermore, moreover, another, likewise, similarly, next, finally, besides, first, second
   - CONNECTORS INDICATING RESULTS: therefore, hence, because, thus, consequently, as a result, for
   - CONNECTORS INDICATING EXAMPLES: for instance, an example of this, for example, take the case of

2. *Activity.* Using Reproduction Page 8, reproduce with spirit duplicator or project with opaque or overhead the paragraph below, written by twelfth grade student Joe Finkelstein. Have students circle all the connecting devices that they can identify in the paragraph. Then go through the paragraph pointing out each connector and discussing with the class how it functions in the paragraph. (Connectors are underscored.)

   The reason for the Philadelphia Eagles' success in the National Football League was new General Manager and Coach Joe Kuharick. Virtually all of the Eagles' weaknesses were filled either by his trades or by his signing of draft choices. <u>For instance</u>, Kuharick saw that the initial need was a pile-driving fullback to complement the break-away running of his speedy halfback, Tim Brown. <u>Hence</u>, Earl Groe was acquired from the

Green Bay Packers. However, his trading was not Kuharick's only accomplishment. He also had the knack of switching players from position to position in order to produce a diversified offense and an aggressive defense. For example, when his star halfback Tim Brown was injured, rookie Jack Concannon was placed in his halfback position. This was an especially interesting maneuver since the use of Concannon, who was a star quarterback at Boston College, gave him not only an excellent running threat, but a continual passing threat as well. Likewise, on defense, players were shuttled in and out, especially at the linebacker position. In this instance Maxie Baugh and Dave Lloyd were alternated constantly, depending on whether the situation called for the quarterback to be rushed or not. Although these accomplishments were great, there was another thing that Kuharick did which was even greater. Because of the Eagles' last place finish each of the past two years, there was much dissension on the Eagles' team. Even the ownership changed hands. Kuharick instilled a new spirit into the team. Now the Eagles were playing to win, as a team, and each individual was not just out for himself. Joe Kuharick did a remarkable job in making a successful team out of one that was struggling in last place just one short year ago.

3. *Activity.* Using Reproduction Page 9, reproduce with spirit duplicator or project with opaque or overhead the paragraph below, which is badly in need of logical connectors. Ask students, working in pairs or individually as you prefer, to put in links wherever they think connectors are needed. Then have the class share and discuss their answers.

> *The continued success of the Red Legs gave rise to several unexpected and not wholly desirable consequences. The team as a whole began to show signs of overconfidence. Their play on the field became just a little sloppy. Their activities off the field began to include certain lapses of training discipline. There were instances of rudeness toward fans who wanted autographs. Four players became loud and boisterous on a commercial airlines flight. They were actually ejected from the plane at the next scheduled landing. The team's playing became less sloppy after the manager imposed a few stiff penalties. He made it clear that the mark of a true champion lay in the ability to handle success as well as failure. He made it clear that any player who behaved in a rude or overbearing manner would be suspended. The team settled down and began to behave more acceptably both on and off the field.*

4. *Activity.* Have students examine paragraphs that they themselves have written for previous activities to see if they would profit from the insertion of logical connectors. Ask them to put a check at any point in the text where a connector would help, and to write the connecting word or phrase in the margin at the end of the line. (It might be helpful to have students keep all written work in a folder so that early work can be used for activities such as this one.)

5. *Teacher Presentation.* If writing is to be coherent and easy to read, writers must develop the habit of consistency. They must be consistent in the use of the same subject throughout the paragraph, in the words used to refer to the same subject, and in the verb tense in which the subject of the paragraph is placed. They must, for example, avoid starting out with "Students are . . ." and then switching to "The student is . . ." and to "He was . . ." If they start out with a plural form of the subject, they must continue with plural forms. And if they are telling a story or summarizing a plot in the present tense, they must stick to the present tense throughout. If students find it difficult to control these inconsistencies in their writing, they will profit from learning to correct them consciously as part of the process of revising.

6. *Activity.* Paragraph A below is incoherent because there is a different gram-

matical subject in almost every sentence. Reproduce or project it (using Reproduction Page 10) and read it aloud with the class so they can "hear" the incoherence. Then ask students (either individually or as part of a total-class discussion) to rewrite the paragraph sticking to one subject throughout. When they have finished rewriting, have some students read their revisions aloud to see if the coherence has been improved. Paragraph B (on Reproduction Page 11) can be used as an example of one way of revising paragraph A to improve the coherence. Repeat the procedure with paragraph C below (on Reproduction Page 12) in which the subject changes so many times the paragraph moves away from the subject of the topic sentence. After students have rewritten paragraph C, you may wish to show them paragraph D, in which the writer sticks more closely to the subject of the topic sentence (available on Reproduction Page 13).

A. *Advance planning is half the secret of a good party. A wise hostess will want to examine her guest list and plan the sort of party those particular guests will most enjoy. Some people like a non-alcoholic punch, while others will feel cheated unless the refreshments include alcoholic beverages of some kind. Food is also a matter the hostess should consider carefully ahead of time. Dieters will not appreciate an array of creamy, high calorie goodies, but neither will the happy eaters enjoy munching carrot sticks and celery. The food, in short, will need to be planned to fit all the guests. Entertainment is also a matter concerning which guests might have a wide range of preferences. Young people tend to want a loud background of rock music, while quiet semi-classical or show music is usually more pleasing to adults. Pencil and paper games delight some guests, particularly adults, but dancing or quiet conversation is the choice of others. All these questions must be solved ahead of time if you are to be sure of a successful party.*

B. *The experienced hostess knows that advance planning is half the secret of a good party. She will want to study her guest list and plan the sort of party those particular guests will most enjoy. She will want to know ahead of time which of her guests might prefer a non-alcoholic punch and which would feel cheated if she did not serve some kind of alcoholic beverage. If she is planning to feed her guests, the hostess will carefully consider what foods will be most suitable for her dieting guests while at the same time she will plan something a bit more palatable than carrot sticks and celery for those guests who eat heartily regardless of calories. The skilled party giver is also aware that guests may well have a wide range of preferences in entertainment. If her guests are all young, she may choose a loud background of rock music for dancing or listening, but if she is entertaining adults, she may prepare a program of show records or light classical music. She will be prepared for the possibility that some guests might enjoy cards or pen and pencil games as well as the likelihood that others would enjoy simply conversing or, perhaps, dancing. She will, in short, be thoroughly prepared to give a very successful party.*

C. *The police officers who patrol the northeast district of the city must cope with problems more numerous and complex than those of any other section of the inner city. The population density is the highest in the city, even though the district itself is the smallest in terms of city blocks. The nineteen eight-story buildings in the Jefferson Street high-rise housing project partially account for the large number of people living in such a restricted ground area. The narrow streets, shallow building lots, and almost hidden alleyways and inner courtyards are so densely crowded with old tenement buildings, multifamily houses, shacks, and sheds that fleeing criminals easily find a haven. Traffic in heroin and cocaine is heavy in the northeast district, and many known criminals live in the area. Glittering pastel Cadillacs are often seen parked amid the litter of the filthy streets, and at any time of day or night the painted street girls may be seen sallying forth to make their way to the more prosperous areas to the south. Known underworld characters live and work next door to pimps and numbers racketeers in this most multi-racial and ecumenical of neighborhoods. Most of the churches which once served the community have boarded up their broken windows and moved to the suburbs, and the school survives only with the help of armed guards. Yet, amid all this social refuse live many helpless, frightened citizens who need and value the help of the police.*

D. *The police officers who patrol the northeast district of the city must cope with problems more numerous and complex than those of any other section of the inner city. They must cope with a population density which is the highest in the city, even though the district itself is the smallest in terms of city blocks. In the center of their patrol area are the nineteen eight-story buildings of the Jefferson Street high-rise housing project, which partially accounts for the large number of people living in such a restricted area. In other parts of the district the police are forced to find their way through a warren of narrow streets, shallow building lots, and almost hidden alleyways and inner courtyards so densely crowded with old tenement buildings, multi-family houses, shacks, and sheds that the fleeing criminal can easily find a haven the police cannot penetrate. Here, also, the police are faced with the city's heaviest traffic in heroin and cocaine, and they must maintain surveillance over the many known criminals who live in the area. They observe with frustration the glittering pastel Cadillacs parked amid the litter of the filthy streets and watch the painted street girls sally forth at all hours of the day and night to take their wares to the more prosperous areas to the south. They try to keep order on the streets where known underworld characters live and work next door to pimps and numbers racketeers, and where they receive little help from any other source. They have watched church organizations which once served the community board up their broken windows and move away, and they give what help they can to the armed guards who patrol the school. Yet, amid all this social refuse live many helpless, frightened citizens who need and value the help of the police.*

7. *Activity.* Paragraph A below is incoherent because there are a number of verbs in the passive voice. As a result the reader is kept in the dark about the *subject* of the verb and the coherent flow of meaning is impeded. Using Reproduction Page 14, reproduce paragraph A or project it and read it aloud with the class so they can "hear" the incoherence. Then ask students (either individually or as part of a total-class discussion) to rewrite the paragraph, putting all verbs in the active form and providing a subject for each verb. When they have finished rewriting, have some students read their revisions aloud to see if the coherence has been improved. Paragraph B (on Reproduction Page 15) can be used as an example of one way of revising paragraph A to improve the coherence by eliminating passive verbs. (Point out that it is not always desirable to eliminate all passive verbs, as it sometimes allows the writer to avoid bringing in other grammatical subjects: "The moment he put his hand into the hole it was seized by. . . .") Repeat the procedure with paragraph C below (available on Reproduction Page 16) which also lacks coherence because of frequent use of passive voice. After students have rewritten paragraph C, you may wish to show them paragraph D, which indicates one way the coherence could be improved (Reproduction Page 17).

A. *As our car was driven through the gate, it was swung shut behind us, and our car was driven on. As we approached the next gate, it also was opened at our command. Our car was eyed with suspicion, but no stones were thrown, and no epithets were shouted that could be heard in the car. We had been promised that the way would be cleared for us, and it must be acknowledged that the pledge was meticulously honored.*

B. *As Pedro drove our car through the gate, the keeper pulled it shut behind us and we drove on down the road. Soon we saw another gate ahead, but in spite of some trepi-*

dation, we were able to pass through immediately upon showing our official pass to the guard. We saw groups of sullen peasants eyeing us with suspicion; but we had received a pledge that the road to the border would be clear for us, and that pledge was meticulously honored.

C. *A garden should be planned very carefully before a single seed is planted. Plans must be made not only for all the space that is available but also for all the time provided by your growing season. Each vegetable must be selected not only because it is enjoyed by your family and recommended by nutritionists, but also because the time taken in growing from seed to table is not out of proportion to the number of vegetables which can be produced by each plant. For instance, zucchini squash takes only forty-five days from seed to table, and once the first squash appears, if every succeeding one is picked before it reaches a length of eight or so inches, more squash will be produced steadily until the vines are killed by frost. It can be seen, therefore, that the space occupied by each zucchini plant is utilized productively. A similar extended productivity can be expected from tomatoes, green peppers, Swiss chard, and broccoli, and these vegetables are, hence, prized by home gardeners. Root vegetables, on the other hand, such as carrots, parsnips or radishes, produce only one vegetable for every seed, and should be planted only when the gardener knows they are well liked by the family.*

D. *Home gardeners should plan their gardens carefully before they plant a single seed. They must plan not only for the space available to them but also for the time the growing season provides. They should select each vegetable they will grow not only because their families like it and because it has nutritional value, but because the time it will take in growing from seed to ripeness is not out of proportion with the number of vegetables each plant will produce. For instance, gardeners should know that zucchini squash takes only forty-five days from seed to ripeness, and that once they pick the first squash the plant will continue to produce right up to frost, as long as they pick each squash before it exceeds approximately 8" in length. Thus, they will utilize space productively by planting zucchini. They should know that they can expect a similar kind of extended productivity from tomatoes, green peppers, Swiss chard and broccoli, but that root vegetables such as radishes, carrots, and parsnips produce only one vegetable for each seed. They will want to be sure their families are fond of such one-shot vegetables before they devote a great deal of limited garden space to them.*

8. *Activity.* Paragraph A below is incoherent because it contains many errors in point of view. The writer did not choose the person and number of the subject and stick to them faithfully throughout. Using Reproduction Page 18, reproduce paragraph A or project it and read it aloud with the class so they can "hear" the incoherence. Then ask students (either individually or as part of a total class discussion) to rewrite the paragraph with a consistent point of view. When they have finished rewriting, have some students read their revisions aloud to see if the coherence is improved. Paragraph B (on Reproduction Page 19) can be used as an example of one way of revising paragraph A to improve the coherence by making point of view consistent. Repeat the procedure with paragraph C below (on Reproduction Page 20), which also lacks coherence because of frequent shifts in point of view. After students have rewritten paragraph C, you may wish to show them paragraph D, which indicates one way the coherence could be improved (available on Reproduction Page 21).

A. *Students often dislike a teacher because they do not understand him or her. It is not uncommon, for instance, for a student to make a negative judgment of a teacher and consequently have a bad experience in his or her other class as a result of a simple cultural difference to which, in all fairness, no blame should be attached. We tend to judge teachers by standards more stringent than those one applies to himself, and, as a* result, to put up artificial barriers which prevent a pleasant and productive relationship from developing between yourself and the teacher. The student is the one who loses in such a situation, and sometimes our loss is a great one, indeed. You will do well to remind yourself that teachers—in addition to being teachers—are husbands, fathers (wives and mothers), wage earners, bill payers, voters, gardeners, and a host of other things. And we will profit from learning to regard them in the context of their total personhood.

B. Students often dislike a teacher because they do not understand him or her. It is not uncommon, for instance, for students to make a negative judgment of a teacher and, consequently, to have a bad experience in his or her class as a result of a simple cultural difference to which, in all fairness, no blame should be attached. Students tend to judge teachers by standards more stringent than those by which they judge themselves, and, as a result, to put up artificial barriers which prevent pleasant and productive relationships from developing between themselves and certain teachers. Students are the ones who lose in such situations, and sometimes their loss is a great one, indeed. They would do well to remind themselves that teachers—in addition to being teachers—are also husbands and fathers (or wives and mothers), wage earners, bill payers, voters, gardeners, and a host of other things. And students will profit from learning to regard them in the context of their total personhood.

C. I have observed that careful young drivers strongly resent the endless criticism heaped on the youthful driver as a class. They feel, and rightly so, that there is every kind of young driver, just as there are all degrees of skill among older drivers, and it is unfair to tar all with the same brush. The young fellow of nineteen who has never so much as had a parking ticket should not be unthinkingly lumped with the relatively small number of careless speed demons who create unfavorable statistics with regard to the youthful driver. One can understand their feelings.

D. I have observed that careful young drivers strongly resent the endless criticism heaped on youthful drivers as a class. They feel, and rightly so, that there are all kinds of young drivers just as there are all degrees of skill among older drivers, and it is unfair to tar all with the same brush. They believe that young fellows of nineteen who have never had so much as a parking ticket do not deserve to be lumped with the careless speed demons who create unfavorable statistics for their age group. I can understand their feelings.

9. *Activity.* Paragraph A below demonstrates how inconsistency in verb tense can reduce coherence. This problem often arises when students are summarizing the plot of a story or movie, or when they are describing an episode from their own experience. You might wish to remind them that it is customary to write plot summaries in the present tense. Using Reproduction Page 22, reproduce paragraph A or project it and read it aloud with the class so they can "hear" the incoherence. Then ask students (either individually or as part of a total class discussion) to rewrite the paragraph, correcting the inconsistencies in verb tense. When they have finished rewriting, have some students read their revisions aloud to see if the coherence has been improved. Paragraph B (Reproduction Page 23) can be used as an example of one way of revising paragraph A to improve the coherence by making verb tense consistent. Repeat the procedure with paragraph C below (using Reproduction Page 24), which also lacks coherence because of frequent shifts in verb tense. After students have rewritten paragraph C, you may wish to show them paragraph D (available on Reproduction Page 25), which indicates one way the coherence could be improved.

A. The children poured on to the beach from the landing boat in a confused and noisy stream. Struggling to find their way to safety and fearful that the boat will pull away *before they are safely ashore, they push and shove against those in the front ranks, heedless of the additional danger this creates. John, who was sitting in the stern of the craft before it reached the shore, was one of the last children to disembark. He looks around frantically, searching for his little sister, Susan, whom he last saw on the dock before they were placed aboard the big ship. Where was she?*

B. *The children poured onto the beach from the landing boat in a confused and noisy stream. Struggling to find their way to safety and fearful that the boat would pull away before they were safely ashore, they pushed and shoved against those in the front ranks, heedless of the additional danger this created. John, who had been sitting in the stern of the craft before it reached the shore, was one of the last children to disembark. He looked around frantically, searching for his little sister, Susan, whom he had last seen on the dock before they were placed aboard the big ship. Where was she?*

C. *The basement looked as if everything that had ever come into it was still there, stacked in random layers through which one moves at one's own risk. Beside the entrance door, on the left, is a leaning tower of crates, some containing whole sets of books which were obviously never even unpacked and some overflowing with an accumulation of daily newspapers whose dates, one can see, stretched far into the past. Nothing seems ever to be thrown out. From the ceiling beams, dimly discernible in the feeble light from my flashlight, hang various sizes of wheels and tires and other parts of what might once upon a time have been unicycles or bicycles. And stacked in unbelievable disorder throughout the whole area were crates, baskets, bins, and boxes holding heaven only knows what and interspersed with, leaning against, and falling upon such objects as statues, paintings, urns, ship models, rolled up carpets, and, far to the back, in regal splendor, a gigantic cigarstore Indian who surveys the accumulated flotsam through unswerving and opaque eyes.*

D. *The basement looked as if everything that had ever come into it was still there, stacked in random layers through which one moved at one's own risk. Beside the entrance door, on the left, was a leaning tower of crates, some containing whole sets of books which had obviously never even been unpacked and some overflowing with an accumulation of daily newspapers whose dates, one could see, stretched far into the past. Nothing seemed ever to have been thrown out. From the ceiling beams, dimly discernible in the feeble light from my flashlight, hung various sizes of wheels and tires and other parts of what might once have been unicycles or bicycles. And stacked in unbelievable disorder throughout the whole area were crates, baskets, bins, and boxes holding heaven only knew what and interspersed with, leaning against and falling upon such objects as statues, paintings, urns, ship models, rolled-up carpets, and, far to the back, brooding in regal splendor, a gigantic cigarstore Indian who surveyed the accumulated flotsam through unswerving and opaque eyes.*

10. *Teacher Presentation.* Point out to students that one sure way to produce incoherent writing is to put together a succession of short, simple sentences as children do. This makes for rough, choppy reading which simply cannot hold a reader's interest for very long. Since not all sentences in a paragraph are of equal importance, there is no need for the writer to give them equal emphasis. When one sentence is less important than another sentence, the less important statement can be made subordinate to the statement that should be emphasized. And in the case of statements of equal importance, it is often good to connect them, rather than letting each statement stand as a short, simple sentence. It is by a judicious combination of connection and subordination that the skillful writer avoids the effect of sloppy, childish writing. Demonstrate this principle to students by reproducing by spirit duplicator or projecting paragraph A below (using Reproduction Page 26), which contains virtually no connection or subordination.

Help students see how awkward and choppy the paragraph is. Then show them paragraph B (available on Reproduction Page 27) in which connection and subordination have been utilized to improve coherence.

A. *I was in the valley. I could not see the old church building. I climbed up on a nearby outcropping of rock. It reached thirty feet above the valley floor. I could see much farther. I could see trees in a bend. I could see trees in a curving line. They were following the river's bend. I could see a hill on the other side of the river. On it I could see the old church building. The steeple caught the sun's last rays. It was white against the darkening evening sky.*

B. *From where I was on the floor of the valley, I could not see the old church building. However, observing a nearby outcropping of rock which reached a height of almost thirty feet, I climbed to its top and discovered that I could see much farther. In the distance, a graceful line of trees followed the river's bend, and on the other side of the river, on a low hill, I could see the old church, its steeple a brilliant white in the sun's last rays against the darkening evening sky.*

11. *Activity.* Have students, working individually or in pairs, rewrite the following paragraph of short simple sentences, using subordination and connection to improve coherence. (The paragraph is available on Reproduction Page 28.)

    He ran up the front steps. He burst through the door. The door slammed noisily against the wall. He didn't stop to close the door. He raced through the rooms. He kept calling Peter's name. His voice was hoarse and frantic with fear. He wanted to find Peter. He was afraid of what he might find. He raced upstairs. He flung open doors to bedrooms and closets. He raced back downstairs. He went down into the basement. A noise, half scream, half groan, burst from him. I stood at the top of the steps. I was afraid to go down. I knew what he had found.

12. *Activity.* Put students in pairs or small groups and announce one topic sentence for all to use. (See list in Teacher Presentation #1 on pages 26–27.) Instruct students to list developmental details that support or specify the topic sentence and put them in logical order for a paragraph. Then have students, working individually, write the paragraph in short simple sentences. Ask them to exchange with one another and have each student rewrite, using subordination and connection and other means of improving coherence to improve the other student's paragraph. Students may be interested in hearing or seeing some of the most dramatically improved paragraphs.

13. *Teacher Presentation.* Explain to students that a basic way for the writer to achieve coherence is to make sure that he or she leaves no gaps in thought. The reader can move successfully and smoothly along the sequence of thoughts the writer has prepared if the writer has been sure to say exactly and completely what he or she means instead of assuming that the reader will be glad to figure it out and fill in the gaps. Only a few readers are willing to go to that trouble (and most of them are English teachers). Few will be interested in a paragraph full of "holes"—places between sentences where more needs to be said but is omitted. At best, the reader will know *generally* what the writer means, rather than exactly, and the paragraph will stagger and stutter along, rather than flowing smoothly and coherently.

14. *Activity.* Using Reproduction Page 29, duplicate paragraphs A and B below with a spirit duplicator (or project them using an opaque or overhead). Have students discuss and agree, if possible, on exactly what the writer meant. Help them see

that because the writer has left glaring gaps in thought, he or she leaves to the reader much of the work of filling in the holes. You might wish to have students work in pairs in trying to figure out the writer's meaning and then have the pairs share their opinions with the class and see if there is agreement. Note that paragraphs C and D (available on Reproduction Page 30) indicate how the gaps might be filled in.

A. *I have always said that "come the holocaust," I would want to be somewhere in the country with my mother. My mother was a country woman, born on a small farm in Missouri near the end of the 19th century. She had many skills her city daughters know nothing of, and she possessed a rich fund of old-time lore. She knew how to do many things that would be important to survival. After all, she was poor all her life. She was also accustomed to fending for herself and solving her own problems. When I was a child there were few things she could not fix more skillfully than could my city-bred father.*

B. *The porch was a shambles. There had been a storm in our absence, and the neighbor's dog had gotten in through a broken window. Apparently there had been a strong wind which played havoc with potted plants and hanging flower baskets.*

C. *I have always said that "come the holocaust," when survival would be the only issue, I would want to be somewhere in the country with my mother. My mother was a country woman, born on a small farm in Missouri near the end of the 19th century. Like all farm women of that time, she had many skills her city daughters know nothing of, and she possessed a rich fund of old-time lore which could mean the difference between living or dying in a time when there would be no stores, doctors, or hospitals, and little medicine. She knew how to find a spring, spear a fish, butcher and skin an animal, set a trap, make soap, and do many other things that would be important to survival. After all, she was poor all her childhood, and poverty forced her and her brothers and sisters to learn many lessons which her more affluent children never had occasion to learn. She was accustomed to fending for herself and solving her own problems, which is a kind of independence we city people often lose, finding it easier to call a plumber or an electrician. When I was a child, I remember, there were few things she could not fix more skillfully than could my city-bred father.*

D. *The porch was a shambles. There had been a storm in our absence, and the wind had blown in a window so that rainwater had drenched the rug and furniture, and the neighbor's dog had gotten in through a broken window, rooted through all the containers and left muddy tracks over everything. Apparently there had been a strong wind, which played havoc with potted plants and hanging flower baskets. Broken planters lay in shattered pieces on the floor and potting soil formed a thick mud over all.*

15. *Activity.* Duplicate Reproduction Page 31 and have students rewrite paragraphs A and B, filling in gaps in thought to improve coherence. Paragraphs C and D (available on Reproduction Page 32) are examples of how the revisions might be made.

A. *I always wanted to go to Harvard. I went to the University of New Mexico. My folks moved to Washington, D. C. I finished my degree at Harvard.*

B. *Eleanor found her schedule to be more demanding than she had anticipated during her two years of working full time and also attending night school to finish her nursing degree. During that time she was promoted to a supervisory position at the hospital. A shortage of critical care nurses often laid on her the responsibility of filling in an extra shift. The hospital more and more frequently sent her to other cities to attend medical workshops and symposia. Her husband, at the same time, was completing his Master of Arts degree. She often felt she was holding her real life in abeyance until she should have her degree.*

C. *When I was a child I always wanted to go to Harvard. My great-grandfather had gone there, and as a small child I heard many tales of Harvard life. My grandfather attended Harvard also and spoke often of his years there. He brought his family to New Mexico in the 1890's and my father attended the University of New Mexico. Dreams of Harvard seemed out of the question when I was eighteen, so I enrolled at the University of New Mexico also. However, because my folks moved to Washington, D. C. during my junior year, I was able to finish my degree at Harvard and thus fulfill my childhood dream.*

D. *Eleanor found her schedule to be more demanding than she had anticipated during her two years of working full time and also attending night school to finish her nursing degree. Had she continued to work simply as a staff nurse, she would, perhaps, have been able to manage without too much strain, but during that time she was promoted to a supervisory position at the hospital and, as a consequence, her responsibilities and her hours devoted to the hospital were greatly increased. One particular hardship stemmed from the shortage of critical care nurses at that time, which frequently required that she, as supervisor, fill in an extra shift in the Intensive Care Unit as well as performing all her usual supervisory duties. In addition, the hospital, evidently recognizing her increasing value as an employee, more and more frequently sent her to other cities to attend medical workshops and symposia. These absences not only made it difficult for her to keep her course work current, but deprived her, as well, of time she would have liked to devote to her personal life. Her husband, during this same time, was completing his Master of Arts degree at a nearby college and was, himself, on such a busy schedule that Eleanor and he sometimes felt that they saw one another only in passing. Small wonder that she often felt she was holding her real life in abeyance until she should have her degree.*

16. *Activity.* Using Reproduction Page 33, reproduce paragraphs A and B below and distribute them to students or project them with the overhead or opaque. Read paragraph A, warning students to be aware of the incoherence caused by gaps in thought. Then read paragraph B so that students can see how the gaps in thought have been filled with "extender sentences" which make the writing both more coherent and more complete. Then, using Reproduction Page 34, duplicate and pass out copies of paragraph C below, which has places provided for students to insert sentences further specifying and extending the sentences they follow. After students have finished, read some of their efforts aloud and emphasize the improvement in both completeness and coherence. Urge the use of extender sentences to help students avoid the effect of a "grocery list" when they put together in final form the list of developmental details they have decided on. Point out that this is developing, not just *listing.*

A. *As Jules Henry commented in his book* Culture Against Man, *ours is an advertising culture in which we must learn that much of what purports to be truth is, instead, partial or total falsehood. Even the small child must learn that all that is advertised is not so. And unfortunately, everyone's youth is filled with more such disillusionments. Yet, in spite of constant disappointments, we retain some residue of faith. We try, over and over, to gain the blessings promised. When we want to be slim, we buy the $8.95 books which promise to tell us how to reduce without inconvenience. And we are hurt and disappointed when we don't lose ten pounds a week as the "doctor" said we would. We continue to try to believe even when it is no longer possible.*

B. *As Jules Henry commented in his book* Culture Against Man, *ours is an advertising culture in which we must learn that much of what purports to be truth is, instead, partial or total falsehood. Even the small child must learn that all that is advertised is not so. The "delicious," "candy-like" toothpaste that he badgered Mom to buy may well turn out to taste more like spearmint flavored chalk. Unfortunately, everyone's* *youth is filled with such disillusionments. Why does the complexion cure not take away teenage blemishes as promised? Yet, in spite of constant disappointments, we retain some residue of faith. Surely, we think, "they" wouldn't make that ad up out of whole cloth. We try, over and over, to gain the blessings promised. We show faith and buy, even when we doubt. When we want to be slim, we buy the $8.95 book which promises to tell us how to reduce without inconvenience. We won't have to give up anything. And we are hurt and disappointed when we don't lose ten pounds a week as the "doctor" said we would. We continue to try to believe even when it is no longer possible. We are like the early saint who cried out in anguish, "I believe, I believe, O, help Thou my unbelief."*

C. *Different breeds of dogs have different qualities that endear them to their owners.*

_____ .

The owners of Irish setters will rhapsodize at length about the aesthetic appeal of their aristocratic animal. _____

_____ .

On the other hand, dachshund owners seem to take particular pleasure in their little fellows' feisty personalities. _____

_____ .

Owners of big, powerful breeds such as German shepherds or boxers take particular pride in their dogs' strength, while at the same time obviously taking pleasure in their loyalty. _____

_____ .

Dog owners, like the rest of us, differ in their tastes and needs, and it is fortunate that such diversity exists among the breeds of dogs.

17. *Activity.* Have students choose a topic sentence from the list on pages 26–27 and write a paragraph, following all the steps outlined previously, except: instruct them to purposely make their paragraphs as lacking in coherence as possible by violating all the principles introduced above. Have students exchange papers and revise the work of their partners—with the original writer of the paragraph evaluating how well the other catches the deliberate errors.

18. *Activity.* Divide the group at random into small groups of three to five students each. Have them work together to write a paragraph (one paragraph per group), following the steps below. (Write steps on board or distribute this list to each student in the group.)

    1. Choose a subject that all in the group know something about.
    2. Compose a topic sentence about this subject, making sure it is narrow enough to be covered in detail in one paragraph.
    3. Jointly come up with a list of developing details that support, explain, illustrate or illuminate the topic sentence.
    4. Agree on the best order for these details.
    5. Check to make sure all details are relevant to the topic sentence.
    6. Compose the sentences containing the developmental details.
    7. Have one member of the group check the paragraph for completeness, adding details where needed.

8. Have one member of the group check the paragraph for coherence, adding connectors and filling in gaps with extender sentences.
9. Have one member of the group check the paragraph for spelling, punctuation, usage, and final form. Then have groups exchange paragraphs and evaluate the work of another group.

ASSESSING ACHIEVEMENT OF OBJECTIVES

On-Going Evaluation

The extent to which students have mastered the individual skills covered under each topic above can be measured by the procedures headed "Evaluation" that appear periodically. Almost any of the activities suggested in each section could also be submitted for evaluation.

Final Evaluation

For an overall evaluation of students' ability to write paragraphs, assign a paragraph to be written in class. List on the board several general subjects from which students can choose, and announce that they are to write a paragraph on some aspect of that subject. Depending on the age and ability level of the students, length requirements can vary from 50 to 200 words. Grade the paragraphs according to criteria such as the following:

1. Has the writer chosen an aspect of the subject that is narrow enough to be developed in detail in one paragraph?
2. Does the paragraph consist of a general statement supported (specified, developed, explained, illuminated) by a series of more specific statements?
3. Are all the specific statements directly related to the general statement, or does the paragraph contain ideas that are off the topic?
4. Has the writer arranged the developmental details in a logical order?
5. Has the writer utilized logical connectors and other devices as needed to improve coherence?

RESOURCES FOR TEACHING PARAGRAPH WRITING

Below is a selected list of resources useful for teaching the skills of paragraph writing. The list is divided into audio-visual materials (films, filmstrips, slide-tape programs, cassettes, etc.), books for students, and books for teachers. Addresses of publishers can be found in the alphabetical list on pages 151–153. Prices, where given, are only approximate since changes occur frequently.

Audio-Visual Materials

Writing: From Assignment to Composition by Arlene Oraby, consultant. Contains two full-color filmstrips plus discussion guide with instructions on how to use the program, discussion questions, and related activities. Outlining, revising, and composition are discussed. This thorough, practical teaching aid provides an excellent foundation for students. Complete kit: $48.50. Guidance Associates.

Paragraph Power (Communication Power). Four full-color filmstrips: "Thinking in Paragraphs," "Topic Sentence Power," "Paragraph Unity," and "Paragraph Development," four LP record sides (tape cassettes optional), sixteen spirit duplicating masters, and script book. Designed with a developmental emphasis to guide students from basic ideas to practical application. Very effective—a fine skill-oriented teaching tool. Appropriate for all students. Complete kit: $45.00 with LP, $49.00 with cassettes. Filmstrip House.

Fundamentals of Writing. Six filmstrip set provides instruction in outlining, choosing a topic, examining sentence and paragraph relations, discussion of introductions and conclusions, the use of transitional devices, establishing unity and creating variety through style. Set includes teacher notes and five sets of student work sheets for use with writing exercises. Complete kit: $52.00. Applause Productions.

Organizing Your Writing. Series of eight filmstrips. Includes key factors on composition: the five steps in writing, outlining, the introduction, the body, and the conclusion, along with pattern of paragraphs and how to make transitions between paragraphs. Set of eight: $65.90. Encyclopedia Britannica Educational Corporation.

Paragraphs. One part of *Composition Skills,* an overhead transparency program. Consists of thirty-eight transparencies in plastic case, duplicating masters, and teacher guide. Excellent materials, appropriate for all students. Complete set: $335.00. Encyclopedia Britannica Educational Co.

Communication Skills: Write It Right. Contains two hundred slides in three carousel cartridges, three tape cassettes, three LP records, Teacher's Guide, and library processing kit. Examples and exercises provide students with a well delineated step-by-step approach to organizing ideas into words, words into an outline, and the outline into a clear, well-written paragraph. Very effective for all students. Educator's price: $159.00. The Center for Humanities, Inc.

Techniques of Paragraph Writing. Filmstrips on: "Planning a Paragraph and Creating a Topic Sentence," "Methods of Developing a Paragraph," "Methods of Organizing a Paragraph, I," and "Methods of Organizing a Paragraph, II." Contains four filmstrips, two cassettes and study guide. Suggested activities and discussion material included. $39.75. Eye-Gate.

Paragraph Techniques. Contains four full-color filmstrips, four LP record sides (or cassettes), four scripts, catalog card kits. The set covers "Focusing on a Topic," "Developing a Topic," "Unifying," and "Writing Transitions." The film features a fifteen year old student learning and modeling, step-by-step, how to write an effective paragraph. Provides good foundation in paragraph writing. $48.00 with cassettes, $42.00 with records. Filmstrip House.

The Paragraph. A discussion of paragraph sense, developing a topic, creating unity and coherence, transitions, and connectives. Four color filmstrips: $26.00. Filmstrip House.

All about Paragraphs and *Paragraphs That Work* by Thomas Gaston. Two filmstrips with records (or cassettes) and guides. Presents the evolution and progression of the paragraph—how and why it became the basic unit of all expository writing. Discussion of topic sentences, the need to substantiate general contentions, and paragraph structure and strategy. Examination of organizational formula (Tell, Explain, Support, Transition). Amusing, entertaining cartoon characters. Suitable as a foundation for all students. $38.50 with records, $39.50 with cassettes. Thomas Klise Company.

Writing a Good Paragraph. Color filmstrip. Emphasizes unity, clarity, coherence, and how to achieve them. Provides detailed explanations of topic sentences, main idea, order of interest, and cause/effect relationships. $20.00. RMI Educational Films, Incorporated.

Books for Students

Composition I by Sara Hickman. Excellent source of materials on a wide variety of paragraph types—descriptive, instructional, factual, narrative, and developmental. Related exercises in paragraph unity, coherence, and emphasis. Flexible, versatile—appropriate for average and advanced students. Paperbound. Educational Publishing Service.

Language Building by Jess G. Berman. Helpful incremental format from parts of speech to sentence structure, to paragraphs to composition to proofreading to story writing. Information on types of paragraphs—informative, instructional, expository, didactic, descriptive, and subjective. Visually attractive, clear and direct. Suitable for slower and average students. Paperbound. Student edition $3.50, teacher edition $5.00. J. Weston Walch.

Paragraph Development by Malcolm Moore. Workbook format. Provides students with interesting, educational practice exercises and clear models to follow. Divides composition into well-delineated, easily manageable sections—the topic sentence, supporting sentences, method of development, special purpose sentences, and special purpose paragraphs. Helpful in encouraging students to really understand paragraph logic, and then practice and apply methods of good composition. Excellent for all students. Paperbound. $1.50. Houghton Mifflin Company.

The Lively Art of Writing by Lucile Vaughan Payne. An excellent guide, provides a multi-faceted analysis of writing from basic compositional problems to the intricacies of advanced writing. Contains sections on the paragraph's purpose, style, structure, and length, along with a valuable discussion of continuity. Suitable for more advanced students. Paperbound. $1.25. Mentor Book Company.

Paragraph Writing by Frank Chaplen. An excitingly concise and illustrative text on paragraph writing. Complete with model paragraphs, informative instructional notes, and tips on how to compose a good paragraph. Excellent exercises, explanations, assignments, notes, and diagrams. Contains substantial sections on "The Controlling Idea and Its Development" along with information on selectivity, scope, content, and emphasis. Appropriate for average and advanced students. Paperbound. Oxford University Press.

Composing with Paragraphs by Sr. Agnes Ann Pastva. Exceptional in its visual attractiveness. Sections on words, sensory awareness, communication, description, expressive impact, style, and composition. An interesting and stimulating work which will motivate students and facilitate learning. Excellent for all students. Paperbound. Cambridge Book Company.

Composition: Models and Exercises by Desmond J. Nunan and Philip McFarland. Part of a five book series. Contains sections on "Finding Ideas," "Choosing Words," "Description," "Narration," "Exposition," and "The Paragraph"—unity, coherence, and development. Provides excellent models, explanations, and exercises richly augmented by interesting suggestions for possible writing activities. Consistent instructional format, concise, well-delineated, easy-to-follow framework. Appropriate for all students. (Teacher's manual

available.) Paperbound. $1.95. Harcourt Brace Jovanovich.

The Five-Hundred-Word Theme by Lee J. Martin, revised by Harry P. Kroitor. Complete, comprehensive chapters on paragraphs, putting the paper together, maintaining unity and coherence. Outstanding in its clarity. Appropriate for average and advanced students. Prentice-Hall.

Twenty Steps to Better Composition: How To Write Clear and Readable Themes, Reports, Letters, and Stories by the authors of READ magazine. A short, informative guide with brief, condensed explanations, practice exercises. Workbook format lets students respond right in the book to many assignments. Especially useful for average or slow students. Paperbound. $.50. Xerox Educational Publications.

Writing Sentences and Paragraphs by Bernard R. Tanner and Craig Vittetoe. Contains a section on paragraphs and paragraph structures. Clear and precise explanations and good learning activities. Paperbound. Addison-Wesley Publishing Company.

The Writer's Handbook by John B. Karls and Ronald Szymanski. A comprehensive writer's guide with sections on paragraphing, paragraph structures and types: introductory, developmental, transitional, and concluding. Succinct definitions and effective explanations. Practice section included. Primarily for better students. Paperbound. $3.21. Laidlaw Brothers.

The Art of Composition by Barbara Pannwitt. One of six books on composition in the *Contemporary English Modules* series. Excellent format—helpful diagrams, examples, charts, and explanations. Teacher's manual available. Complete with prepared lesson plans. Paperbound. Silver Burdett Company.

Planned Paragraphs by J. Rowe Webster. Contains numerous examples of effective well-written paragraphs and provides fundamental principles and suggested steps toward putting these into practice. Helpful to students in grades seven to twelve. Paperbound. $.90. Educator's Publishing Service.

Developing Ideas by Paul O'Dea. Aimed primarily at grade 9. Sequential format provides opportunities for students to become actively involved in learning. Contains models, explanations, assignments, and evaluation devices. Incorporates twelve important composition principles on the paragraph. Hardcover $4.25, paperbound $3.48, teacher's guide $.66. SRA.

Steps to Better Writing by Gene Stanford. A self-teaching self-checking workbook. Contains all the instructions and explanations that students require and allows them to check their own work against an answer key. Breaks down basic writing skills into small, logical steps; the student practices each step before moving on to the next. Especially suitable for grades 7–10 or slower and average students in upper grades. Excellent, Paperbound. $2.10. Holt, Rinehart and Winston.

3

Teaching Students to Write Expository Essays

This chapter focuses on the skills needed for writing the kind of composition most frequently assigned in high schools—the multi-paragraph essay of opinion. The activities in this chapter follow logically those of the preceding chapter on paragraph writing. In fact, it is assumed that the student has mastered paragraphs before beginning work on essays.

The process of writing an essay should be a fairly orderly one, with the student consciously undertaking each step, rather than simply putting ideas down on paper as they occur. First of all, assuming that students have freedom to choose their own topics, they should choose something to write about which they know well. They then must settle on a thesis (an idea *about* the subject) and restrict it to manageable size. Next, students must organize the paper in a way that is logically consistent with its thesis. They then write the paragraphs for the paper, using transitional devices to help readers find their way through the essay, and giving special attention to the introductory and concluding paragraphs.

The activities in this chapter are arranged in a sequence parallel to the steps writers must take in planning and writing the essay. Some parts of the sequence—or some individual activities—are likely to be too difficult for less mature or less able students and can be omitted at the teacher's discretion. In general, however, following the activities sequentially will provide most students with thorough instruction in expository writing.

OBJECTIVES

As a result of the learning experiences in this chapter, students should be able to:

1. List at least ten topics that are appropriate for a paper of five to ten paragraphs and that they know thoroughly enough to write about.
2. Restrict a subject to a size appropriate for the length of paper to be written.
3. Explain the difference between a subject and an idea about a subject.

---

4. Compose a thesis statement that is limited, precise, and unified.
5. Analyze a thesis into its parts.
6. Organize an essay in a way that derives logically from the thesis.
7. Supply transitional devices as needed to make the organization of the essay apparent and improve its coherence.
8. Write an introduction of the anecdotal type, the outline type, and the funnel type.
9. Write at least two kinds of concluding paragraphs.
10. Describe, step-by-step, how one goes about writing an essay.
11. Write an effective essay of at least five paragraphs.

LEARNING EXPERIENCES

TOPIC I: CHOOSING A SUBJECT

1. *Activity.* Divide the class into small groups of no more than five students each. Challenge each group to make a list of things they know about and could write about. Here are some topics to get the groups started:

   early memories of home, starting to school, grade school, junior high, senior high, problems of school, pleasures of school, teachers one can learn from, teachers one can't learn from, having to take subjects I don't like, getting into trouble, discipline, and family.

   Suggest that the groups use the brainstorming technique in this activity by attempting to generate as long a list as possible without commenting on or evaluating one another's contributions. After fifteen or twenty minutes, reconvene the entire class and have groups share their lists. Instruct one student to write them down as they are read or have the groups submit their lists to you, so that a total list can be reproduced using spirit master and given to each student. Instruct students to keep the list in their notebooks or in a folder in the classroom to be referred to later.

2. *Activity.* Divide the class into small groups of three to five students each. Give all groups a subject (such as "problems of school") from the list generated in the activity above. Challenge the groups to list *everything* they know about this subject. After ten or fifteen minutes (or longer), reconvene the total class and see which group has the most items on its list. Continue to brainstorm in the total class for even more items on the same topic. Reproduce the total list of items, as you did above, and distribute it to students to keep for use in a later activity.

   Here is a sample list, using "problems of school" as the topic:

   Having to take required courses

   Not being allowed to choose preferred teachers

   Too much homework

   Absence of places to be alone

   Difficulty of making friends

   Time schedule too tight—no free times

   Behavior at assemblies

   Vandalism

Library overcrowded

No facility for student smoking

Inadequate parking

Unfair grading by many teachers

Thefts out of gym lockers

Conflict between "jocks" and "freaks"

Poor food in the cafeteria

Only seniors being able to have one pass-fail course

Closed campus

Difficulty in getting permission for independent study

All teachers giving tests at midterm or term end

Too much emphasis on grades

Too much emphasis on college prep only

Failure to provide career advice or training

Discriminatory enforcement of rules

Refusal to encourage student participation in curriculum planning

Student behavior and sloppiness in cafeteria

Inadequacy of homeroom system

TOPIC II: RESTRICTING THE SUBJECT

1. *Activity.* Reproduce and distribute to each student the list of all the things they know about one subject (from Activity #2 above). Point out that this long list of subtopics indicates that there is a lot they can "say" about the subject. Suggest that they discuss for a few moments how they would go about writing an essay on all this material. They may conclude that it is simply too much for one paper.

     Then ask the class what problems they would have if you assigned them to write one paragraph on the subject. They will realize, one hopes, that there is far too much for one paragraph. Therefore, suggest that they find one "piece" of information in their list that might be suitable for one paragraph. Have them compose a sample topic sentence or two and quickly brainstorm how that topic sentence might be developed.

     Next, have the group find a larger "piece" of the material they have listed which could be turned into an essay with three parts (which could be turned into three developed paragraphs).

2. *Teacher Presentation.* Use Reproduction Page 35 to make a transparency for overhead projector or a spirit master for making copies of a diagram for each student. Use the diagram to explain how a large (very abstract) subject can be broken down into a small (less abstract) subject by becoming increasingly specific. For example, you might label the largest square "books" and the next smaller square in the lower left corner "children's books," pointing out that you've chosen one aspect of the large topic and thus have become more specific. Then label the next smaller square with an even more specific subject, such as "heroes and heroines in children's books." Finally, label the smallest square with a still more specific subject,

such as "values transmitted through the example set by heroes and heroines in children's books."

Erase the labels and give students another example of how a large subject can become ever more specific: cars - Fords - old Fords - 1927 Ford - engine of 1927 Ford - ignition system of 1927 Ford. (You may have to draw still smaller squares to accommodate the most specific subjects.)

Then suggest a very general topic—such as education—and have students suggest how it can be cut down in size by becoming progressively more specific. Label the squares in the diagram with their contributions.

3. *Activity.* Give students, individually or in small groups, several large subjects (cars, education, pets, family, etc.) and tell them to change each to a small subject suitable for a short essay.

4. *Activity.* Using Reproduction Page 36, give students the following list of ideas which are vastly unlimited and challenge them to cut the ideas down to the scope desirable for a paper with only three or four developed paragraphs. You might wish to have students work in twos or threes and then come together to share their answers with the total class. Possible restricted ideas for each of the general ideas are underscored, but of course many others are possible.

1. *Health is important. Good health is essential to a happy life. Protein is the foundation of a healthful diet.*

2. *The topography of the continents has a pronounced effect on their weather patterns. The Mississippi Valley provides a channel for Canadian polar air.*

3. *War, in the past, has been a reasonably effective means of settling international problems. Television may well make war obsolete. Conscientious objection to war is on the rise in America.*

4. *Malnutrition is found in all classes of people all over the world. Many American high school students choose a diet notably lacking in life supporting nutrients. In America, bread is far from the staff of life.*

5. *America is entering the postindustrial age. Cars should be made to go no more than 75 miles per hour.*

6. *Traffic deaths in the United States demonstrate the American urge to self-destruction. Drivers convicted of driving while inebriated should be given a prison sentence if ever convicted a second time.*

7. *It is possible for young people to take a conscious, significant part in assisting their own psychological growth. Amateur sports offer an excellent outlet for a person's competitive impulses.*

8. *Modern medicine has performed miracles in conquering diseases which once were scourges of humanity. Many famous personages of history wasted away from what we now know was tuberculosis. Every child should have finished an immunization program by the third or fourth grade.*

9. *Great men have not always been successful fathers. A good father always has time to spend with his children. A child needs to know he is important to his parents.*

10. *In the United States, there is much more prestige to being youthful than to being old. Television commercials sell youth.*

11. *In the history of wars is written the story of the human species' greatness and its baseness. Children who grow up seeing actual war on television will not have the romantic concept of war that their parents had in their youths. Hollywood sometimes makes war seem like lots of good, clean fun.*

12. *The "good old days" were not always so good. Instant foods taste good only to people who don't remember Grandma's cooking.*

13. *Many people act as if old age were something that could never happen to them.* *Voters are often negative toward spending tax money for programs to help the elderly.*

14. *The automobile is one of the major causes of air pollution.* *California was the first state to pass a law requiring control of automobile exhaust pollution.*

5. *Activity.* Using Reproduction Page 37, give students the list of ideas below, which are limited enough to be the topic sentence of a paragraph. Challenge them (perhaps working in twos or threes) to enlarge them to ideas big enough for a five or ten paragraph paper. Possible enlargements are given in parentheses.

1. *A boy can learn much from owning a dog. (Children learn many important lessons about life and death from association with pets during their preschool and early school years.)*

2. *I lost a friendship by being thoughtless. (Life has taught me that successful human relations depend on mutual thoughtfulness.)*

3. *The water of the lake was a deep, dark blue. (The lake and its wooded shorelines made a scene of unsurpassed beauty.)*

4. *I navigated the dark stairway cautiously. (I entered the old tenement building like a traveler embarking on a strange and perilous journey.)*

5. *The otter is the most playful of animals. (Play is the natural learning activity of young animals, including children.)*

6. *The whooping crane is one bird that apparently has been saved from extinction by timely conservation efforts. (Many of the species of animals threatened with extinction can be saved only through controlled and protected breeding programs.)*

7. *The new member of Congress soon learns to give a little in order to get a little. (Politics, it is said, is the art of the possible.)*

8. *One should never betray a friend's confidence. (Friendship is an art.)*

9. *Ice cream has a good deal of nutritive value, even if it is fattening. (Not all desserts are nutritional no-no's.)*

10. *Too much sun can cause skin cancer. (Cancer is a disease that is a product of the way we live.)*

11. *Smoking by young people is increasing. (People seem to have an infinite capacity for ignoring medical advice.)*

12. *Young people are pushed to choose careers before they are halfway through high school. (Young people of our society are under strong pressure to achieve and to succeed at an ever earlier age.)*

13. *Today, young people seem to learn their social values from their peers rather than their families. (The functions and influences of the American family are undergoing rapid and significant changes.)*

14. *Some children in the early grades seem unduly eager to please their teachers. (Children's patterns for winning love and approval are well established by the time they start school.)*

15. *When making assignments, a teacher encourages students' growth by offering as many options as possible. (Schools should offer each student the freedom to grow in the direction of his or her own unique capacities and interests.)*

6. *Activity.* Using Reproduction Page 38, give students the ideas listed below and have them indicate what size composition it would take to develop each: a) a library, b) a shelf of books, c) a book, d) a chapter, e) a five to ten paragraph essay, f) a three paragraph essay, g) one paragraph.

1. *The apple is a remarkable fruit.* *shelf*

2. *Drinking eight glasses of water a day is beneficial to health in a number of ways.* short essay

3. *Achieving psychological maturity can also be called mastering the art of loving.* book

4. *The history of the human race is revealed most truly in its art, architecture, literature, and music.* library

5. *It does not matter if people are free, so long as they think they are.* chapter

6. *The fall of Rome has been so instructive to people of all subsequent generations that if it had not occurred, it would have been invented.* long essay

7. *Suicide has a long and respected history in Japan.* book

8. *Tomatoes should not be planted in the same spot two years in a row.* paragraph

9. *Dogs are more expensive to feed than cats.* paragraph

10. *We will cherish our old people only when our society has changed so that people become loving and lovable.* chapter, book

11. *There are still a number of prestigious careers for which a college education is not at all necessary.* long essay

12. *Religion and humanity have co-existed from the beginning.* library

13. *Fat people often lack self-esteem.* paragraph

14. *Obesity is a serious health problem in the United States.* chapter

15. *It is possible to rear thin children and thus eradicate the problem of obesity.* book

16. *Counting calories is the surest and safest way for the nutrition-wise person to lose weight.* short essay

17. *The functions and effects of cholesterol in the human blood comprise a complex and poorly understood subject.* shelf

18. *We human beings have gained a great deal of knowledge about the workings of our bodies.* library

19. *Obesity is hardly an asset to a happy social life.* short essay

20. *The human soul has never been located, but it has been the subject of conjecture and study for thousands of years.* library

21. *The early Christian church was indebted to many of the other so-called miracle religions for much of its form and substance.* shelf

22. *"Progress" is a difficult term to define.* short essay

23. *Modern art has developed in directions quite unrelated to the tastes and understandings of the public for whom it has, presumably, been created.* book

24. *The tiger in captivity can never be considered an entirely trustworthy animal.* short essay

25. *Bear baiting, a popular spectacle in the London of Shakespeare's time, was a brutal sport.* paragraph

26. *The English bull dog was bred for bear baiting.* paragraph

TOPIC III: TURNING A SUBJECT INTO A THESIS

1. *Teacher Presentation.* Point out to students that even though a subject has been cut down to a manageable size (that is, reduced in abstractness), it is still not suitable for an essay until the writer takes a stand with relation to the subject. For example, the general subject of cars could be reduced in size as follows: cars -

old cars - old cars on major highways with high speed traffic - accidents caused by old cars. But then the writer must take one more step and convert the subject into an idea *about* the subject. For example: Cars older than fifteen years should not be allowed on express highways with high speed limits. This statement of the writer's point of view toward the subject can be called a "thesis sentence" or simply a "thesis."

To clarify the difference between a subject and a thesis, use Reproduction Page 39 to make a transparency for overhead projector. Explain to students (if you did not use Teacher Presentation #2 on pages 61–62) that the largest square represents a large subject. Label the large square with some very general subject, such as "education." Then point out that the next smaller square represents a somewhat restricted subject related to the general subject, for example, "high schools." Write "high schools" in the square labeled "somewhat restricted subject." Then point out that the next smaller square represents even smaller subjects related to high schools, perhaps your own high school. Write the name of your school in the square labeled "even smaller subject." Then point out the smallest square is a very restricted topic, such as "this composition class," which is a small part of the larger topics. Label the smallest square accordingly.

Then explain that the next step for the writer after he or she has reduced the subject in size is to take a stand in relation to that small subject. Write a thesis such as "People who don't learn to write are handicapped in their future lives."

Give the class another example of how the writer must take a stand in relation to the subject after cutting it down to size. Again label the squares with increasingly specific topics, such as dogs - little dogs - dachshunds - pet dachshunds - children's pet dachshunds. Then label the arrow with a statement that shows the writer's point of view on the small subject. For example, "Dachshunds make playful pets for active little boys who like to wrestle."

Point out that the thesis should have the following characteristics:

1) It should be expressed as a declarative sentence, not as a question or merely a word or phrase.
2) It should not be simply a self-evident fact ("Many Americans enjoy apple pie"), but should be at least somewhat arguable ("Apple pie is America's favorite dessert").
3) It should not be simply a statement of personal preference ("I like apple pie"), but should be a statement of the writer's opinion on an issue that includes more people than just the writer ("Americans should eat more apple pie in order to stay healthy").

2. *Activity.* Give the class a general subject from the list below and have them first reduce it in size (perhaps by drawing successively smaller squares as you did in the Teacher Presentation above) and then compose a thesis indicating a point of view toward the smallest subject. Or divide the class into two groups, one to reduce the subject in size, the other to compose the idea about the restricted subject. Use one or more of these general subjects:

education	*music*	*motorcycles*
politics	*cars*	*varsity sports*
canoeing	*camping*	*religion*
food	*dating*	*dieting*

From Subject To Thesis

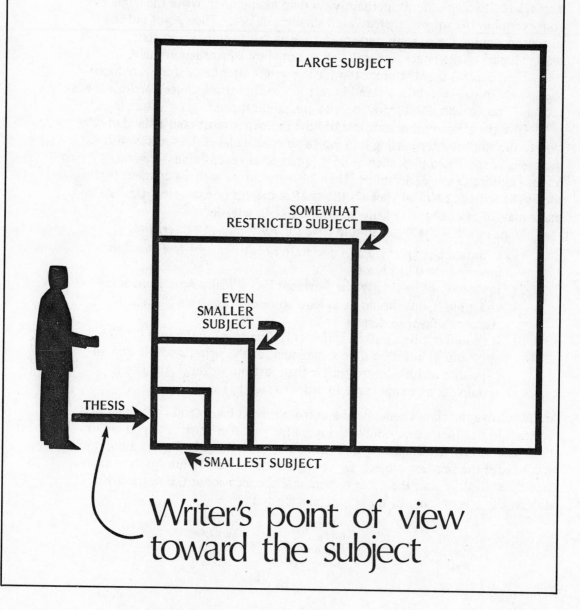

LARGE SUBJECT

SOMEWHAT RESTRICTED SUBJECT

EVEN SMALLER SUBJECT

THESIS

SMALLEST SUBJECT

Writer's point of view toward the subject

fashion	*gardening*	*health*
war	*hair*	*travel*
aviation	*poverty*	*law and order*
human relations	*free enterprise*	*communications*
art	*vacations*	*city life*

3. *Activity.* Have students individually choose a large abstract term from the list below and reduce it to a thesis by cutting its size and then indicating a point of view toward the smallest subject. Have them write down each step in this progression, as shown below:

> *Abstract term:* education
>
> *Steps in reducing the subject in size:*
> secondary education
> my high school
> my sophomore year
> my sophomore math class
> sophomore math was a waste to me
> the teacher was always hurrying so we would finish the book
>
> *Thesis:* In teaching beginning algebra, it does the student more good if the teacher allows the students time for full comprehension than if the teacher worries about "finishing the book."

Then allow students to share and compare their steps and their resulting thesis sentences. They will probably be surprised at the similarities of their thought processes in some cases and the difference in others. Have students save the results of this activity in their folders for later reference. Use one or more of the following terms:

loyalty	*hope*	*death*
love	*courage*	*goodness*
justice	*hatred*	*faith*
maturity	*prejudice*	*security*
peace	*friendship*	*pain*
loneliness	*happiness*	*fear*

4. *Activity.* Using Reproduction Page 40, give students the following list of subjects that have already been restricted in size and have them compose a thesis sentence based on each. Then have them share their results with the total class. It will be interesting to see the similarities or differences in the final statements arrived at by the different students. Or, if you prefer, have students work in small groups and arrive at thesis sentences cooperatively. Make sure students save the results of this activity for use in a later activity.

> *winter in my community*
> *deep sea fishing in Florida*
> *my sophomore English class*
> *experiences playing football in high school*
> *learning to drive at school last year*
> *thefts in the boys' locker room*
> *snorkeling in clear water streams*
> *the Cherokee Indians' trek to Oklahoma*
> *being poor in this country*

voting for the first time

making one's own clothes

a raft trip at the bottom of the Grand Canyon

changes in rock music

high school dress codes

old people in poor health

quiet, shy students

living in a high crime area

5. *Activity.* Working with the total class, take an abstract term, write it on the board, and have the class take the steps necessary, as explained in the Teacher Presentation above, to turn it into a usable thesis statement. See how many times, in how many directions, they can do this for the same term, arriving each time at a thesis sentence suitable for a paper with three or four developed paragraphs. Let the students choose the beginning abstraction or general subject area, or provide it for them from this list: politics, sports, dating, parent/child relationships, growing up, love. Have students save the results of this activity.

6. *Activity.* Divide the class into small groups of three to five persons each. Give each group this list of general subjects:

apples	*being sick*	*friends*
telephoning	*getting up early*	*television*
movies	*going steady*	*being popular*
drag racing	*teachers*	*swimming*
backpacking	*parents*	*seafood*
New York City	*good grades*	*tourists*

Ask each group to come up with two ideas (thesis statements) about each subject or some aspect or part of each subject. Supervise the work of the groups closely to be sure they have learned the difference between a thesis and a personal expression of like or dislike. Save the lists of ideas for use in Activity #7 below.

7. *Activity.* With the lists generated in Activity #6 above, have each group decide which of the two theses about each subject is "bigger" and would require the longer essay to develop it in detail. Or have them determine how long they think each essay would have to be to cover the idea completely.

8. *Activity.* Explain to students that an easy way to arrive at a thesis about a subject is to relate it to another subject. For example, the subject "loving families" can be related to the second subject "crime" to produce the thesis, "A loving family is a major preventive to crime." Using Reproduction Page 41, give students the following chart and have them name the second subject that has been related to the first subject to produce the thesis. Answers are underscored here but do not appear on the Reproduction Page.

subject	thesis	second subject
loving families	*A loving family is a major preventive to crime.*	crime
football	*Football teaches lessons of good citizenship and group awareness.*	membership in society
football	*Strategies of football are similar to military tactics.*	war
basketball	*Basketball is more exciting than football for spectators.*	football

teen years	The teen years encompass some of the most important and consequential decisions a person will ever make.	life decisions
apples	An apple a day keeps the doctor away.	good health
grade chasing	Chasing the grade is not always the best way to get good grades.	good grades
good human relations	Good human relations always thrive on open and honest communication.	communication
loyalty	People owe their highest loyalty to their own personal values, not to any person who would ask them to go against them.	personal values
dress making	People who can make their own clothes will usually have better clothes for less money.	economy
vitamin C	Taking high quantities of Vitamin C can help one avoid the common cold.	getting colds
careful driving	Motorists owe their passengers the courtesy of careful driving.	courtesy
good manners	All courtesy and so-called "good manners" are based on simple thoughtfulness.	thoughtfulness
TV advertising	TV advertising makes it clear that there is something terribly undesirable and unattractive about growing old.	growing old

9. *Activity.* Give students, working in twos or threes or individually, the following list of pairs of subjects (available on Reproduction Page 42) and ask them to construct a thesis for each that relates the two subjects. A sample answer for each is given in parentheses below; students' answers, however, will vary.

1. human beings - tornadoes — *(What human beings can put together, a tornado can take apart.)*

2. girls - basketball — *(It's a rare girl who can hold her own on a boys' basketball team.)*

3. cats - people — *(Independent people seem to prefer cats as pets.)*

4. young men - women's liberation — *(Some young men seem fearful of the new expectations concerning male roles being verbalized by leaders of the women's liberation movement.)*

5. sleep - teenagers — *(Many teenagers habitually sleep far less than doctors recommend.)*

6. crime - unemployment — *(As unemployment increases, so does crime.)*

7. modern society - peace of mind — *(Life in modern society is not very conducive to peace of mind.)*

8. European public transit - Americans — *(Europeans seem more disposed than Americans to utilize public transportation.)*

9. spring - float trip — *(Spring is a perfect time to take a float trip on a gently flowing, scenic stream.)*

10. *Activity.* Use Reproduction Page 43 to give students the following list of thesis sentences composed by joining two subjects. Have them identify the two subjects that have been joined by drawing a line under each.

1. *Regular applications of fertilizer are necessary to the maintenance of a good blue grass lawn.*

2. *A gray and <u>overcast day</u> is a fine time to settle down with a <u>good book</u>.*
3. *<u>Wicker furniture</u>, with its light and airy design, is suitable for decorating a <u>screened porch</u>.*
4. *<u>Breakfast</u> should provide one-fourth or more of one's <u>nutritional needs</u> for the day.*
5. *Many <u>plants</u>, as well as animals, are on the growing list of <u>endangered species</u>.*
6. *Much of the <u>white bread</u> we purchase at the market has little <u>food value</u> beyond calories.*
7. *During the Sixties, <u>hair</u> became a symbol of <u>cultural differences</u>.*
8. *To many young people, the <u>driver's license</u> looks like a veritable <u>ticket to freedom</u>.*
9. *Every <u>kitchen</u> should have a <u>singing bird</u> to keep the cook cheerful.*
10. *People who keep <u>cats</u> for pets but who also like <u>birds</u> should attach bells to the cats' collars.*

11. *Teacher Presentation.* Explain to students that a thesis sentence should be checked to make sure it is *limited*. That is, a good thesis covers only what the writer intends to discuss in the essay. The writer should examine the thesis sentence carefully and qualify any statements that are too sweeping to be supported. For example, the thesis sentence, "Missouri is a great vacation state," is probably too sweeping for most essays (although it might make an excellent headline for a travel promotion leaflet). The writer of this thesis should ask questions such as: all of Missouri? for everyone? all kinds of vacations? all the time? After asking such questions, the writer might arrive at a better thesis: "The Ozark country in southern Missouri is an excellent summer vacation spot for those hardy souls who enjoy hot weather, camping, canoeing, and hiking."

Give students another example of a fairly sweeping thesis sentence, such as "Dogs are wonderful pets," and help them ask the necessary questions to limit and qualify the statement: All dogs? for all people? in all ways? Then have students formulate a more qualified thesis as a result of answering these questions. One such sentence would be: "The poodle makes a companionable pet for an elderly person living in a small apartment."

12. *Activity.* Give students the list of sweeping thesis sentences below (using Reproduction Page 44) and have them limit and qualify them by asking questions such as: all? everyone? always? everywhere? all kinds?

1. *Poverty is not as bad as it is thought to be.*
2. *Being rich is destructive to human character.*
3. *All politicians are just looking for a chance to get their hands into our pockets.*
4. *Surfing in Hawaii is something everyone can enjoy.*
5. *Hooking rugs is an excellent hobby.*
6. *Lawns should be mowed at least once a week if they are to be kept in good condition.*
7. *Music, after all, never hurt anyone.*
8. *The gravest problem facing mankind today is inflation.*
9. *The ideal vacation includes sunshine, sports, a change of scenery and plenty of good food.*
10. *It is impossible to be well educated without some travel experience.*
11. *Everyone loves a frisky kitten.*

12. *It's a wonderful treat to have someone else do your work for you.*

13. *Young people enter senior high school with much fear and trepidation.*

14. *Seniors, in their arrogance, ignore the lowly underclassmen.*

15. *Students find it hard to talk freely with teachers.*

13. *Teacher Presentation.* Explain to students that they should check a thesis sentence to make sure it is precisely worded. They should be sure that every word in the thesis can be interpreted only in the way it is meant by the writer. For example, "St. Louis is an exciting town for sports lovers," is a precise thesis only if the writer intends to deal with both excitement of spectator sports in St. Louis and excitement of participation in sports in St. Louis. If the writer intends to deal with only the excitement of spectator sports, the phrase "sports lovers" should be replaced with the more precise term "fans." Students should see that precise wording is simply one more way of limiting the thesis until it is an *exact* expression of what the writer intends to cover in his or her paper.

14. *Activity.* Using Reproduction Page 45, give students the list of imprecise, and hence misleading, thesis sentences below. Ask them, working as a total class, in small groups, or individually, to identify the weak spots (words that could be taken more than one way, or unqualified terms about which they have questions) and then to rewrite each sentence to make it more precise.

EXAMPLE:

> *Catcher in the Rye* is a dirty book and should be banned. (dirty? entirely banned? everywhere? to all people?)

1. *Love makes the world go around.*
2. *Miami is a great place to go for holiday fun.*
3. *The free parts of the world are the only parts worth living in.*
4. *All good citizens of a democracy will welcome a chance to fight for liberty.*
5. *Patriotism demands that we respond to our country's needs.*
6. *A girl must behave like a lady if she wishes to be thought well bred.*
7. *The whole world loves a lover.*
8. *If one is not moving ahead, one is falling behind.*
9. *Most Americans are imbued with an old fashioned ambition to get ahead.*
10. *Americans have always been devoted to the land.*
11. *Loyalty is one of the noblest of human virtues.*
12. *A great portion of the world's population lives in poverty.*
13. *Every individual should devote at least a portion of his or her life to the pursuit of beauty.*
14. *According to an old adage, "Neatness and system are heaven's first laws, and cleanliness is next to godliness."*
15. *Professional football can do a lot for any major city.*
16. *A country wishing to remain free must be prepared to do battle with those who would destroy its liberty.*

15. *Teacher Presentation.* Explain to students that an essay should deal with only one overall idea. If a thesis sentence contains two or more ideas, the writer has several options:

1. Sever the two ideas and write two papers
2. Combine the two ideas through pointing out a causal relationship, making a comparison, contrasting them, subordinating one to the other, etc.
3. Subordinate both of the ideas to a larger thesis which is general enough to include both ideas

For example, the thesis *"Tennis began as a rich man's game, and also has caused the rise of a profitable industry,"* can be handled by

1. *Severing:* One paper on "Tennis began . . ." and another on "Tennis has caused the rise of . . ."
2. *Combining:* "Tennis has come a long way from a rich man's pastime to a game so popular that it forms the foundation of a million dollar industry."

As another example, the thesis "Dogs are man's best friends, and cats are good friends, too," can be handled by

1. *Severing:* One paper on "A dog is man's best friend" and another on "Cats are good friends to their owners."
2. *Subordinating one part to the other:* "Contrary to the old saying about dogs, cat lovers insist that it is actually the cat who is a person's best friend."
3. *Contrasting:* "Dogs may stay with you to the bitter end, but cats keep you on your toes."
4. *Comparing:* "The much maligned cat has many of the same arts of friendship that make the dog so popular as a pet."
5. *Subordinating both to a larger generalization:* "There are only two animals who have developed sufficient adaptability to human beings' urban life style to be safely and conveniently kept as house pets." Or, "The pet industry of America is dominated by two animals, the dog and the cat." Or, "The slang of America would be must poorer if it were not for cats and dogs."

16. *Activity.* Using Reproduction Page 46, provide the class—working as a total group, in pairs, in small groups, or individually—with the following list of both unified and ununified thesis sentences. Have students identify the unified ones and correct the ununified ones by severing them, unifying them by finding a relationship between the various parts, or by subordinating both parts to a higher generalization large enough to include them both.

1. *All too often the father is not an important figure in the ghetto family, and juvenile delinquency is a serious urban problem.*
2. *Like the extremes of poverty, an excess of wealth can be destructive of good human values.*
3. *Recent political events have revealed the dishonesty of many politicians and a movement should be started to identify the good, honest politicians in America.*
4. *If you learn a few labor saving devices, gardening need not be hard work, and it can also be profitable.*
5. *Cooking, like any creative work, is done best by those who enjoy it and can afford to buy the best ingredients.*
6. *While Americans are accustomed to a diet whose foundation is meat, more of the Earth's inhabitants eat a diet based on cereals.*

7. *New York is the biggest city in the United States, and San Francisco is the most cosmopolitan.*

8. *Dogs are always eager to please, and cats are independent.*

9. *In Denmark the cultural differences between the generations seem even greater than in the United States.*

10. *There were people who saw the Beatles as a Communist menace and were sure that long hair was a mark of moral degradation.*

11. *People who get up early know that dawn shows beautiful colors unlike those of the sky at sunset, when dramatic cloud formations catch everyone's attention and inspire poets, who in these days more often see the sunset than the sunrise.*

17. *Activity.* Have students bring to class three or more thesis sentences which they have consciously made either unified or ununified. (They might wish to base these on thesis sentences constructed for previous activities and filed away for future use.) Have them, one at a time, put them on the board so the class can approve or correct them. Or, if you prefer, students could work in pairs, exchanging lists, signing their own names on their own thesis statements, and on their corrections or acceptances of their partner's statements. These would then be handed in for grading.

18. *Teacher Presentation.* Summarize for students the characteristics of a good thesis sentence:

    1. It is a general statement with which there can be disagreement. In other words, it is not a simple statement of fact which needs no support, nor a personal observation with which no one can disagree, nor a statement of truth so self-evident that there is really no reason even to say it.

    2. It is restricted. That is, it is cut down in size to fit the scope of the assignment, remembering that the task of the writer is to develop in detail, and that if the subject is large and the assignment asks for only three paragraphs, it will be impossible to completely cover the subject in detail.

    3. It reflects the author's point of view. The author takes a stand in relationship to the subject rather than just planning to write about it in general.

    4. It is unified. It introduces one and only one idea.

    5. It is precise. It is stated in words that can be interpreted in only one way.

19. *Activity.* Give students the following list of thesis sentences, using Reproduction Page 47, and have them determine whether they meet the criteria for a good thesis outlined in the Teacher Presentation above.

    1. *I love apple pie.*

    2. *The word "feline" refers to cats.*

    3. *It seems to be true, as George Orwell said, that "all animals are equal but some are more equal than others."*

    4. *A child can learn the lesson of responsibility from owning a dog.*

    5. *Swimming has always been my favorite sport.*

    6. *Many people between the ages of eight and eighteen play baseball.*

    7. *Baseball fascinates as much by its possibilities for strategy as by its demonstration of athletic skills.*

8. *The trials of life tend to be overwhelming for many people.*
9. *A well reared cat is an endlessly entertaining pet.*
10. *There are not as many kings and queens in the world today as there were one hundred years ago.*
11. *Physical education classes are a feature of almost all American schools.*
12. *Football is an excellent sport.*
13. *There is a big difference between friendship and romance.*
14. *Young women today have an ever widening range of career opportunities open to them.*
15. *Movies are fine entertainment.*
16. *Not only are boys and girls sharing gym classes and home economics classes, but re-allocation of educational funds and revision of traditional curricula are foreseen as consequences of the women's movement and some educators are strongly opposed to the changes coming about.*

20. *Activity.* Have students revise each of the thesis sentences from the previous activity which they considered to violate the criteria of a good thesis sentence.

21. *Evaluation.* Many of the previous activities could be submitted for grading, if you wish. However, since many of them may be assigned as homework or may be completed by students working in small groups, a more carefully controlled measure of the individual student's ability to construct an effective thesis sentence may be desirable. To assess students' ability to construct an effective thesis sentence, write on the board a list of general subjects such as parents, hobbies, personal qualities, good citizenship, etc.—and give the following instructions:

"Imagine that you have been assigned to write an essay of approximately five paragraphs on one of these topics. Choose a topic, and construct a thesis sentence for that essay, applying everything we have discussed about what makes an effective thesis sentence. You will have no more than twenty minutes to write and turn in your thesis sentence."

Apply the following criteria when grading:
1. Has the student chosen a topic he or she knows well enough to write an essay about?
2. Is the thesis sentence a complete declarative sentence and not a phrase or question?
3. Is the thesis sentence limited enough in scope to be developed in detail in an essay of approximately five paragraphs?
4. Is the thesis sentence broad enough in scope to require an essay to develop, or is it merely a good topic sentence for a single paragraph?
5. Does the thesis sentence indicate that the writer has taken a stand in relation to the subject? That is, is it at least somewhat arguable? Or has the writer simply stated a fact, a self-evident truth, or a personal preference?
6. Is the thesis sentence unified? That is, does it introduce only one subject?
7. Is the thesis sentence precise? That is, does it contain no words that can be interpreted in more than one way?

TOPIC IV: ORGANIZING THE PAPER

1. *Teacher Presentation.* Explain to the class that after they have formulated a proper thesis sentence, the next step is to plan what they are going to do to explain, support, amplify, and develop that thesis. To do so, writers must ask themselves, "What are the parts that I must develop to cover my thesis entirely?" The thesis statement itself will determine the proper technique of division. Sometimes a thesis sentence clearly reveals its parts, as when it asserts that there are, say, many *causes* of something, or that there are many *ways* to do something, or many *results,* or a number of *great women,* or whatever. One knows at once what will be the parts of each of these thesis sentences.

   Not so simple are statements of ideas dealing with concepts or extrapolations rather than facts. For instance, a thesis such as, "If humanity is to survive, we must develop techniques or institutions for the purpose of effecting anticipatory change, a task for which we have shown little or no capacity in the past," must be carefully examined to identify the parts that must be covered in an essay. A little study makes clear that here is a recommendation based on an observation of humankind's past history and an evaluation of our present situation. The parts, hence, are: 1) how human beings have failed to achieve change in the past before great catastrophes forced them to; 2) a look at present circumstances which will no longer permit such behavior if humanity is to survive; and 3) suggestions for ways of developing the means for anticipatory change.

2. *Activity.* One by one put on the board as many of the following thesis statements as you believe suitable for the level of your class. Help students see the parts into which each one must be divided if a complete essay is to be written.

   1. *The Civil War had many causes besides the move to free the slaves.*

      Parts: causes—probably categorized as economic, social, political, etc.

   2. *Uninterested high school students might devote themselves more seriously to their school work if they had more of a hand in planning their own courses of study.*

      Parts: 1) facts and statistics indicating the problem of uninterested students
      2) evaluation of why students are uninterested
      3) recommendation of how to re-interest them
      4) prediction of favorable results

   3. *The dachshund is a better apartment pet than the collie.*

      Parts: list of qualities making up the difference, such as size, kind of hair, living habits, etc.

   4. *It is a wise parent who knows how much freedom to grant an adolescent offspring.*

      Parts: 1) pitfalls in giving not enough freedom
      2) pitfalls in giving too much freedom
      3) wisdom of falling in between—giving enough freedom to show trust and develop maturity, but not enough to convey neglect and encourage dangerous or unacceptable behavior

   5. *There are many techniques for . . .*

      Parts: different techniques

   6. *There are many reasons why membership in the Republican Party is declining.*

      Parts: reasons

7. *Complete and honest communication among all members of a family is essential if they are to have a happy life together.*

   Parts: 1) *description of unhappy status of family when communication is poor*
   2) *description of happy family status when communication is good*
   3) *suggestions for improving communication in order to achieve happier family relationships*

8. *One sure way to win friends is to become a person people are comfortable around.*

   Parts: 1) *why we feel uncomfortable with some people and try to avoid them*
   2) *why we feel comfortable with others and seek their company*
   3) *how to make people feel comfortable so they will seek us*

9. *A smoking lounge should have been provided at the high school several years ago.*

   Parts: 1) *present situation concerning the smoking lounge*
   2) *occurrences and situations of the past years that could have been avoided*

3. *Activity.* Ask students, one by one, to put on the board thesis sentences they have written (perhaps from a previous activity which they have saved in their folders) and see if class members can divide each into the proper parts for a complete essay.

4. *Evaluation.* To test students' understanding of this important skill (or to give them further practice), provide them with the following list of thesis statements (using Reproduction Page 48) and see if they can successfully divide them into the parts that must be covered if a complete essay is to be written. Point out that they need not know anything about the subject matter being introduced to identify the parts of each thesis.

1. *It is a mistake to provide a smoking lounge at any public high school.*
   Parts: reasons why

2. *In personal conversation we often use our own speaking for purposes other than to reveal ourselves or convey information.*
   Parts: real purposes behind our speaking

3. *Despite the absence of immediate victory, there are benefits derived from devoting oneself to a losing cause in which one sincerely believes.*
   Parts: benefits derived

4. *It is difficult to identify any beneficial consequences of war which could not have been achieved by more peaceful means.*
   Parts: 1) *beneficial consequences of wars—examples needed*
   2) *peaceful means by which these same positive outcomes could have been achieved*

5. *There are many lessons that young people could learn from old people if they lived more closely together.*
   Parts: 1) *lessons a young person could learn*
   2) *styles of living that would promote such learning*

6. *Many Americans behave as if they considered themselves immune to the dire consequences of which they are warned by doctors, scientists, policemen, and safety experts.*
   Parts: 1) *behavior contrary to doctor's warnings—smoking, etc.*
   2) *behavior contrary to scientists' warnings—DDT, etc.*
   3) *behavior contrary to police's warnings—hitchhiking, etc.*
   4) *behavior contrary to safety experts' warnings—boating without life jacket, etc.*

7. *Life becomes richer and more rewarding as we learn to break down the obstacles to free and open intercommunication.*

Parts: 1) *free intercommunication enriches life*
2) *barriers exist to prevent intercommunication*
3) *how to overcome barriers*

8. *The history of the American Revolution as it is presented today is a far cry from the simple story of a battle for human liberty that most of us learned in grade school.*

Parts: differences

9. *A civil war is one of the most horrifying of all human conflicts.*

Parts: ways in which it is horrifying

5. *Teacher Presentation.* Explain to the class that once the writer has determined the parts of a thesis, the next step is to arrange those parts in the best order. The writer attempts to arrange the parts in an order which will be logically satisfying to the reader while fulfilling the purpose of the author. Thus, the best internal organization of each essay will depend on the nature of the thesis. For example,

1. If the thesis indicates parts such as examples of ways or methods, reasons, causes, results, or arguments, then the author's task is to arrange these parts in a climactic order, that is, from least to greatest in terms of length, interest, significance, complexity or persuasiveness. Thus, the writer builds the reader's response throughout the essay to a climax at the end.

2. If the thesis is one in which the parts are not explicitly identified but are implied by the meaning of the statement, a general rule might well be to move in the order of
   a) facts
   b) evaluation or opinion
   c) suggestion or recommendation
   Thus, one builds support on a foundation of fact and prepares the reader for agreement. A good example is the thesis sentence about uninterested students which was introduced in Activity #2 above.

3. If the thesis is one indicating that a contrast is to be developed, the author should determine the common elements of the subjects which are to be contrasted and arrange them in as appropriately climactic an order as possible. Example: Most high school seniors look back at themselves as ninth graders and are amazed at the changes in themselves. Parts arranged in order of increasing importance: a) physical, b) social, c) values and interests, d) intellectual, e) self-concept.

4. If the thesis is highly argumentative, the author should be prepared to identify the contrary arguments and dispose of them adequately by developing his or her own arguments. Otherwise, the author may well leave readers unconvinced, with unanswered questions and unrefuted arguments. Two ways to organize such a paper are:
   a) Identify the major opposing arguments in at most two paragraphs at the beginning of the essay and devote the remaining major portion of the essay to developing your own arguments that refute all of these.
   b) Identify each contrary argument and develop your own argument opposing it in separate paragraphs throughout the essay, as in a debate. Sample paragraph: "While there are reasonable people who assert that . . . it is my contention that they overlook a major flaw in this view . . ."

If the author will keep the reader in mind at all times, as well as his or her own exact purpose in approaching the reader, it should not be too difficult to put the parts of an essay in an order which will satisfy both writer and reader.

6. *Activity.* Using Reproduction Page 49, provide students with the following list of thesis sentences and their parts and have them, working in groups of three or four, determine what they consider to be the most climactic order. You may, of course, prefer to have students work individually so you may more surely ascertain the grasp of each student.

1. *Thesis:* As a result of numerous disastrous experiences on blind dates, I am convinced that no right-minded young man should ever go on a date with a girl he doesn't already know.

   Parts: (numerous disastrous experiences)
   - _____ a. Girl was so nervous she threw up in the car and cried all the way home.
   - _____ b. Girl was 5'10" and made me feel like a pigmy.
   - _____ c. Girl argued violently over everything I said, including the value of rock music, health food, politics, sexual revolution, college education, communes, and my way of dressing.
   - _____ d. Girl wouldn't talk about anything.
   - _____ e. Girl didn't know anything about sports.

2. *Thesis:* Lionel Farber's life was a demonstration in itself of how a criminal is created.

   Parts: (events in Farber's life)
   - _____ a. His father, a convicted murderer, was executed.
   - _____ b. His mother deserted the family when he was four.
   - _____ c. He had a disfiguring birthmark on half his face.
   - _____ d. He was brutalized by a neighborhood gang as a child.
   - _____ e. He was unsuccessful in school.
   - _____ f. His older brother, his model and a petty criminal, was his only friend and support.

3. *Thesis:* The new college freshman's first semester is a time when he or she is forced to make successful adjustments to many new demands.

   Parts: (new demands)
   - _____ a. The freshman is forced to regulate his or her own life with no help.
   - _____ b. Classes are harder, and teachers are more demanding.
   - _____ c. The person is away from home and family, perhaps for the first time.
   - _____ d. There is a roommate, a stranger the student must live with.
   - _____ e. Unfamiliar environment is confusing.
   - _____ f. He or she must choose companions and make friends.

4. *Thesis:* Persons who achieve renown in one field often show great talent or competence in others.

   Parts: (multitalented people)
   - _____ a. Albert Schweitzer: medical missionary, expert on Bach and organs
   - _____ b. Albert Einstein: violinist, scientist
   - _____ c. Thomas Jefferson: inventor, statesman
   - _____ d. Eugene McCarthy: baseball player, poet, politician
   - _____ e. Winston Churchill: painter, statesman
   - _____ f. Ben Franklin: diplomat, printer, journalist, inventor

5. *Thesis:* Careful study has suggested certain circumstances which predispose a marriage to failure.

   Parts: (causes of failure in marriage)
   - _____ a. Deep devotion to different religions by the pair.
   - _____ b. Coming from home broken by divorce.

    _____ c. *Wide divergence in cultural or educational backgrounds.*
    _____ d. *Emotional immaturity of one or both people.*
    _____ e. *Short acquaintance before marriage.*
    _____ f. *Insufficient financial means.*
    _____ g. *Parental disapproval.*

6. *Thesis:* **The least experienced person can, with advance preparation, give a successful dinner party.**

   Parts: (steps in preparation)
    _____ a. *Plan arrangement of the table the day before.*
    _____ b. *Choose menu you already know how to cook.*
    _____ c. *Plan dishes that don't require last minute activities.*
    _____ d. *Polish silver well in advance.*
    _____ e. *Be sure table cloth and napkins are ironed the day before.*
    _____ f. *Plan in advance which serving dish will hold which item on the menu.*
    _____ g. *Choose records to provide congenial background music.*

7. *Thesis:* **A hospital is not the place to go for a rest.**

   Parts: (unnerving elements of hospital life)
    _____ a. *They wake you up to give you a sleeping pill.*
    _____ b. *After lunch, when you'd like a nap, it's visiting hours.*
    _____ c. *Constant stream of nurses, interns, etc.*
    _____ d. *Bathing you constantly.*
    _____ e. *Blood tests, samplings.*
    _____ f. *Nurses up at dawn.*

7. *Activity.* Put students into groups of three to five students each or work with the total class in one group. Ask each student to prepare a thesis sentence that explicitly indicates its parts. (They may wish to utilize a thesis they constructed for a previous activity.) Then ask the students to make a list of from four to six parts for their thesis statements, arranged on the page in random order as in Activity #6 above. Finally, have students exchange papers and try to arrange the lists of parts in an order that agrees with what each author had in mind. If you have an opaque projector, you could project each thesis and list of parts and let the entire class choose the best order.

8. *Activity.* Distribute to students the following list of thesis sentences (using Reproduction Page 50) with parts that are *not* explicitly identified. Do one or two as examples on the board for the benefit of the whole class and then let students work at dividing the statements into their logical parts and listing them in proper order. They may work individually or in pairs, as you prefer. Then let the entire class go over the list together to check each student's understanding.

   1. *Good study habits go a long way toward producing good grades.*

   2. *Some young people seem to know everything not to do to win friends.*

   3. *Being an only child has certain advantages.*

   4. *Even with the best intentions, many parents of adolescents alienate their children.*

   5. *The high school principal must be an expert in many fields besides teaching.*

   6. *Student honor codes are rarely successful in high schools.*

   7. *Disciplinary measures in school should be aimed at teaching and helping the students, rather than punishing them.*

   8. *Much dating in high school is an exercise in ego building, rather than a matter of true friendship or love.*

9. *A long engagement period increases the likelihood of a successful marriage.*
10. *A good correspondent writes letters which are a pleasure to receive.*
11. *A particularly admirable kind of courage is demonstrated by the capacity to endure.*
12. *Many lessons one should learn during the years in school have little to do with academic knowledge.*

9. *Evaluation.* Repeat the procedure in Activity #8 above, but with the following list of thesis sentences (available on Reproduction Page 51) and with students working individually.

1. *The decision of what college to attend must be based on a number of considerations.*
2. *Our failures often teach us more than our successes.*
3. *The high school drop-out creates many problems that will plague his or her future.*
4. *Based on all we know today, human society does not enjoy the prospect of a long and increasingly joyous future.*
5. *Punishment is seldom the most effective technique for teaching young people the guidelines for socially responsible behavior.*
6. *A valuable rule to live by is expressed in the question, what if everyone behaved as I am behaving.*

TOPIC V: PROVIDING TRANSITIONS

1. *Teacher Presentation.* Explain to students that it is the author's task to provide as much assistance as possible to the reader working his or her way through an essay. The author must be concerned with seeing to it that the reader does not get lost among the developmental details and fail to follow the idea sequence which has been prepared for him or her. That is, the author must strive to keep the reader informed about the organization of the paper. Perhaps the best way to keep the reader on the right path (aside from simple clarity and directness of language) is to provide "sign posts" wherever they might be helpful, much as the highway planner puts signs wherever there is a chance a driver might miss an important turn or overlook an intersection.

These signposts may take the form of deliberate transition sentences or even entire paragraphs at those points in the essay where the writer is concluding one section of the essay and moving to the next.

Such transitions may also be as simple as the addition of one word, such as the summing-up word "then" or the moving-on word "next." Or they may be an entire paragraph summing up the previous section and introducing the next. Whatever their form and length, the purpose of such signposts is simply to point the reader to the next part of the author's idea-structure and to assure the reader's easier comprehension of the essay.

One much used technique of achieving easy transitions through the structural framework of the essay is the use of leading questions. In the first part of her article "Let Us Speak to One Another," Ardis Whitman specifies at length the importance of communication in our lives. Reaching the second part of her essay, she asks, "Why, then, if communication is so important in our lives, are we unable to . . .?" and after discussing barriers which keep us from freely communicating, she goes on to ask, "But is there nothing we can do to improve the quality of our . . .?" Then she discusses possible ways to improve communication.

Following is a list of possible wordings for transitions. Along with an adaptation of the material above, they appear on Reproduction Page 52. You might want to duplicate and distribute this list to students for their discussion and use. Or you might prefer just to put each example on the board or project it with the overhead projector and lead the class in discussing them, asking students to take notes. Examples of transition devices include:

1. *It is evident, then, that the Gallic Wars proved Caesar's military genius.*
2. *In spite of these powerful arguments, there were still many dissenters.*
3. *Administrators, however, are not the only ones disturbed by this problem.*
4. *Not only must students solve these financial problems, but they are faced, also, with new and difficult academic challenges.*
5. *Having seen how the early Popes handled this problem, let us turn to the Popes of later centuries and see whether they were as successful.*
6. *We will go either to the movies or to the game.*
7. *Having considered the Renaissance, let us now move on to the Baroque.*
8. *We decided, finally, to cancel the meeting.*
9. *No discussion of literature would be complete without mentioning Shakespeare.*
10. *Granting that this viewpoint has some validity, we still question its overall viability.*
11. *In light of this evidence, then, why is it that so many people continue to smoke?*
12. *Let us turn, now, to some other more positive issues.*
13. *In concluding this presentation of photography, let us discuss lighting.*
14. *Answers, as we shall see, are not easily formulated.*
15. *Hemingway is not the only author who deals with this theme.*
16. *The third and last example to be discussed involves the Supreme Court decision on euthanasia.*
17. *Let us consider, on the other hand, the benefits of vocational training.*
18. *The answers, nevertheless, remain to be seen.*
19. *Ice cream is fattening; yogurt, conversely, is quite low in calories.*
20. *We should mention, in addition to the facts already presented, that there were two witnesses.*

2. *Activity.* Have students make up transition sentences and paragraphs like those on the list above and have them share them with the class. Let the other students try to guess the place in an essay where the transition would be suitable (i.e., what has gone just before and what will follow).

3. *Activity.* Have students look in books and magazines (preferably non-fiction) that they have read recently or are reading now and identify transitional devices the author has used to ease the reader's passage through an idea-structure. Suggest that students choose expository prose for this assignment, since the transitions are likely to be more apparent here than in fiction. Have students bring their examples to class and explain them to one another. It's probably best to let students choose the reading material they wish to examine for transitions, rather than imposing on them a teacher-chosen model.

4. *Evaluation.* To test students' ability to provide necessary transitions between the parts of an essay, administer the following two-part test, which is available on Reproduction Page 53. Answers are given below.

Part I.   Identifying Transitions

Instructions: In each group below you are given a sentence that you are to imagine is the last sentence in a paragraph, and two sentences from which to choose the first sentence of the next paragraph. Circle the letter of the sentence in each group that provides the smoothest transition. Underline the transitional or connecting devices.

1. *A simple misunderstanding, then, can become a major stumbling block to communication between teenagers and parents.*

    a) *Embarrassment plays a considerable part in the lack of communication between generations.*

    b) *Embarrassment also plays a considerable part in this lack of communication between generations.*

2. *Reading a textbook assignment actively, therefore, is an excellent way to use your study time most effectively.*

    a) *Another effective study habit is that of raising the right questions as you read.*

    b) *You should learn to raise the right questions as you read.*

3. *Courses at the high school level are generally difficult, and students are often expected to work on their own.*

    a) *On the other hand, the junior high program is organized quite differently.*

    b) *The junior high program is organized quite differently.*

4. *But, in general, students who are interested in school take more active roles in school affairs than apathetic students, for they run for offices, work hard on committees, help to make plans and formulate ideas, and interact with administrators and teachers.*

    a) *As a result of this more active role, interested students develop faster socially.*

    b) *Interested students often develop faster socially than students who are not interested in school.*

5. *We are not surprised, therefore, to learn that almost all teenagers are deeply interested in increasing their skills in human relations.*

    a) *Most young people are willing to work hard at any task which seems to contribute to group cohesiveness.*

    b) *One form this interest takes is a willingness on the part of most young people to work hard at any task which seems to contribute to group cohesiveness.*

6. *As a result of this experience, she never again cared to get on a horse.*

    a) *She turned her attention to bird watching, a safe pastime for one who loves the outdoors.*

    b) *She still loved the outdoors, however, and soon settled on bird watching as an outdoor pastime somewhat safer than horseback riding.*

7. *With these instructions, she was finally able to finish step three with no further difficulty.*

    a) *Step four, however, was another problem entirely.*

    b) *Step four presented a problem.*

8. *After a great deal of hard work, she was able to turn in the completed paper on Thursday.*

    a) *Having managed to complete her English assignment for the week, she next turned her attention to her overdue biology reports.*

    b) *She turned her attention to her overdue biology reports.*

9. *We can see, then, that this method is relatively simple and requires little technical training.*

(a) There are three _other_ methods of which, unfortunately, _this_ cannot be said.
b) There are three difficult methods which require lengthy technical training.

10. She was, in short, the most beautiful girl he had ever seen.
 (a) _But_ it was not her physical beauty which drew him to her.
 b) He was not drawn to her because of her physical beauty.

Part II. Writing Transitions

Instructions: In each group below you are given a sentence that you are to imagine is the last sentence in a paragraph, and another sentence which is the first sentence in the next paragraph. Rewrite the second sentence to provide a better transition between the paragraphs.

1. _Thus, the American woman accepted the domination of her husband for many years, apparently without question or regret._
 Many American women will no longer accept domination passively.
 Better opening sentence for the second paragraph: But many American women will no longer accept this domination passively.

2. _The materials were assembled and I was ready to begin work immediately._
 I attacked the Spanish translation, which I dreaded the most.
 Better opening sentence for the second paragraph: First I attacked . . .

3. _In fact, I was so far behind I was afraid I would not be able to finish the course._
 I had a deep interest in the next course in the sequence, so I caught up and finished the course on time.
 Better opening sentence for the second paragraph: However, I had a deep . . .

4. _Having learned this hard lesson, I was never again tempted to take something that did not belong to me._
 It was hard for me to learn the lesson that I should always tell the truth.
 Better opening sentence for the second paragraph: An equally difficult lesson for me . . .

5. _This particular incident contributed to the mutual hostility which finally led to the outbreak of fighting._
 An incident which brought two soldiers into personal conflict increased the tension on both sides.
 Better opening sentence for the second paragraph: The tension on both sides was also increased by an incident . . .

6. _If all these considerations are taken into account ahead of time, it is clear that the actual arranging of the buffet will present no problems on the day of the dinner._
 Care must always be exercised in planning the guest list.
 Better opening sentence for the second paragraph: Equally important is that care be exercised in planning the guest list.

TOPIC VI: CONSTRUCTING INTRODUCTIONS AND CONCLUSIONS

1. _Teacher Presentation._ Explain to students that an introductory paragraph is, like a transitional paragraph, a _functional_ paragraph and not a _developed_ paragraph, which presents a topic sentence and develops it in detail. The introductory para-

graph has the special function of introducing the reader to the central idea of the essay.

Generally speaking, the length of an essay determines the length of the introduction. A thesis sentence that can be supported with only three or four developed paragraphs requires only a single introductory paragraph. But an essay with six or eight major supporting points, each of which is explained in one or more paragraphs, may require two or even three paragraphs to adequately introduce the thesis.

In any case, the introduction should contain the thesis sentence in some form. Thus, the reader knows at the very outset of the essay what point the writer is trying to make and is not kept in the dark as to the writer's purpose. On the other hand, the writer can be somewhat subtle in introducing the thesis, and should avoid at all cost such awkward statements as, "In this essay I shall attempt to show that . . ." or "My thesis is that . . ."

Four common types of introductions are described below, and a sample of each is provided. This material can also be found on Reproduction Page 54, if you wish to duplicate and distribute it to students.

1. *An anecdotal introduction relates an incident which demonstrates or exemplifies the author's thesis. It is usually quite brief, points clearly and directly to the thesis and easily culminates in a statement of the thesis. Its major advantage is in capturing the reader's interest both by its content and by its easy and informal style. This opening is more likely to be favored for articles written for popular consumption than for formal scholarly works. Here is an example of an anecdotal introduction:*

Thelma Gray and Lucy Taylor, both fifteen years old and known for their adventurous spirits, said goodbye to their mothers on a sunny morning in May, 1976, and set out for their bus stop at the corner. They were invited to a picnic and swimming party at a suburban park a few miles away. Clutching their bathing suits and bright beach towels, they hurried toward a fun-filled day with their friends. Thelma and Lucy, however, never reached that park and never saw their friends again. By nightfall their bodies had been found beside a seldom used road in an isolated area of the county near the park. Both had been bludgeoned to death. Police, reconstructing the young women's last day, determined that they were two more on a growing list of girls who had decided to hitch-hike and who had paid the ultimate price for their decision. Chief of Police Erwin T. Miller had tears in his eyes as he announced the cause of the teenagers' deaths and pleaded with other girls to heed police warnings against hitch-hiking. "People," he said, "who accept rides with strangers run the risk of losing their lives in the same tragic manner as these two poor girls."

2. *The outline introduction includes a statement of the thesis along with the major parts to be covered in the essay. This introduction is not suitable for a brief essay, but may be very helpful to introduce a long essay on a difficult and complex subject. In such cases it is often helpful for the reader to know in advance exactly what aspects of a subject the author plans to develop and in what order. Thus, the reader is equipped with a "roadmap" through the essay. Here is an example of the outline introduction:*

The American Civil War is often described as the bloodiest and most tragic experience in the nation's history. The very nature of civil war, with family members divided by differing loyalties and friend estranged from friend, is, of course, sufficient reason to regard such a war with particular horror. However, a study of the toll in human suffering in the war between the North and South requires close examination of the specific aspects of the conflict. This present study will attempt to show that immediate battlefield losses, serious as they were, represented only a minor portion of the human suffering caused by the war. An examination of actual direct casualties (dead and injured) for both the North and the South will comprise the opening sec-

tion. *Succeeding sections will examine in turn the prisoner of war camps of both North and South with their grossly inadequate living facilities, diet and medical provisions; military hospitals and other medical establishments, with emphasis on the primitive nature of facilities and technology; and legal and historical records of cases in which individuals of one side or the other were accused of wreaking atrocities on helpless persons in their power. The final section will deal with sufferings of civilian populations in areas where the two armies fought, foraged, and scorched the earth. The miseries of the American Civil War, we shall see, fell on soldier and citizen alike.*

3. The <u>contrast introduction</u> *is especially appropriate when your thesis contradicts or modifies a commonly held belief or assumption. It begins with several sentences explaining the commonly held opinion and then presents the thesis as the opposite of this belief or assumption. Here is an example of the contrast introduction:*

> *Most people assume that learning to ski is not extremely difficult. They imagine the process consists of little more than strapping on two long boards, pushing off at the top of a hill, and gliding gracefully and effortlessly to the bottom. However, learning to ski is more difficult than these people realize, and requires long hours of practice, extremely good physical condition, and a lot of determination.*

4. The <u>funnel introduction</u> *is very useful and common. The writer identifies the general subject area in the opening sentence, making some generalization aimed at arousing interest and, perhaps, establishing a bond of common awareness and knowledge with the reader. The author narrows the subject down step by step, sentence by sentence, to the specific aspect of the general subject and the specific viewpoint towards it that forms the thesis. In other words, the funnel introduction begins with a very broad general idea and continues with ideas that are more and more specific, until it arrives at the thesis sentence—the most specific idea in the introduction. Since it becomes more and more narrow from top to bottom, this kind of introduction is given the label "funnel." (Draw a rough sketch of a funnel on the board or even a simple inverted triangle to help students visualize the form of this paragraph.) Here is an example of the funnel introduction which you might wish to copy into the diagram you have drawn on the board:*

> *The life of a teenager in modern America is not always pleasant. He or she is faced with a multitude of conflicts and problems, many of which seem almost impossible to overcome. Most of these problems center around school, which is not surprising considering that the teenager devotes an average of eight hours a day to school and school-related activities. One of the primary problems created by school is the intense pressure for good grades.*

2. *Activity.* Using Reproduction Page 55, give students the seven introductory paragraphs below and have them determine which method was used for constructing each introduction—anecdotal, contrast, funnel, or outline.

Paragraph I.

> *Since of all the animals the human animal alone is capable of reasoning, it would seem to follow that above all animals human beings would be able to plan and execute a regimen for living that would result in vigorous health and a harmonious, productive life. That this is far from the case is evident to the most casual observer. The lowliest of animals, unaided by anything remotely resembling human intelligence, manage, more successfully than we, to eat what is good for them, sleep as much as their bodies require, exercise enough to stay agile and remain through life a functional part of nature's harmonious whole. Human beings get low marks in all these achievements. Our sophisticated intellect, far from being an aid to promotion of health, spurs us to destructive behavior in terms of food, drink, sleep, exercise, work and play. An examination of human behavior with regard to these lifelong activities might well persuade one that good health is better promoted by animal instinct than by an intricate and miraculous brain.*

Paragraph type _____

Paragraph II.

Friendship is an art which requires more than common skill and commitment. It requires, in its highest form, knowledge of the mysteries of human motivation and a willingness to accept one's friends in terms of their own inner conceptions of themselves instead of by their all too often imperfect external expressions of self. This kind of knowledge and this capacity for acceptance are not easily gained, and are most often the consequences of long experience and practice. For young people, therefore, who are at the beginning of their practice of friendship, a simpler capacity must suffice. This can be found, I believe, in the deliberate development of the quality of loyalty. Of all the components which are important to a rich, long lasting friendship, loyalty is the most essential.

Paragraph type _____

Paragraph III.

I wanted, more than anything, to be invited to join a sorority when I entered high school. I was sure that to be left out of this magic circle of popular girls would mean the absolute end of my hopes for teenage happiness and social success. Imagine my excitement, therefore, when I received invitations to rush parties from three different clubs. And imagine the frenzy of preparations I entered into, the endless efforts to insure the acceptability of my face, figure, hair, clothes, small talk, and table manners. I was to be whatever each club wanted me to be, perfect in all respects and equally pleasing to all. As it happens, I did join a sorority but not, it soon became apparent, because I was perfect in all respects. On the contrary, my making over began the day I joined. In time the magic circle became a restricting cage and I longed to exercise my own standards and search for my own goals. Many a young girl, I suggest, learns as I did that the important task of becoming one's best self is seldom served by unthinking efforts to become what others want you to be.

Paragraph type _____

Paragraph IV.

From the beginning of history myths have abounded in which some magical elixir of youth or good health or long life has been hoped for, searched for, and, as some tales would have it, discovered and lost again. Such natural phenomena as geysers or sulphur springs have been thought to produce miraculously restorative waters, and people have traveled long distances to drink foul tasting potions in the hopes of regaining health or retaining youthful vigor. Even today, we are not far removed from our grandparents' faith in the "tonic" sold by the traveling medicine show. We buy billions of dollars worth of highly advertised, medically questionable elixirs of one kind or another and at the same time undervalue and ignore the true fountain of life which pours out its gift in almost endless supply all around us. Water, the most accessible of all drinks, is also the most essential to human health, and yet, it is a rare person, indeed, who drinks as much water as he or she should. Every adult, according to current medical knowledge, should drink at least eight full glasses of water a day for maximum support of health.

Paragraph type_____

Paragraph V.

A successful wedding, even a relatively small one, is generally the result of careful planning. There are, in fact, so many considerations to be kept in mind that it is common for the bride-to-be to hire a bridal consultant. Many girls, however, cannot afford such a consultant or, even if they can, prefer to do their own planning. Such an independent young woman might find helpful the following brief but complete collection of traditional and innovative ideas for planning a wedding. Her entire delightful task is covered, beginning with ideas for announcement of the engagement and written invitations to the wedding, and continuing through choices of wedding clothes; selection of attendants and conventions pertaining to their participation and the bride's obligations to them; choice of location, whether religious or social; decorations, including suggestions for color *schemes, uses of flowers, candles and other lighting; personal flowers for the bride as well as the two mothers, any grandmothers and the various attendants; options available as to the ceremony itself, including readings and music; and the reception following the ceremony, be it large or small. Armed with such complete and helpful advance information, the least experienced young woman can take pleasure in planning her own wedding.*

Paragraph type _____

Paragraph VI.

Choosing a puppy to be a family pet is a happy and exciting occasion, but one which requires serious advance consideration. Many circumstances relate to the making of the proper choice, and the consequences of ignoring any of them could be expensive, inconvenient, and disappointing. The prospective owners should make a careful study of the suitability of the pet to the environment it will be living in, both as a puppy and as a full grown dog. They should learn about the dispositions and habits of the various breeds they are considering, with special concern, first, for the welfare of the children in the family, and, second, for the feelings and safety of neighbors and others who might visit the house. They must be aware of the demands that proper care of their puppy will make on their time, energy, and funds, and they must be sure that their selection is compatible with their actual situation. Thus, informed and knowledgable, the family should be ready to choose a pet which can add to the happiness of the household for many years.

Paragraph type _____

Paragraph VII.

Great-grandmother Margaret, as she expected to be called, was my father's grandmother, and although she had lived with us as long as I could remember, my affection for her was tempered by a large measure of nervous respect. She was too distant, too dignified, for me to feel entirely at ease in her company. When she disappeared from our house one night without any explanation, I took for granted that she would be back, and when she did not return I began to wonder if others in the family might disappear also. I timidly questioned my mother, who assured me that no one else in the family would leave and that even Great-grandmother Margaret had not really left, but was still watching over us from up in Heaven. This failed to reassure me. For some weeks I felt as if a stern, ghostly eye were, indeed, watching me, and it was a long time before I was free of a vague feeling of anxiety. The memory of this experience leads me to believe that small children should be carefully prepared for the experience of a death in the family and that when a death actually occurs, they should receive careful and reassuring explanations.

Paragraph type _____

3. *Activity.* Using Reproduction Page 56, give students the pairs of sentences below. In each pair, one sentence is a large generalization and the other is a thesis statement related to it. Have students connect the two into a properly constructed funnel introduction by supplying the intervening sentences. In small groups students might trace the necessary steps to bring the generalization down in size to the thesis statement. Then each student could write his or her own version and they could be compared for fluency and completeness.

　　1. *Generalization: If there is one truism in our society which receives almost universal acceptance, it is the one which expresses our belief that experience is the best teacher.*
　　　Thesis: Increasingly, we are putting our older people out to pasture and depriving ourselves of contributions they could be making.

　　2. *Generalization: Puppy love is the rather condescending name adults give to the romantic feelings of very young people.*
　　　Thesis: Parents should be aware that the feelings of young people involved in a first love affair may well be as intense as any they will ever experience.

3. *Generalization:* Nature is a great healer.
   Thesis: We must fight the constant efforts of powerful industrial forces to encroach on our great wilderness sanctuaries.

4. *Generalization:* No person will be truly educated without reading constantly for pleasure.
   Thesis: The best way for parents to be sure their child is a reader is to be readers themselves.

5. *Generalization:* Values are learned primarily in the home.
   Thesis: Parental example is the most powerful teacher of values.

6. *Generalization:* The first year away at college is both an adventure and a challenge.
   Thesis: The college freshman's first task is to learn to organize his or her time.

7. *Generalization:* Mother Nature is our best teacher.
   Thesis: People could improve their health if they would listen more attentively to the signals their bodies provide for them.

8. *Generalization:* The times are changing.
   Thesis: Within two decades some regulation on the manufacture and use of automobiles will be recognized as essential.

9. *Generalization:* Loneliness is the most painful of human emotions.
   Thesis: For emotional health an individual should engage in three different kinds of human relationships: intimate, casual and nurturant.

10. *Generalization:* Many people feel a need to be different from others, to stand out from the crowd.
    Thesis: True individualism need not preclude a comfortable acceptance of most group styles, customs, and conventions.

4. *Activity.* Using Reproduction Page 57, distribute to students the funnel introductions below, all of which contain flaws, and ask the class to test them for coherence (too big gaps in thought between the sentences) and consistent direction from the opening generalization to the thesis sentence. Also ask them to comment on the suitability of the opening generalization in terms of its actual relationship to the thesis: did the writer jump too far, and did she jump in an unnatural or unwarranted direction?

1. *Americans have always claimed to be devoted to quality education for all youngsters. Many school districts are currently caught in the fiscal squeeze, with costs rising rapidly and property taxes proving inadequate as a source of revenue. More and more parents claim that the schools are not doing a good job of preparing students to make their way in society, while educators suggest that parents are failing to do their part in influencing their children to behave acceptably in an educational setting. In the light of such an impasse, it is not surprising that parents are often unwilling to vote for increased costs to themselves for their children's schooling. When class sizes get too large, quality education becomes impossible.*

2. *Young people are taking an increasing interest in planning their own education. Students feel that they know best what they should be studying and should, therefore, be allowed a dominant role in establishing course requirements and evaluative criteria as well as actual lesson plans. In theory one can hardly quarrel with this viewpoint, but in practice several considerations must be kept firmly in mind if such student participation is to be fruitful.*

3. *Some people seem to have a natural gift for friendship. They are thoughtful; they remember birthdays and other important occasions. They seem to have an unusual ability to sense the feelings of others and to avoid trespassing on the private moods of their friends. After all, one doesn't always want to be with others or reveal what one is feeling, even to a friend. Sometimes one simply wants to be left alone. A person may not be upset or depressed, but may just feel a need for solitude. Solitude is essen-*

tial to us all in some degree, and everyone should try to spend some quiet time alone each day.

4. *Clothes make the man, or so the saying goes. But what do they make him, one might well ask. His necktie must make him uncomfortable and his coat must make him hot, particularly if he remains faithful to it in summertime. His shirt collar and cuffs must make him feel stifled, his vest must make him feel padded, and his belt must make him feel like a package tied around the middle. The rebellion against such clothing as the right way, the only way to array oneself to face the world is not surprising; in fact, to many it seems long overdue. More and more men are gaining the courage to flout traditional standards for masculine dress and are daring to wear comfortable and colorful clothes to even the most formal business occasions. They are also beginning to wear their hair at casual lengths that please their sons and dismay their barbers. Men have gradually gotten used to hair styles that horrified them ten years ago. They would have been hard put to explain their horror in rational terms, but it was quite evident that their responses were to hair as a symbol rather than to hair as something real.*

5. *Activity.* Give students the thesis statements below (using Reproduction Page 58 if you wish) and have them construct anecdotal introductions leading to them. Caution students not to think of the thesis as a topic sentence and attempt to develop it with a narrative. Instead, they should narrate an incident that leads to the thesis; thus, the thesis sentence should usually be the last sentence, not the first, in their introductions.

   1. *The best camping trips are those that follow careful planning.*
   2. *Tourists should remember that bears in state parks are not always as friendly as they seem.*
   3. *What seems like a very small fib can have disastrous consequences.*
   4. *There is no denying the fact that mothers often do know best.*
   5. *A lesson worth learning is that sometimes a lesson cannot be taught; one must learn it for oneself.*
   6. *Simple courtesy makes life more pleasant for everyone.*
   7. *Parents should be aware that the example that they set speaks more loudly to their children than any words they say.*
   8. *If parents will listen carefully, they will find that their children have much to teach them.*

6. *Activity.* Using Reproduction Page 59, give students the following outline for a rather complex essay and have them construct an outline introduction for it. This assignment could be done as homework, with the students bringing their introductions to class to share with others. It may be interesting to them to see how similar and how different they are.

WRITING AN OUTLINE INTRODUCTION

Thesis: World War I provided only a glimpse of the contribution the airplane would make in such later wars as World War II.

    I. Planes used for actual combat
      A. Fighter planes
        1. Numbers of planes, makes, etc.
          a. World War I
          b. World War II
        2. Missions accomplished and results

        a.   *World War I*
        b.   *World War II*
    3. *Quality of aircraft as compared to enemy aircraft quality*
        a.   *World War I*
        b.   *World War II*
    4. *Assessment of value to war effort*
        a.   *World War I*
        b.   *World War II*

  B. *Bombers*
     (same subdivisions as above)

II. *Transport planes*
  A. *Personnel transport*
    1. *Planes available*
        a.   *World War I*
        b.   *World War II*
    2. *Men carried, numbers, where, when, success*
        a.   *World War I*
        b.   *World War II*
    3. *Assessment of importance to war effort*
        a.   *World War I*
        b.   *World War II*
  B. *Transportation of equipment*
     (same subdivisions as above)

III. *Reconnaissance planes*
  A. *Long range*
    1. *World War I*
    2. *World War II*
  B. *Combat support*
    1. *World War I*
    2. *World War II*
  C. *Spy planes*
    1. *World War I*
    2. *World War II*

IV. *Aircraft industry in America*
  A. *World War I*
  B. *World War II*

7. *Activity.* Give students, using Reproduction Page 60, the following list of thesis sentences and have them construct contrast introductions for essays based on them. Remind students to begin their introductions with a popular misconception that their thesis contradicts.

  1. *Ballet dancing requires that performers be in top physical condition. (Assumption thesis contradicts: Ballet dancing looks effortless.)*

  2. *Accepting praise gracefully requires skill. (Assumption thesis contradicts: Receiving a compliment is always a pleasure welcomed by anyone.)*

  3. *On many occasions, honesty is not the best policy. (Assumption thesis contradicts: Honesty is always the best policy.)*

  4. *If one is always cautious, one misses some of life's greatest joys. (Assumption thesis contradicts: You should always look before you leap.)*

5. *Harry Truman was perhaps America's most effective President of recent times.*
   (Assumption thesis contradicts: Harry Truman, a rather uncultivated, uneducated
   specimen of the common man, accomplished very little.)

8. *Activity.* Have students choose one of the thesis sentences they developed in previous activities or give them a list of thesis sentences to choose from. Have them write an introduction for one thesis, using any method they choose. Have them read their introductions to the class, and let the rest of the class attempt to determine which type of introduction the writer constructed. Have the writer justify the choice of type of introduction.

9. *Evaluation.* To test students' abilities to construct an effective introduction, have them choose one of the thesis statements below (also available on Reproduction Page 61) and write an introduction for it. After grading the introductions, return them to the students and have all students who wrote an introduction for the same thesis sentence move their desks into a circle, read their paragraphs to the group, and discuss similarities and differences in their approaches.

   1. *One learns, as years go by, that there is always another day; there is always a new chapter beginning as the old one ends.*
   2. *Young love is at least as serious and meaningful as the love of older persons.*
   3. *One must develop his or her own ways of achieving peace of mind.*
   4. *In the long run, your best friend is the one who is honest with you.*
   5. *The development of missiles and rockets in both Russia and America rested on work done in Germany before and during World War II.*
   6. *Both the South and North stand convicted of poor treatment of prisoners during the War between the States.*
   7. *The most significant war prizes of World War II were the minds of captured German scientists.*
   8. *Where the white man went on his explorations, he took not only white culture and religion, but also white diseases and white weapons.*

10. *Teacher Presentation.* Explain to students that the concluding paragraph, like the introductory paragraph, is a *functional* paragraph, not a *developed* one. That is, it does not present a topic sentence and develop it with details. The conclusion gives the essay a neat, rather than an abrupt, closing, so that the reader is not left hanging after the last supporting point has been made. Students often find conclusions difficult to write. The following suggestions and sample conclusions (available on Reproduction Page 62 for distribution to students) should be helpful:

    1. The conclusion can be a *summary* of the main points made in the essay—a reminder of the thesis and the arguments that the writer has used to support it. A summary conclusion is usually most suitable for long and complex essays—often those for which it is also helpful to provide the outline introduction (see Teacher Presentation #1 above).
    2. The conclusion can be an "upside-down funnel." That is, it can begin with a restatement of the thesis and then enlarge the idea with statements that become more and more general to show the setting which gives the idea significance.
    3. For shorter essays, a separate conclusion is not always needed. It is possible to include in the last supporting paragraph an extended

clincher sentence in which you echo the thesis sentence and make some sort of significant final statement.

4. Since concluding paragraphs often sound tacked on, make special attempts to link the conclusion to the paragraph that precedes it by repeating an appropriate key word or idea and by utilizing the other connecting devices discussed previously.

Here are some sample conclusions written for the same essays for which the introductions in some of the previous activities were written:

I. *When the evidence is all in, then, the arguments against hitchhiking are overpowering. People who do not heed them take a grave risk. Indeed, Thelma Gray and Lucy Taylor might be alive today if they had realized that the stranger's invitation to ride was in reality an invitation to tragedy.*

II. *So much, then, for the human being's superiority! It looks as if the animals have us beat on every aspect of health. When it comes to sleeping, eating, drinking, exercising, and maintaining activity throughout life, we might as well be mindless. Certainly we act as if we are.*

III. *Young people who develop these qualities and who learn to be truly loyal to friends will never find themselves friendless. They will have learned the skill most important to the art of friendship.*

IV. *Now the family is ready to start looking for that perfect puppy, the one who will bring pleasure to the entire household for many years. Good luck!*

V. *Many of the fears of childhood are, perhaps, unavoidable. The world, after all, is a big and fearful place, and there is much the child can learn only from experiencing it. However, the destructive fear which sometimes accompanies the early experience of death can be avoided or, at least, minimized if parents are sufficiently alert to their child's emotional needs. Properly prepared by loving and sensitive parents, there is no reason why a child's first knowledge of death cannot be a constructive, psychologically maturing experience.*

11. *Activity.* Have students look at essays in their favorite newspapers and magazines and identify the way that the authors introduce their central ideas and how they conclude their essays.

12. *Activity.* Have students write a conclusion for an essay based on the thesis sentence they used for Activity #8 or Activity #9 above.

13. *Activity.* Distribute to each student a copy of an essay from which the conclusion has been omitted. Have students read it carefully and write a conclusion for it. Then show them the original conclusion and let them discuss how theirs differ from it.

TOPIC VII: WRITING THE COMPLETE ESSAY

1. *Teacher Presentation.* Point out to students that so far they have concentrated on learning the various individual skills needed for writing a good essay. They are now ready to write an entire essay from beginning to end. Suggest that they help you list on the board the steps a writer should go through in writing an essay. Elicit answers from the total class. The result should be something like the following (which can be duplicated using Reproduction Page 63):

1. Choose a topic you know well.
2. Narrow the topic down to a subject limited enough to be developed in detail in an essay of the length you plan to write.
3. Write a thesis sentence that indicates your point of view in relation to the restricted subject.
4. Check to make sure your thesis sentence contains only one idea.
5. Check to make sure your thesis sentence contains no words that may be interpreted in more than one way.
6. Analyze the thesis to determine what are the parts that must be developed in order to cover the thesis entirely. Write down the parts in list form.
7. Decide on the best order for the parts of the thesis.
8. Begin to write the essay, one paragraph at a time, starting with the introduction.
9. For each developed paragraph, construct a topic sentence and make an outline of the specific details before starting to write it.
10. Write a conclusion.
11. Check to make sure you have provided transitions as needed to guide the reader through the paper.
12. Proofread the rough draft to make sure it contains no errors in usage or spelling.
13. Copy the essay over and submit it to the teacher or distribute it to other students to read.

2. *Activity*. Give the class a short list of general subjects—such as loneliness, space exploration, smoking, TV violence, good teachers (or see the list under Activity #3 below). Instruct them to write an essay on some aspect of one of these subjects. For average students, you may wish to distribute the checklist above and suggest that students check off each step as they finish it. More advanced students may not need the check list if they were attentive during the Teacher Presentation. This assignment can be done as homework, with students working entirely on their own. On the other hand, there is undoubtedly value in having students pair up and exchange papers after completing each step, so that they can get help and feedback from one another. Having students work together in this fashion is particularly valuable when they are first beginning to write complete essays.

3. *Activity*. Give the class the following list of general subjects to choose from and have them write an essay of at least five paragraphs. When the essays are finished, divide the class into groups of four or five students each. Have the members of each small group exchange papers until all members of each group have read the papers of all other group members. Instruct the small groups to make suggestions for improvement in the papers they have read, attempting to make every paper from their group as good as possible. After all students have made suggestions, have the authors of the papers revise them and turn them in for grading.

vacations	*required courses*	*religion*
homework	*popularity*	*pornography*
summer jobs	*human relations*	*censorship*
public health	*losing weight*	*self-discipline*
self-reliance	*advertising*	*propaganda*

tropical fish	*horsemanship*	*drag racing*
honesty	*communal life*	*country living*
pollution	*scenic rivers*	*white water*
sky diving	*public transportation*	*bigotry*
float trips	*back packing*	*motorcycles*

ASSESSING ACHIEVEMENT OF OBJECTIVES

On-Going Evaluation

The extent to which students have mastered the individual skills covered under each topic above can be measured by the procedures headed "Evaluation" in each section. Almost any of the Activities suggested in each section can also be submitted for grading.

Final Evaluation

For an overall evaluation of students' abilities to write an expository essay, assign a short essay to be written in class. List on the board several general subjects from which students can choose and instruct them to write an essay of, say, four to six paragraphs. Require them to underline the thesis sentences in their essays before submitting them for grading. Grade the essays according to these criteria:

1. Has the writer chosen a topic he or she knows well?
2. Has the writer narrowed the subject adequately?
3. Does the thesis sentence indicate that the writer has taken a point of view in relation to the subject?
4. Is the thesis unified?
5. Is the thesis precise?
6. Is the essay logically organized?
7. Does the essay contain extraneous material that does not support or amplify the thesis?
8. Is the introduction effective?
9. Does each developed paragraph contain a topic sentence developed with specific details arranged in a logical order?
10. Does the essay have an effective conclusion?

RESOURCES FOR TEACHING THE EXPOSITORY ESSAY

Below is a selected list of resources useful for teaching the skills of expository writing. It is divided into audio-visual materials (films, filmstrips, slide-tape programs, cassettes, etc.), books for students, and books for the teacher. Addresses of publishers can be found in the alphabetical list on pages 151–153. Prices, where given, are only approximate, since changes occur frequently.

Audio-Visual Materials

How to Write an Effective Composition: Organizing and Writing an Essay by Morris Schreiber. One side of an LP record. Gives a concise summary of the steps in writing an essay, similar to those outlined earlier in this chapter. Probably most useful for an individualized instruction program or small groups rather than the entire class. Folkways Records.

Organizing an Outline, Writing an Opening Paragraph, Writing Paragraphs, Editing and Rewriting. This series of filmstrips, under the series title *Composition*, is particularly suited to less capable students. Captions rather than recorded narration. Set of four: $26.00. Filmstrip House.

Composition Starters: Argumentation and *Composition Starters: Exposition* by Bruce Reeves. Two sets of four film loops (silent) and cards with questions and suggestions for writing. Students can choose from a number of possible assignments for each film loop. The loops are all taken from Walt Disney nature films and deal with topics such as "Lions Hunting Gnu" and "Hawk Attacking Rattlesnake." Doubleday Multimedia.

Organizing Your Writing. A series of eight filmstrips with captions, rather than recorded narrations, on the following topics: "The Five Steps in Writing a Composition," "Outlining a Written Composition," "The Main Parts of a Written Composition," "The Introduction of a Written Composition," "The Body of a Written Composition," "The Conclusion of a Written Composition," "The Patterns of Paragraphs," and "Making Transitions in Written Composition." Could be used for a presentation to the total class or for individualized instruction. #11140. Series: $65.90. Encyclopaedia Britannica Educational Corporation.

The Techniques of Theme Writing. A series of four sound filmstrips (records or cassettes) that explore four aspects of expository writing: the beginning, the arrangement of paragraphs, the transitions between paragraphs, and the ending. Series of four filmstrips with two cassettes: $39.75, four filmstrips with two records: $39.50. Individual filmstrips: $7.50, individual cassettes: $5.95, individual records: $5.75. Eye Gate House.

Writing: From Assignment to Composition. Two sound filmstrips with records or cassettes. Part I, "Outlining the Composition," deals with selection and delineation of the topic, organizing an outline to suit content, achieving a logical flow of thought, and the major first-draft challenge of getting something down. Part II, "Rewriting the Composition," covers topic sentences and paragraph structure, sentence length and design, elimination of unnecessary thoughts and words, and means of achieving coherence, tone, unity. Discussion guide included. $48.50. Guidance Associates.

Steps to Better Writing. Series of five sound filmstrips (records or cassettes) that present the essentials of composition in a clear, clever way. The five areas covered are as follows: "Writing Your Way to an Oscar" (establishes that writing must be approached as a systematic process), "Worrying Your Way to a Purpose" (clarifying subject, audience, purpose, role, main point), "Planning Your Way to a Paper" (how and why to outline), "Writing Away to an End" (writing the first draft), "Revising Your Way to an A" (rewriting). Highly recommended. Series: $96.00; each filmstrip: $21.50 with record, $22.50 with cassette. Thomas Klise Co.

Writing a Good Theme. Sound filmstrip. Part One explains and shows by examples an essay in terms of development of the introduction, the body, and the conclusion. Part Two explains and shows by examples an essay in terms of unity and coherence. Sound on records or cassettes. $30.00. RMI Educational Films.

Writing a Short Theme. Sound filmstrip presenting a step-by-step procedure for organizing and writing a good essay. Establishes a number of criteria for evaluating a theme and shows by examples how to distinguish between good and bad themes. Sound on records or cassettes. $20.00. Westwood Educational Productions.

Books for Students

A Short Guide to Writing Better Themes by Ann R. Morris. Composed chiefly of college freshman essays which the student can use as models. Discussion questions call the student's attention to various aspects of each model; a writing assignment follows each. Suitable only for advanced students in upper grades. Paperbound. $2.00 (less school discount). Everett/Edwards, Inc.

A Composition Practice Book by Zan L. Skelton, Jr. Provides, as the title suggests, opportunities for the student to write many compositions of various types, from paragraphs through the term paper. For most assignments space is provided right in the book for the student to write responses, with the book serving as a convenient reference file of compositions and corrections throughout the year. Suitable for average students from grade nine up. Paperbound. $4.00. J. Weston Walch, Publisher.

Twenty Steps to Better Composition by the staff of READ Magazine. A real bargain, considering the low price and excellent contents. Covers all aspects of expository writing from word choice to paragraphs to essays. Workbook format lets students respond right in the book to many assignments. Especially useful for average or slow students. $.50. Paperbound. Xerox Education Publications.

Organization and Outlining by J. F. Peirce. Focuses chiefly on patterns of organization and the various types of outlines, but also includes brief sections on other aspects of expository writing. Probably not useful as the sole text in any composition course, but individual students could be referred to this book for extra explanations and practice. Paperbound. $4.00. Arco Publishing Company.

The Art of Composition by Barbara Pannwitt. A brief, rather superficial introduction to basic aspects of expository writing. Packaged in a visually attractive, compact little paperback. One of a series of "Contemporary English Modules" with a single teacher's guide for all composition titles. Another title in the series, *The Persuasive Writer* by Deborah Stevens, is somewhat more substantial. Paperbound. Silver Burdett Company.

The Freshman Writer by Michele F. Cooper. An excellent "how to survive" book that college-bound high school students may find useful. Includes sections on writing about literature, the term paper, and essay exams. Emphasis is on giving the reader the bare essentials rather than extensive practice. Paperbound. $1.95. Barnes & Noble.

How to Write Themes and Term Papers by Barbara Lenmark Ellis. A survival guide, similar to the book described above, but more appropriate for high school students. Contains only explanations, no exercises or assignments. Paperbound. $1.95. Barron's Education Series.

The Lively Art of Writing by Lucile Vaughan Payne. A superb basic composition text for high school students. Gives very little attention to paragraphs, but treats all other aspects of expository writing thoroughly. May be somewhat difficult for slower students or those in grades below eleventh. Available in both hardbound and paperbound editions. Paper: $1.25, Mentor. Hardbound, Follett Publishing Company.

The Five-Hundred-Word Theme by Lee J. Martin and Harry P. Kroitor. Intended for college freshmen, but very appropriate for capable high school students. Takes much the same approach as the material in the preceding section of this chapter. Clear explanations, many examples, useful exercises and activities. Paperbound. Prentice-Hall.

Composition Workshop by Herbert M. Rothstein, Peter Beyer, Frank Napolitano. A series of small workbooks without grade level designations, so that they can be used for multi-level individualized learning in the classroom. Includes explanations and activities dealing with words, sentences, paragraphs, and longer forms. Excellent for average students. Clearly delineates skills to be mastered and provides opportunity for practice. Students record their progress on a chart at the back. Paperbound. Prentice-Hall.

The Writer's Handbook by John B. Karls and Ronald Szymanski. Opens with an extensive glossary of terms and topics related to writing, which students might find useful for reference purposes. More useful, though, is the "Writer's Guide," which contains explanations of various aspects of the writing process and practice activities. Suitable for average students. Paperbound. $3.21. Laidlaw.

Composition: Models and Exercises by Harold Fleming, Allen Glatterhorn, Philip McFarland, Desmond J. Nunan, and Diane Wilbur. A series of five books covering roughly grades 7–12 but since they carry no grade-level designation, the teacher can be flexible in choosing the book appropriate for the needs of the class. Each book contains examples of professional writing, guided student analyses of the writing skills illustrated in these examples, and composition assignments applying these skills. Teacher's manual for the series. Paperbound. $1.95. Harcourt Brace Jovanovich.

Steps to Better Writing by Gene Stanford. A self-teaching, self-checking workbook. Contains all the instructions and explanations that students require and allows them to check their own work against an answer key. Basic skills of writing are broken down into small, logical steps; the student practices each step before moving on to the next. Especially suitable for grades 7–10 or slower and average students in upper grades. Paperbound. $2.10. Holt, Rinehart & Winston.

Books for Teachers

Some of the titles listed above as appropriate for more capable students are also very useful as teacher resources even if they are too difficult for use as a student text. See especially: *A Short Guide to Writing Better Themes, Organizing and Outlining, The Freshman Writer,* and *The Five-Hundred-Word Theme.*

Teaching Written English Today by W. K. Jones and A. J. Francis. A collection of teaching strategies useful for a variety of grade levels. Paperbound. $5.00. J. Weston Walch, Publisher.

4

Teaching the Research Paper

At one time no student graduated from high school without writing at least one, usually several, formal research papers, complete with footnotes in MLA style. Today, the popularity of the research paper as a learning experience for all students is waning. Many teachers question whether it is the best way of using valuable time in the English class, time that might be utilized teaching more basic skills that all students—even those not going on to college—need to master.

But even teachers who question the importance of the formal research paper acknowledge that students need a rudimentary understanding of how to collect a wide range of information on a topic, how to organize that information into an effective presentation, and how to give credit for ideas that are not one's own.

This chapter,[1] therefore, focuses on introducing students to the process of compiling and presenting information on a topic, but does not presume to give students the thorough, comprehensive mastery of research skills that are probably best taught at the college level. The emphasis is on finding information in the library, choosing and narrowing a topic, systematically collecting information on the topic, and presenting the information in a well organized manner. Whether to have students master a particular system of footnoting, for example, is a decision that must be made by individual teachers, based on the system they prefer and their knowledge of their own students.

OBJECTIVES

As a result of the learning experiences in this chapter, the student should be able to:

1. Utilize the *Readers' Guide,* card catalog, Dewey Decimal System, dictionaries, encyclopedias, and other reference books to find information in the library.

---

1. Adapted from teaching materials prepared by Robert Evans, English Department, Perry Junior High School, New Hartford, New York, and used with permission.

2. Choose and narrow a topic for a research project.
3. Systematically gather information from a variety of sources.
4. Keep efficient records of the sources of information.
5. Organize the information he or she has collected into an informative or persuasive essay.
6. Utilize a logical system for giving credit for ideas that are not one's own.

LEARNING EXPERIENCES

TOPIC I: LOCATING INFORMATION IN THE LIBRARY

1. *Teacher Presentation.* Point out to students that there is simply too much knowledge for anyone to ever remember it all, but that if they develop the ability to locate information, particularly in the library, they can have easy access to much of the knowledge of the human race. To do this, they must have a working knowledge of the library—the way it is organized, sources of information, and location of information in the various areas. With this information, a student will find the library to be a tool at his or her disposal, rather than a vast complicated jungle of books, magazines, shelves, chairs, and librarians.

   Begin with a presentation of the basic headings of the Dewey Decimal System, either by utilizing an overhead transparency made from the chart on Reproduction Page 64 or by distributing copies of the chart reproduced by spirit duplicator. As an example of how the DDS subdivides the general categories into subtopics, write the following chart on the board:

   900–999 History, Geography and Biography
   910 General Geography
   920 General Biography
   930 History of Ancient World
   940 History of Modern Europe
   950 History of Modern Asia
   960 History of Modern Africa
   970 History of North America
   980 History of South America
   990 History of Rest of the World

2. *Activity.* As an alternative to simply telling the students how the DDS is organized, ask students to divide all the knowledge areas in the world into 10 categories. See if they come up with any of the ones in the Dewey Decimal System. Point out similarities and differences.

3. *Activity.* After presenting the ten major DDS categories to the class, have students, working individually or in small groups, try to expand on what would be found in each category, perhaps by listing at least five topics that would be found in each one. Have students meet in small groups and compare their work, discussing any items in one anothers' lists that they think are out of place.

4. *Activity.* To help students remember the main categories of the DDS for their own use, have them compose a sentence of words that begin with the same letters

as the DDS categories. For example: *G*eorge (General works, 000) *P*urdy (Philosophy and psychology, 100) *R*ode (Religion, 200) *S*ix (Social sciences, 300) *L*arge (Language, 400) *P*igs (Pure Science, 500) *A*cross (Applied science and useful arts, 600) *A*cres (Arts and recreation, 700) of *L*ovely (Literature, 800) *H*ills (History, geography and biography, 900).

5. *Activity*. Assign students at random to small groups of four to five students each. Distribute copies of a worksheet containing the following questions and have each group come to agreement on one set of answers to submit:

   1. List the Dewey Decimal classifications and their numbers.
   2. From the accompanying map, put the location number of each category of the Dewey Decimal System after its heading in question 1 above. (See Activity 16 for suggestions for preparing map of your school library.)
   3. Indicate the Dewey Decimal System category in which each of the following would most likely be found:
      A. Book on Catholicism
      B. Book on water skiing
      C. Book on astronomy
      D. Book of plays
      E. Encyclopedia
      F. Book on engineering
      G. A bibliography
      H. A thesaurus
      I. Book on government
      J. Book on psychology.
   4. True or False
      A. The Dewey Decimal System classifies all books in the library.
      B. Painting, photography and music are all found in the 700's.
      C. Some books may be classified into two or more categories of the Dewey Decimal System.
      D. Dictionaries are found under General Works (000's).
      E. Each Dewey Decimal classification has its own subclassifications.

   Or, alternatively, the questions above can be utilized as a quiz to determine how well students have mastered the basic concepts of the Dewey Decimal System.

6. *Teacher Presentation*. Less able students may profit from an explanation of the parts of a book, so that when they locate a book that might contain useful information they will know how to find the information they seek in it. Choose a general nonfiction work and, using the opaque projector if possible, show students the title page, preface, chapter headings, illustrations, tables, maps, appendix, table of contents, glossary, bibliography, index, author, illustrator, publisher, copyright notice and other parts of the book, explaining how each can be helpful to readers in finding what they are looking for.

7. *Activity*. For many of the Teacher Presentations about locating sources of information, the school librarian is an obvious choice of guest speaker. In inviting the librarian to visit the class, make sure to be specific about the particular skills you want the students to master and provide him or her with some notion of the ability and maturity level of the class. Even if you choose not to invite the librarian to speak to the class, enlist his or her cooperation when teaching the research

paper, since many of the Activities require the use of library facilities. After fully understanding what you are doing, the librarian is better able to be helpful to students learning about the library.

8. *Activity.* Bring to class reference books of all kinds as may be found in the library. Hand these out to students, with the requirement that each student examine the book he or she has been given and report to the class the nature of that book, its title, makeup, and usefulness. The student will make a brief report; for example, "This is a book entitled *Roget's Thesaurus.* It is like a dictionary but it lists synonyms for all kinds of words. It would be useful for writing papers or creative writing when another word or better word is needed."

9. *Activity.* After students have had an introduction to major reference books and their contents, give them a mystery to solve that requires them to track down information in a wide variety of reference works. Here is the approach English teacher Paul Janeczko took with this Activity:[2]

"For more than five years Interpol has been trying to track down one of its most notorious enemies, a man by the name of Jon P. Ulbrec Zyanaka. Al Dreman, an American now in charge of the Berlin office of Interpol, considers Zyanaka to be one of the most influential international criminals the world has ever known. Zyanaka's interests were in all fields of crime, but his most successful ventures had been in the traffic of illegal drugs."

So begins "Interpol Case #101," an imaginary story that we used to give our ninth and tenth graders some practical experience in using some basic reference tools. To continue with our story:

"Dreman had heard through the grapevine that Zyanaka was ready to receive a shipment of pure heroin worth more than three million dollars. One Saturday as Dreman was going over some clues in the case, he received a phone call from his new partner, Zak J. Nepaluco who told him that he had found Dale Thanmur dead in a back alley near The Wall. Thanmur, an American, was one of Interpol's top informers. Dreman questioned Nepaluco:

'Did he have anything on him?'

'Yes, he did. He was carrying some scraps of papers with some strange sort of scribblings on them.'

'Anything else?'

'Nothing else.'

'Did he say anything to you before he died?'

'Yes. I got to him just before he died. He muttered a few phrases, but they were like the scraps of paper; they didn't make any sense to me.'

'What did he say?'

'I wrote them down right away so I wouldn't forget them. I figured it would be better if you saw them. It's safer than me saying them over the phone.'

'Good idea, Zak.'

'I'll be right there and we can both see if we can make any sense out of them.'

'Fine. I'll see you in a little while.'

Nepaluco hung up and Dreman waited for him to arrive. 'Maybe,' he thought, 'just maybe this is what we've been waiting for.'

Dreman and Nepaluco spent that entire night going through the information that Thanmur had on him when he met his fate. After much talk, they were finally convinced that they had all the information they needed to find when and where Zyanaka was going to make his big pick up."

2. Paul Janeczko, "Interpol Case #101: Getting Students to Use Reference Works," *English Journal* 61 (October, 1972), 1048–50. Copyright © by the National Council of Teachers of English. Reprinted by permission of the publisher and Paul Janeczko.

What followed this little story was an explanation of the task at hand. This game, it must be pointed out, was preceded by a full explanation of what some specific reference works contain and how to use them profitably. The rules of the game were quite simple:

"You are about to attempt to solve a mystery. You are to gather information in an effort to beat Dreman and Nepaluco to the discovery of the time and location of Zyanaka's drug delivery. All of the information can be found in our library in the following reference works:

Encyclopedia Americana
Encyclopaedia Britannica
Collier's Encyclopedia
National Geographic World Atlas
Guinness Book of World Records
Dunlop Illustrated Encyclopedia of Facts
The New York Times Encyclopedia Almanac
Information Please Almanac
Webster's Third International Dictionary (unabridged)
. . . and the card catalog

"After you have gathered the information, you should try to see if there is something important about the information. Be careful. Don't overlook something that may appear insignificant. The persons who can make the best conclusions from the information will be the ones to solve the mystery.

"After you have exhausted clues 1, 2, and 3, come to see me and I will give you your next clue. There are ten clues in all; I will give you one at a time. You may take an educated guess at any time, but each incorrect guess will cost you one point. You will start with ten points and work your way down from there.

"You must also keep very detailed notes of your information which must include the books you used as well as the process you used. These will be very helpful in reviewing your case.

"Interpol Case #101 does have a solution and you can find it if you get accurate information and then try to reason carefully.

"Good Luck! You have no time limit on this problem although I would like to talk with you each day to evaluate your progress. Also, please don't hesitate to come to me if you meet a problem."

The clues, their sources, and their meanings are as follows:

#1: *GREENLAND, TRISTAN DA CUNHA, ST. HELENA (We wanted them to realize that these were all islands. Any encyclopedia.)*

#2: *THE NUMBER OF REVOLUTIONS AROUND THE EARTH MADE BY RUSSIAN SPACECRAFT VOSHUD 1 ON FEBRUARY 12, 1964.*

#3: *THE AVERAGE TEMPERATURE FOR FEBRUARY IN MOBILE, ALABAMA (The answer to this clue and the previous clue are the longitude and latitude of the place we were looking for. The New York Times Encyclopedia Almanac.)*

#4: *MARJORY BARTLETT SANGER (Miss Sanger wrote a book entitled Mangrove Islands. This information was meant to reinforce the idea that we were looking for an island. Card catalog.)*

#5: *CARTOGRAPHY ("The study of maps and map making" was meant to put the students onto the idea that a map has more to it than land and water. Webster's Third.)*

#6: *THE HARPER ENCYCLOPEDIA OF SCIENCE, PP. 648-9 (These pages carry a definition and explanation of longitude and latitude.)*

#7: *OUT TO SEA WHERE IT IS COLD/YOU FIND THE WHITE GOLD (This corny rhyme was meant to tell them that we were looking for an island and that it was probably in the north.)*

#8: *WHAT GOES UP, MUST COME DOWN/WHAT OPENS MUST CLOSE:/LIKE A SUBWAY AND A WORLD'S FAIR/IN NEW YORK CITY (The subway in New York City opened on October 27, 1904 and the World's Fair closed on the same date in 1940. This was the date of the pick up. Information Please Almanac.)*

#9:   *IF YOU GO FARTHER THAN 300 KILOMETERS, YOU'VE GONE TOO FAR (The point of reference for this one is Berlin since that is where our action takes place. Atlas.)*

#10:   *HALFWAY BETWEEN AARHUS AND MALBORK,/BUT CLOSER TO BOSTOCK AND KOTOBREZ (Again, the atlas will allow them to zero in on the correct location: Bornholm Island.)*

10. *Teacher Presentation.* Make a transparency from Reproduction Page 65 ("Sample Entries from the *Readers' Guide"*) or reproduce it and distribute it to students. Use these sample entries to introduce students to the purpose and use of the *Readers' Guide.* Include the following points in your explanation:

    1. The *RG* indexes magazine articles from approximately 130 magazines.
    2. It first appeared in 1900 and is now published twice monthly.
    3. The *RG* is published cumulatively, listing magazines of the current month only for two months, while the third month includes all entries for the previous two months.
    4. There is a bound annual or two-year cumulation at the end of the year.
    5. An abridged *Readers' Guide* (begun in 1935) indexes approximately 40 magazines.
    6. Articles may be found under either an author entry or a subject entry.
    7. Often one subject may be followed by many divisions or subheadings.
    8. All abbreviations are to be found in the front of the book.
    9. To find events of a specific date, look in the *Readers' Guide* that contains that date.
    10. To find current topics, or topics of uncertain dates, begin with the latest issue and work back.

    Also explain how to obtain a back issue of a magazine in your school library. Other basic information about the *Readers' Guide* can be found in a useful booklet, "How to Use *The Readers' Guide to Periodical Literature* and Other Indexes," available free from the H. W. Wilson Company, 950 University Avenue, Bronx, New York 10452. You might wish to obtain enough copies of this booklet to distribute to all students. A set of up to fifty copies is free; additional copies may be purchased at two cents each.

11. *Activity.* Reproduce the worksheet on Reproduction Page 66 ("Worksheet on the *Readers' Guide"*) and distribute to students. Have them complete the worksheet either individually or in small groups.

12. *Evaluation.* To determine how well students understand the use of the *Readers' Guide,* or to give them additional practice, reproduce the "Quiz on the *Readers' Guide"* that appears on Reproduction Page 67 and distribute it to students. Or make an overhead transparency and conduct a total class discussion of the questions.

13. *Teacher Presentation.* Explain to students the three types of cards found in the card catalog, using a transparency made from Reproduction Page 68 ("The Card Catalog"), or make a spirit duplicator master and reproduce the page and dis-

tribute it to students. Students should be able to identify the three types of cards and should know the pertinent information found on each—author, title, subject, call number, pages, illustrations, publishers, and publishing date.

14. *Activity.* Using Reproduction Page 69, duplicate the "Worksheet on the Card Catalog" to give students practice in using information about the card catalog. You will probably wish to let them work in pairs and then compare answers with another pair of students when they have finished. Or this can be used as a quiz, with students working alone.

15. *Activity.* Have students discuss in groups the things that happen in the school library that make studying difficult or things which happen that irritate a student who wishes to work. Then have them consider the following list of ways to help others in the library and see if their ideas are reflected here:

   1. Do your work quietly.
   2. Return books on time.
   3. Return books to their proper place after using them (proper area, shelf, alphabetical sequence, etc.)
   4. Treat books with care.
   5. Do not mark or cut up magazines.
   6. Learn and follow the rules of your library.

Then have the students draw up their own list of library user guidelines. This could be done by the entire class and posted in the library as a reminder.

16. *Activity.* Draw on a spirit master a simple map or diagram of your school library. Place a number on the map at the location of each major source of information, such as card catalog, magazine section, *Readers' Guide,* magazine storage, newspapers, vertical file, atlases, almanacs, dictionaries, encyclopedias, other reference books, each of the major categories of the Dewey Decimal System. Duplicate enough copies of the map for each student to have at least one. Utilize one or more of the following approaches to help students become familiar with the physical layout of the library:

   A. Have students fill in all the numbered areas of the map with the name of what is located there.
   B. Have students make a list of the various areas of the library that correspond to the numbers on the map. Have them match these with the proper number.
   C. Working in teams, have students race to see who can correctly identify the areas of the library first.

17. *Activity.* Assign students to pairs or let them choose a partner. Have each student write down some topic of interest to him or her and give it to his or her partner. The partner's job is to find a magazine article on that subject listed in the *Readers' Guide,* write down the information needed to locate the magazine, find the article and give it to the partner. The magazine is then to be read and returned by the partner interested in that topic.

18. *Activity.* Assign students to pairs or let them choose a partner. Have each person choose a drawer from the card catalog and find a book listed therein that interests him or her, marking it with a piece of paper or a paper clip. The student

then gives the card drawer to the partner, who writes down the information from the card that is needed for finding the book. He or she looks for the book, turns it over to his or her partner, and at the same time receives the book the partner has been looking for.

19. *Activity.* On the following page is a list of twenty-five pieces of information that could be located fairly easily in one school's library. Prepare a similar list for your library using any items from our list that can be located in your library, if you wish. Duplicate it and distribute it to students. Utilize it in one of the following ways:

   A. As an individual assignment, with each student finding the information on his or her own.
   B. As the focus for class discussion, deciding where the best place to look for each item would be.
   C. As a scavenger hunt, with the class divided into groups of five, with groups competing against one another to find the correct answers first.

20. *Activity.* Have each student choose a topic that is of particular interest; the procedures in Activities #4 and #5 on page 108 will help students who can't think of one. Then tell them to locate all possible sources of information on that topic, using both the library and any outside sources. (The topic must be fairly narrow or the number will be too large.) Have students either photocopy the source (if it's a magazine in the library) or if possible clip the actual article itself (from old newspapers and magazines at home). The object is to compile a file of articles that can be utilized in the classroom by other students. (See Activity #10, page 104.)

21. *Activity.* With the approval of your school librarian, have students work for a week in the library, either before or after school or during study halls or free time. They can be useful in returning cards to books, replacing books on the shelves, getting magazines for students, straightening the book shelves and magazine stacks, signing out books, adding to the vertical file, and many other activities.

22. *Activity.* An exciting, comprehensive approach to developing library skills can be found in *Search*, an "interaction unit" published by Interact, Inc. Students work in teams to complete a number of activities similar to some of those suggested above, all the while accumulating points in a race against other teams to earn the highest number of points. Included is a "Problem-Solution Competition" in which teams create brief library research problems for another team to solve. See the resources list at the end of this chapter for further information.

23. *Evaluation.* On Reproduction Pages 70 and 71 are sample tests for measuring students' understanding of basic concepts related to finding information in the library. They can either be used as quizzes, or they can be assigned to students to work on in small groups as learning experiences.

TOPIC II: PREPARING FOR RESEARCH

1. *Teacher Presentation.* Explain to students that researching a topic is a process very well described by the word "research" itself. It consists of searching and

Group _____ Period _____

SCAVENGER HUNT

Give the answer or the exact place where the information was found.

1. What does "vacada" mean in Spanish?

2. What is an "amphilinidea" in science?

3. Give three synonyms for the noun "jinx."

4. What college did Dick Gregory attend?

5. What is the population of Deer Park, Ohio, as of 1970?

6. Who said, "A jest breaks no bones?"

7. What is the title of a March, 1970 magazine article on air traffic control?

8. How many railroads have served Utica, New York?

9. Name two baseball novels by John Tunis.

10. Give the address and birthdate of Barbra Streisand.

11. Give the date and the cause of the sinking of the *Maine*.

12. Name the play presently on Broadway in the Shubert Theater.

13. What is the tuition for Drew University?

14. What are the dates of the 1970 magazine articles on Oral Roberts University?

15. Identify the world's longest railway tunnel (name or length).

16. Name the first word on page 233 of the book *Moon of Three Rings*.

17. Who won the Academy Award for best actress in 1935?

18. Name the author of "Crystal Moment," a poem.

19. Give the title of an illustrated book on hippies.

20. Who was on the cover of October 24, 1976 *New York Times* Magazine?

21. Give the 1960 population of Syracuse, New York.

22. Give the author and call numbers of a boy scout book on automobiles.

23. Identify the author of a magazine article on pork.

24. Who wrote the opera *Carmen*?

25. What is the first word on page 303 of *Little Women*?

searching again to find information necessary to explain or prove a point. The search is for information above and beyond what the writer already possessed. However, writing a research paper is more of an organizational task than a writing task. The researcher must have a plan of action to assure that the job is done thoroughly and efficiently. By proceeding in a systematic, step-by-step fashion, the researcher will be successful in going from a vague idea of what he or she wants to write about to a finished paper which has been researched, organized, and put together in a proper form.

2. *Activity.* Ask students to help you list on the board the steps a writer might need to go through in preparing a research paper: "Imagine that your science teacher assigned you to write a paper about pollution. How would you go about doing it?" Elicit from students their ideas about the procedure for researching a topic; then distribute the guidelines entitled "Ten Steps for Writing a Research Report" (see Reproduction Page 72), or you can make an overhead transparency and project the guidelines as you discuss them with students.

3. *Teacher Presentation.* Emphasize to students that before they can start researching a topic in earnest they must have a clear idea of what their paper is going to deal with. If they have the freedom to choose a topic, the task is fairly easy. All that is required is to select something that one is interested in learning more about or feels strongly about. Activity #4 and Activity #5 suggest several ways of selecting a topic if one can choose freely. But if the topic has been assigned by a teacher, the process is a little more difficult. What one has to do is to determine some aspect of the topic that is interesting or appealing. This may require some informal preliminary research to learn something about the topic in order to discover some part of it that one is curious about or concerned about.

4. *Activity.* To help students choose a topic for a research paper, have them answer the following questions:
    A. List three things you would like to be doing right now if you weren't in school.
    B. What are some things you have wondered about—things like, "I wonder why . . ." and "I'd like to know more about . . ."?
    C. What are the three biggest problems facing the world today? our nation? our community? our school?
    D. What would you like to be able to do better?
    E. What have you always wanted to try?

Any of these questions could be the basis of small group discussions in which students share ideas, explore their own ideas and beliefs in more detail, and are stimulated to consider new points of view which may not have occurred to them. Several topics appropriate for research projects are likely to emerge in the mind of each student.

5. *Activity.* Duplicate the list of topics on Reproduction Page 73. Instruct students to circle the three topics that they would like to find out more about. Then have them place check marks next to three topics about which they hold strong opinions.

6. *Teacher Presentation.* Explain to students that whether a topic has been assigned by the teacher or has been left up to the student to choose, it is almost always

necessary to narrow it to manageable size. As an example, have students imagine they were assigned to write a paper about "pollution." Point out that this topic is too broad (e.g., air pollution, water pollution, litter, oil spills, sewage, automobiles, factories, garbage disposals, glass recycling, etc.). Then have them choose one subtopic and break it down even further by thinking of a particular aspect of it. For example, for "oil spills," they might mention "Whose responsibility is it to clean up oil spilled by a tanker in the ocean?" For "glass recycling" they might mention "Ways to organize a glass recycling program in your community." Underscore the fact that a topic like "Ways to organize a glass recycling program in your community" is an appropriate topic for a research paper because it is focused and of manageable size, whereas the original topic ("pollution") is too big.

7. *Activity.* Working with the total class, ask volunteers to tell the class one of the items from the "Ideas for Research Papers" list that they either circled or checked. Then have the entire class suggest ways to narrow that topic until it is of manageable size.

8. *Activity.* Assign students at random to small groups and have them tell the group one topic they chose from the list of "Ideas for Research Papers." Then have the group brainstorm all the possible subtopics that could be the focus of a research paper.

9. *Activity.* If students need more practice and instruction in limiting a topic for a paper, utilize the teacher presentations and activities dealing with this topic in Chapter 4.

10. *Activity.* Have students choose one idea that struck them as interesting or intriguing in Activities #4 and #5 above. Ask them to narrow it down to one aspect that is limited enough in size that it can be adequately dealt with in a single paper. When they have finished, have them find another student who has finished and compare results, checking to make sure their partners have sufficiently narrowed their topics.

11. *Teacher Presentation.* Since a research paper generally attempts to persuade the reader to accept some point of view (although some papers may be simply informative), students should be encouraged to formulate a thesis statement—one single declarative sentence that states the writer's point of view on the topic. For example, "Unless drastic steps are taken, automobile pollution will become an extremely serious problem." Point out that a statement such as this is somewhat arguable (i.e., not everyone would agree to it), whereas a statement such as "Grass is green," is not likely to arouse much debate.

12. *Activity.* Have students choose several ideas that interest them from Activities #4 and #5 and narrow them to manageable size. Then have them formulate a thesis statement for a research paper on that topic. When they have finished, assign them to small groups to share and compare their results.

13. *Teacher Presentation.* Suggest that students jot down all they already know about a topic they have chosen for a research paper before they begin systematic research. This will save them work in looking for information they already have, and will give them ideas about what information they need to collect.

14. *Activity.* Have students choose one or more thesis statements that they formulated for Activity #12 above and list everything they already know that could be used to support it. Then have them make another list of the things that they think they might need to find out in order to support or explain their thesis sentence.

TOPIC III: GATHERING INFORMATION

1. *Teacher Presentation.* Point out to students that from this point on in the process of collecting information for their papers, the material they find will belong to other people. The students are only borrowing or using it to help them prove a point. Therefore, the proper (and legal) thing to do is to give credit to all sources of information. This is done through context notes, footnotes for quotations and paraphrases, and bibliography entries which will be explained in more detail later.

   Also suggest ways that students can go about finding information that will be useful in writing their papers. If they have mastered the earlier section on use of the library, they will need little more than some reminders; otherwise, they may need explicit guidelines.

   1. List all authors, titles and subjects suggested by your topic. Look these up in the card catalog and list the call number, author, and title of each book on the topic listed in the catalog.
   2. Using the Dewey Decimal outline, find shelf location(s) of books on your topic. Use the index of all books in this section to locate material on your topic. Ask the librarian if there are similar books on reserve which you should look at.
   3. Is there a possibility that there are pamphlets or newspaper articles on your topic in the vertical file?
   4. Look up your topic in at least two encyclopedias. Use the index.
   5. Look up your topic in the *Readers' Guide* and list all magazine material on cards.
   6. Use any other reference books that might have material related to your topic.
   7. Don't overlook the current issues of magazines and newspapers which will not have been listed in the *Readers' Guide* and other references.
   8. Are there sources other than the library that you should consult? Can you secure information from interviews, for example, or from public records?

2. *Teacher Presentation.* Explain to students that as they search for and find information related to this topic, they need to do more than just read the material they find. They must record it for future use in writing the paper, since they can't rely on memory alone to store all the details they'll be reading. Keeping records, then, is an important part of research. Two kinds of records are particularly necessary: 1) notes of the ideas the writer has located that may be worth including in the paper, and 2) information about the sources of these ideas. Both types of records are best kept on 3x5 or 4x6 index cards so that the writer can rearrange their order when planning and writing the paper.

3. *Teacher Presentation.* Reproduce the "Sample Note Cards" that appear on Reproduction Page 74 and distribute to students—or, preferably, make a transparency and project it using the overhead projector. Point out that the paragraph at the top is part of a magazine article on page 57 of its issue. The two cards have been used to record details from this passage that the researcher may later wish to incorporate into his or her paper. Emphasize that every note card should include the following (and point out each on the sample cards):

   1. A heading indicating the subject of the notes. Only one subject (piece of information) should be written on a card. Use a different card for each new idea, even if it appears in the same article. Stress that the researcher does *not* attempt to put all notes about one article on a single card!
   2. The page number of the article where the passage appeared.
   3. A number in the upper right-hand corner indicating which source the idea came from. Thus all note cards from a given source would be designated with the same number. (This number will also appear on the bibliography card on which all the information about the source appears—more about that later.)
   4. Either a quotation, indicated by quotation marks, or (in your own words) a paraphrase of an idea from the article, indicated by parentheses. Point out to students that the first sample note card contains a direct quotation from the article; the second contains a paraphrase.

4. *Activity.* Reproduce and distribute the "Worksheet on Notetaking" that appears on Reproduction Page 75. Have students assume they are writing a paper on automobile pollution, with the thesis statement, "Unless drastic measures are taken, automobile pollution will become an extremely serious problem." Have them imagine that the passages on the left side of the worksheet are a portion of page 57 of a magazine article on automobile pollution they have found in the library. This is the third source of information they have used. Have students fill in the "cards" on the right hand side with either direct quotations or paraphrases of the passages on the left. Remind them of the information that every note card should include (Teacher Presentation #3 above). Have students work individually. When everyone has finished, call on volunteers to tell the class how they filled out the cards. Answers will vary, of course. The class should try to determine whether each volunteer has filled out the cards correctly.

5. *Activity.* Distribute to each student a copy of a magazine and tell them to choose an article that they are at least somewhat interested in. Give each student several index cards or have them draw facsimiles on their own paper. Have them record on the cards ideas from the article they have read, imagining that the article is a relevant source of information for a paper they are writing on that topic. When they have finished, have students meet in small groups. Each student will select one of his or her cards to submit to the group for checking. The groups should consider the following questions in evaluating the cards:

   1. Has the researcher indicated the subject of the information at the top of the card?
   2. Does the card indicate what page the information appears on?

3. Does the card indicate whether this is a quote from the article or an idea expressed in the researcher's own words?
4. Does the card indicate which source the information comes from? (Each student can use an imaginary number.)

6. *Teacher Presentation.* Explain to the class that it is essential that a researcher keep careful records of the source of each piece of information, so that he or she can give credit to the source. Using someone else's ideas or words without giving credit is known as "plagiarism," an act that is unethical at least and at worst illegal. Therefore, every time the researcher makes notes of an idea or quotation from a source, he or she should indicate where it was obtained. To avoid having to write down the same information (title, author, etc.) over and over when the same source is used for several ideas, a single card can be filled out for each source and each note card can carry a number that matches the number of the bibliography card.

Using Reproduction Page 76, duplicate and distribute to students the handout on "The Bibliography." Read through it with them and suggest they keep the handout to refer to in future Activities that require them to fill out bibliography cards.

7. *Activity.* Distribute to each student at least five index cards or have them draw five facsimilies on their own paper. Write the following list on the board or project it for the class to see, and have students fill out a bibliography card for each item, following the instructions on the handout "The Bibliography." When all students have finished, draw sample "cards" on the board and fill them in correctly. Suggest that students determine whether their cards match those you have drawn on the board.
   1. Magazine dated January 21, 1965. Article entitled "The Last Oil Well," by Will Hineline. *Time* magazine, pages 17–18.
   2. Book entitled *No Air to Breathe* by Sidney Frayberg. Published by Rayce Books, Princeton, New Jersey, copyright 1972.
   3. Encyclopedia Americana, volume 16, pages 446–48, subject is pollution, copyright 1967, Americana Company, Chicago, Illinois.
   4. Interview with Jake Scott, Newark City Council, April 18, 1974, Newark, New Jersey, in which he told you that he is opposed to any governmental regulation of automobile manufacturing, even if it helps to control pollution.
   5. A *Miami Dispatch* newspaper article entitled "Gasoline Shortage Cuts Tourism," by Ray Randall, May 5, 1975. The article appeared on page one of section A, since Miami depends so heavily on tourism to boost their economy.

8. *Activity.* Using Reproduction Page 77, duplicate and distribute the "Worksheet on Bibliography Cards." Assign students at random to groups of three, and have them fill out seven index cards (distributed by you or drawn by the students) with the information from the worksheet.

9. *Activity.* Have students choose any topic that interests them (see Activity #4 and Activity #5 on page 111 for suggestions) and to locate in the library or elsewhere at least two books, three magazine articles, and one encyclopedia entry on the topic. For each, they are required to fill out a bibliography card following the

instructions given in previous activities. Either collect these for checking yourself or have students exchange with a partner for checking.

10. *Activity.* It is possible to give students practice in compiling information and making note cards and bibliography cards without having them go to the library to secure the information first-hand. The "casebook" is a commercially produced collection of articles on a single topic, from which students can draw information for use in writing a research paper on some aspect of that topic. Most casebooks are prepared for use in college composition classes and are thus too advanced for most high school students. An alternative, according to Edward Deluzain in an article in *On Righting Writing,* is to compile your own case folders, manila folders containing newspaper and magazine articles on a particular topic. In compiling a set of these folders, he suggests that the teacher give each person in the class the task of choosing a topic of interest and finding copies of articles that relate to it (see Activity #20 on page 106). The teacher could supplement the articles located by students with others that he or she encounters. The folders could be kept on file in the classroom and students could be assigned to choose the one that interests them most, to formulate a thesis statement related to it, and to compile information using only the sources in the folder. This approach, although not a substitute for students actually visiting the library, is a way to give the class additional practice in gathering information if the library is too crowded or if other conditions restrict students' free use of the library.

11. *Activity.* If you anticipate having students write a complete research paper as part of the learning experiences for this unit (and you undoubtedly will), there are at least two different ways you can make the assignment. One is to have them choose a topic and collect information after completing the Learning Experiences for Topics I, II, and III but before beginning the Learning Experiences for Topic IV. They would thus be able to put into practice what they have learned immediately after completing the activities. The second approach is to complete Learning Experiences for Topic IV before beginning work on an entire research paper on a topic of one's own. There are merits to either approach, and the teacher will have to decide which is best suited to the particular class.

TOPIC IV: ORGANIZING AND WRITING THE PAPER

1. *Teacher Presentation.* Refer the class to the handout on "Ten Steps for Writing a Research Report." If they have been through the Activities for the preceding Topics, they will have mastered the first five steps. This Topic deals with the final steps: taking the raw material assembled through research, organizing it into a logical form, and writing a paper that conveys the information clearly and persuasively. The first concern is to examine all the ideas that have been collected and sort them into categories—with related ideas together. Since only one piece of information has been written on each note card, it is a fairly easy task to spread out the cards on the floor or on a table and begin to sort them.

2. *Activity.* Using Reproduction Page 78, duplicate and distribute to the class the "Outlining Worksheet" and have them complete it working individually. Then have them meet in small groups and compare answers.

3. *Activity.* Reproduce and distribute the fictitious note cards that appear on the "Note Card Worksheet" on Reproduction Page 79. Have students arrange them in a logical order to support the thesis statement, "Unless some drastic measures are taken, automobile pollution will become an extremely serious problem." Have them work either individually or in small groups, numbering the cards in the order they feel is most effective. Then discuss with the total class the approaches that various groups took.

4. *Teacher Presentation.* In preparation for students' writing a complete research paper, give them specific instructions on the proper form for footnotes and bibliography. Since most teachers have their own preferences, we have not attempted to specify one particular form here. Consult the Books for Teachers section at the end of this chapter for suggestions on finding further information.

5. *Activity.* Using the same "Worksheet on Bibliography Cards" that was used for Activity #8 on page 112, have students write footnotes in proper form for each item and compile a bibliography in proper form.

6. *Activity.* Assign students to write a research paper of a length appropriate for the age and ability level of your class. Have them submit to you for checking (or evaluation) each of the following as they are completed. This requirement will assure that, if a student has not done one step of the process correctly, the error will be caught before the student goes on to the next step.
   1. The subject of the paper. This should be the "narrowed down" topic, not the general topic.
   2. The thesis statement for the paper—a declarative sentence that indicates the writer's opinion or point of view toward the topic.
   3. Note cards and bibliography cards for all information collected for the paper.
   4. An outline or rough draft of the paper.
   5. The final paper.

You might wish to have each student choose a partner to give each step a preliminary check before it is turned in to you. This will give the student a "last chance" for improving the work before submitting it.

ASSESSING ACHIEVEMENT OF OBJECTIVES

On-Going Evaluation

The extent to which students have mastered the individual skills covered under each topic above can be measured by having them submit for grading those experiences marked "Evaluation" or those marked "Activity" that appear near the end of each section. Almost any of the Activities suggested in each section could also be submitted for grading.

Final Evaluation

For an overall evaluation of students' ability to write a research paper, the most logical procedure, of course, is to assign a research paper as suggested in

Activity #6 above. Before students begin work, explain what criteria you will measure the paper against in grading it. You will probably wish to include the following among your criteria:

1. Has the writer chosen a topic that is narrow enough to be explained or supported in detail in a single essay?
2. Has the writer researched the topic thoroughly, using a variety of sources rather than just one or two?
3. Has the writer organized the information logically?
4. Has the writer been meticulous in giving credit for ideas that are not his or her own and in indicating all direct quotations?
5. Has the writer followed a consistent style in footnotes and bibliography?

RESOURCES FOR TEACHING THE RESEARCH PAPER

Below is a selected list of resources useful for teaching the skills of researching and writing a paper. The list is divided into audio-visual materials (films, filmstrips, slide-tape programs, cassettes, etc.), books for students, and books for the teacher. Addresses of publishers can be found in the alphabetical list on pages 151–153. Prices, where given, are only approximate, since changes occur frequently.

Audio-Visual Materials

Using Reference Materials More Efficiently. Four filmstrips giving detailed instructions in locating reference materials and using them in essays, compositions, and reports. Explains the use of the dictionary, periodicals, biographies, quotations, encyclopedias, almanacs, and other indices. Set: $32.95. Applause Productions.

How to Write Reports. Six filmstrips with three records/cassettes. Explains footnotes, bibliographies, writing and presenting information, and the differences between writing a paper and a book report. Clear, direct, easy-to-understand. $59.75 with cassettes; $59.00 with records. Eye-Gate.

Constructing Reports by Ruth G. Strickland. Six filmstrips dealing with "digging for facts," "selecting a theme," "building reports," "painting with words," "finishing reports," and "using reports." Suitable for junior high only. Set: $49.50. Encyclopaedia Britannica Educational Corp.

How to Write a Term Paper. Part of a series entitled *Conquering Composition.* Set on term paper includes four filmstrips, four LP records/cassettes, and four scripts. Presents the true-to-life photographed experience of three students, their writing assignment, and how they tackle it. Explains library research, resources and references, note taking, organizing and writing, and preparing the final draft. Thorough and interesting. Appropriate for all students. Set: $42.00. Filmstrip House.

Writing a Research Paper. One filmstrip, one cassette, and one copy of each of the two guides. This complete teaching package provides instruction in library research, note-taking, documentation, and writing the paper. Interesting, clear, and informative. $25.00. The Reading Lab., Inc.

Books for Students

Research: An Introduction by Robert Ross. Contains a thorough guide from initial planning to final copy—researching, planning, gathering, and organizing. Includes forms for documenting notes and writing bibliographic entries. Useful for more advanced students. Paperbound. $2.95. Barnes and Noble.

Preparing the Research Paper by Lorraine F. Dangle and Alice H. Haussman. Concise instructions on correct bibliographic form, note taking, direct quotations, footnotes, title page, actual writing, and preparing the final paper. Also included: self-evaluating checklist. A good choice for the average student. Paperbound. $.45. CEBCO/Standard Publishing.

The Skills of Research by Norman L. Haider. Contains sections on narrowing the topic, uses of the card catalog, the *Readers' Guide* and other sources of information, note taking, and organizing the material. A sample research paper is provided. Fine for the average student. Paperbound. Silver Burdett.

The Hutchinson Guide to Writing Research Papers by Helene D. Hutchinson. A comprehensive work. Examines choice of topic, range of scope, exploring resources, research steps, library skills. Valuable diagrams, summary charts, indices, annotated bibliographies included. A rather complex work, most suitable for advanced students. Paperbound. $3.98. Glencoe Press.

The Freshman Writer by Michele F. Cooper. A guide to writing first-year college papers. Deals specifically with length, style, subject matter, choosing a topic, library skills, determining a thesis, composing an outline, writing the paper, editing, and preparing the final draft, footnoting, and typing. Helpful diagrams and samples. Suitable for advanced senior high and college students. Paperbound. $1.95. Barnes and Noble.

Guide to Writing Term Papers by Albert A. Theriault, Jr. Provides instruction in planning, topic selection, outlining, library tools, reference materials, bibliographic documentation, quoting and writing. Sample term paper provided. Valuable visual aids and models throughout. Suitable for average and advanced students. Paperbound. Amsco School Publications.

A Manual for Writers of Term Papers, Theses, and Dissertations by Kate L. Turabian. Discusses the parts of the paper, documentation, spelling, punctuation, abbreviations, numbering, and typing the paper. Focuses on specifics; general step-by-step information is not given. Suitable for advanced students only. Paperbound, $2.25; Hardcover, $5.95. The University of Chicago Press.

Writing Term Papers and Reports by George Shelton Hubbell. Excellent systematic instruction in choice of subject, reading and note taking, organization of materials, outlining, writing, documenting, and revising. Sample term paper provided. Valuable models and examples throughout. Ideal handbook for advanced students. Clear, direct, easy to use. Paperbound. $1.50. Barnes and Noble.

The Research Paper Guide edited by Anthony C. Sherman, Robert B. Ewald. A guide to effective, precise writing. Contains chapters on topic and outline, discovering research sources, rough draft, revisions, documentation, bibliography and footnotes. Sample paper included, plus valuable writer's checklist. Easy-to-follow format. Paperbound. $1.00. Pendulum Press, Inc.

How to Use the Readers' Guide to Periodical Literature and Other Indexes. A helpful guide designed to teach students to use important resources. Includes practice exercises as well as explanatory material. Skill oriented. Ideal for all students. Paperbound. H. W. Wilson Co.

Ten Steps in Writing the Research Paper by Roberta H. Markham. Reduces the complications normally associated with writing research papers—delineates ten easy-to-follow steps. Systematic and succinct. Suitable for average and advanced students. Paperbound, $1.75; hardcover, $4.75. Barron's Educational Series, Inc.

How to Write Themes and Term Papers by Barbara Lenmark Ellis. Contains a section on the research paper. Paperbound, $1.95. Barron's Educational Series.

Writing and Researching Term Papers and Reports by Eugene H. Ehrlich and Daniel Murphy Explains the use of reference books, procedures for note taking, outlining, writing, editing, and documenting. Annotated sample research paper and comprehensive bibliography of reference books provided. Appropriate for average and advanced students. Paperbound. $1.50. Bantam Books.

How to Write Reports, Papers, Theses, Articles by John P. Riebel. An informative guide to writing effective, technically correct papers. Practical and clear. Paperbound. $5.00. Arco Publishing Co., Inc.

Writing a Research Paper, Manuscript Form and Documentation by Eliot D. Allen and Ethel B. Colbrunn. Explains choice of topic, using the library, note-taking, outlining, writing, pagination, margins, quoting, footnotes, and bibliographies. Sample pages and models provided. Paperbound. $1.50. Reading Laboratories, Inc.

Preparing the Research Paper by Phillips G. Davies and Samuel J. Rogal. Includes sections on topic selection and scope, preparation, taking notes, planning, and documenting. A sample research paper is included, along with suggested topics for the research paper. Valuable visual aids and diagrams. Excellent guide for all students. Paperbound. Educators Publishing Service.

Researching and Reporting by Robert and Mary Lou Burch. Probably the best single book for the average student in grades 7–12, particularly considering its low cost. The first section is written like a short story: three students and a beleaguered teacher select a topic, decide upon sources, forage through the library, and put it all together. The second section includes explanations, activities, diagrams, and checklists to guide the student in preparing his or her own paper. A free teacher's guide includes three worksheets that can be reproduced and distributed to students. Highly recommended. Student book, $.50. Xerox Corp.

About Writing Reports. Visually interesting but somewhat superficial guide to selecting a topic, researching, using the library, compiling a bibliography, organizing ideas, outlining, note-taking, quoting, paraphrasing. Emphasis is on easy-to-follow examples. Particularly useful for the "turned off" student. Paperbound. Channing L. Bete Co.

Books for Teachers

Some of the above titles listed as appropriate for more capable students are also very useful as teacher resources even if they are too difficult for use as a student text. See especially: *Research: An Introduction* by Robert Ross, *A Manual for Writers of Term Papers, Theses, and Dissertations* by Kate L. Turabian, and *Writing a Research Paper, Manuscript Form and Documentation* by Eliot D. Allen and Ethel B. Colbrunn.

Research Paper Project. A series of worksheets for use in the senior high school. Can be used as the basis for explanations to the class, even if you do not choose to reproduce the worksheets and distribute them to students. Paperbound. $.50. New York State English Council.

Search: An Interaction Unit Introducing

Library Skills. A complete teaching unit on library skills, emphasizing student involvement and interaction. Students work together on Learning Objectives (L.O.'s) in the areas of understanding the library's contents, using a book, and using the *Readers' Guide.* Highly recommended. Interact.

5

Teaching Students to Revise

Most good writing proceeds in three stages: prewriting (planning), writing (producing a rough draft), and revision (making improvements and correcting errors). Unfortunately, many times the first two stages are given proper emphasis, but the last is neglected. All too often students dash off a rough draft of a writing assignment and then, with no particular plan for proofreading or revision, correct a gross error or two and simply copy the whole thing over in a neater, more legible form, and hand it in, feeling they have done their best.

But the truth is that they seldom come near doing their best work. Revision is a skill which can contribute almost as much to the finished product as does the first rough writing, and in order to get full benefit from this process, student writers should be consciously aware of weaknesses to look for in their rough drafts; know how to spot and correct errors in spelling, punctuation, and usage; and know what stylistic problems are likely to plague their writing and how to correct them.

OBJECTIVES

As a result of the learning experiences in this chapter, students should be able to:

1. Identify and correct misspelled words in their own compositions.
2. Identify and correct ineffective punctuation in their own compositions.
3. Identify nonstandard usages in their own compositions and change them to standard usages.
4. Identify poor organization in their own compositions and improve it.
5. Identify poor development in their own compositions and improve it.
6. Eliminate clichés that appear in their own writing.
7. Eliminate any unnecessary words and phrases so as to make their writing as concise as possible.

LEARNING EXPERIENCES

TOPIC I: USING A GUIDE TO REVISION

1. *Teacher Presentation.* Prepare a Revision Guide or Proofreading Checklist by choosing those sections or items from the "Complete Revision Guide" compiled below which you consider most appropriate for your students. For younger students you may wish to limit yourself to paragraphs, and to include other, more basic items, such as "Have I indented the first line of the paragraph? Have I kept my margins straight?" You may wish to add a short line at the beginning of each item for students to check off after examining their work for each type of problem and correcting any mistakes they find. Reproduce and distribute to students copies of the check list and require them to use it as a guide whenever preparing a writing assignment.

A COMPLETE GUIDE TO REVISION

I. *Expository Writing*
  A. Organization
    1. Do I introduce my subject or thesis idea clearly and precisely, so the reader will know exactly what the essay is to be about?
    2. Do I divide my thesis into its logical parts (its factors), and do I then arrange these parts in a logical order such as sequential, chronological, or climactic?
    3. Do I state each of these parts in a topic sentence that is then developed by at least one paragraph?
    4. Do I have an introductory paragraph and a conclusion?
    5. Are there transitions where necessary throughout the essay, so the reader will have no trouble following the organization?

  B. Development
    1. Is the topic sentence of each paragraph developed in adequate detail? Is every general statement made more specific by detailed statements?
    2. Does each paragraph develop only one topic idea? Are there irrelevant details in any paragraph? Do I get off the subject?
    3. Do the details in each paragraph follow a logical order, or do they simply appear in what seems to be random order? Could the order of sentences be improved?
    4. Do the sentences in each paragraph flow smoothly one to the next? Do I help the reader by use of connectors and other transitional devices? Do I combine clauses and use subordination to make my sentences smooth and coherent?

  C. Style
    1. Do I know, for sure, the exact meaning of every word I've used?
    2. Have I used any slang or nonstandard language?
    3. Have I used the most precise direct words? Have I said exactly what I mean?
    4. Do I vary my sentence constructions to avoid dull, mechanical writing?
    5. Have I eliminated all clichés and stale metaphorical language?

II. *Creative Writing*
  A. Words
    1. Do I use label words when I should be describing?
    2. Do I use words that fit the mood I am creating?
    3. Do I use vivid, active, feeling words that will engage the emotions and suspense of the reader?

B. Details
   1. Do I use details that convey the essence of my characters?
   2. Do my descriptions of characters contain any irrelevant details that serve no purpose?
   3. Do my descriptive details help the reader to visualize what I am portraying?
C. Realism
   1. Do my characters seem real?
   2. Are the situations believable?
   3. Do the characters talk in language consistent with their age , status in life, inner nature and values?
   4. Do all characters behave consistently with the nature, condition, and values they are described as having?
   5. Do I use sufficient detail in describing actions and events so that these happenings come alive for the reader?

III. *Mechanics for All Writing*
   A. Spelling. Is every word spelled correctly?
   B. Punctuation.
      1. Is every comma used for a valid reason?
      2. Are there places where I need a comma and have not put one in?
      3. Does every sentence end with a period, exclamation point, or question mark?
      4. Does every sentence begin with a capital letter?
      5. Are all quotations properly punctuated?
      6. Do I ever join two complete sentences with a comma?
      7. Is every colon, semicolon, and dash I used justified?
   C. Grammar and Syntax
      1. Does every sentence have a subject and a predicate?
      2. Does each subject agree in number with its predicate?
      3. Is every verb in the proper form and tense?
      4. Does every pronoun have an antecedent?
      5. Is every pronoun the proper number, gender and case?
      6. Are my modifiers properly placed so it is obvious what or who is being modified? Have I left some modifiers dangling, with no subject identified?
      7. Does every sentence convey a clear meaning?

2. *Activity.* Using Reproduction Page 80, duplicate the student-written essay below and distribute a copy to each student, or make an overhead transparency and project it for the whole class to view. Have the class, using the proofreading check list you prepared for Teacher Presentation #1 above, identify ways the student could inprove the essay. The activity could be conducted with the total class, to introduce the use of the proofreading check list, or you could have students work individually, checking the essay against the revision guide and marking weaknesses that should be corrected. They could then share with the total class what they discovered. Or students could work in small groups of three to five pupils each, using the check list to discover weaknesses in the essay.

Cars I Would Not Want to Own
John Richardson
(10th grade student)

There are over a quarter of a million automobiles sold in the United States each year. Many types are available; foreign cars and American cars, convertables and sedans, big cars and little cars. This variety is the result of the wide range of tastes of the driving population. There is three kinds of cars which doesn't suit my taste at all, and which I would never own. One type is impractical, another is little and ugly, and a third is poorly made.

An example of an impractical car is the Excalibur SS, perhaps you have never seen one of these cars. It bears a strong resemblance to the Dusenberg of years ago or to an old MG, early 1951 or 1952. One of the things I don't like about it are that it only comes in a convertable model. That's fine in the summer or on a sunny day, but when it rains or when winter comes, its rather impractical. Winter is perhaps the roughest though. Mainly because the car is not even equipped with a heater. And the softtop has plastic side windows and a plastic rear window that leaks and yellows in the sun and becomes briddle with age. This car is fitted with a 327 cubic inch engine from the Corvette Stingray. The car does not weigh more than 2000 pounds, compared to the Corvette, which weighs approximately 3200 pounds this year. With over 350 horsepower and so little weight, the Excalibur is very dangerous, you can't come near controlling it on accelleration around curves or on a panic stop. Combining these shortcommings with a $10,000 price tag, you have a very impractical car.

A car that I wouldn't want is one of those ugly little foreign "bugs" you see everywhere. The Volkswagen is a good example, this simply isn't my idea of a car with good looks. In addition, its to small for safety. If you were hit in the side by a large car or by a truck, you'd be finished. You also can't ride for great distances in comfort, because the engine is to noisy and the interior is cramped. Another shortcomming is that Volkswagen's are to common. I don't want a car that every mothers son has, and if you look around any large parking lot in this city, you are bound to see at least ten Volkswagen's. Besides being so common, this car is to underpowered for freeway driving. Its almost impossible to pass a car on the expressway at sixty miles per hour, if there is a stiff crosswind blowing, you would think you were on a roller coaster. This is both unpleasant and unsafe.

The third type of car that I wouldn't like to own is one that is cheaply made. Ford Mustangs fall into this class—my family owned one once, and before we got rid of it the muffler fell off at least five times. By the time we sold it six months later, there was rattles in every corner. Meanwhile, the paint had started peeling off, to say nothing of the first layer of chrome on the bumpers. To top it off, whenever the driver made a hard left turn, the door on the passenger's side would fly open. My uncle own a Cougar, and it doesn't have these problems.

3. *Activity.* Without indicating the name of the author, of course, reproduce one or more compositions written by students in your class. Then follow the instructions for Activity #2 above.

4. *Activity.* When a paper is due to be handed in by your students, use class time to work through your revision guide. Have students read their papers several times, each time checking a different item in turn. When students have checked all of one category of skills—punctuation, for instance—they should write the word "punctuation" at the end of the paper and put their initials beside it to show they have done so. They should follow this procedure through the entire check list.

If you do not wish to take class time for such revision (particularly as some students may discover a need for more time for re-writing after such a thorough and enforced proofreading), you may wish to reproduce a large supply of your revision checklist so that you can give a copy to each student whenever a major assignment is due, with the instruction that every item on the list be checked by the student while using the guide to proofread and revise the paper. Students could attach the guide to the paper when turning it in, with each item checked off.

TOPIC II: CORRECTING ERRORS IN MECHANICS

1. *Teacher Presentation.* Using Reproduction Pages 81 and 82, duplicate the two lists of words that are often misspelled, "Look Alikes/Sound Alikes" and "Spelling Demons." Go over the lists with the class, discussing the types of spelling errors that frequently creep into student writing. Then assign students to study the lists as homework.

2. *Activity.* Play the spelling game described below. The game is designed to help students spot spelling errors when they appear in sentences, and thus improve their proofreading skills. The heart of the game is a series of sentences, some of which contain no spelling errors, though most contain errors listed on the two handouts mentioned in Teacher Presentation #1 above. The object is for students to find the errors by carefully reading the sentence in much the same way that people proofread their own writing. Thus what appears to be a "game" is really serious practice in spotting and correcting spelling errors. After discovering an error, students must give the correct answer and explain and support the correction. This is to insure that any given answer is not just a lucky guess. Also, by explaining the correction, students educate their peers and reinforce their own understanding of the correct answer.

   The game can be used in several ways. Two come to mind at once. First, by preparing one set of materials the teacher has an activity for use by four or five students while the rest of the class works on another activity. These could be students who have finished other work and are ready for a change of pace, or they could be students who need extra work on spelling. Second, if the teacher prepares six to eight sets of materials, the entire class, divided into small groups, can play the game so all can gain proficiency in spotting spelling errors.

   The components of the game appear on Reproduction Pages 83–86, in addition to being shown below. To prepare the materials for one game set:

   1. Photocopy the 178 sentences that appear on Reproduction Page 83. Cut out each sentence from the photocopy and, using cellophane tape, mount it on a 3" x 5" index card. Shuffle the cards so they are not in any specific order.
   2. Photocopy the game board that appears on Reproduction Page 84 and mount it on an 8½" x 11" piece of cardboard. Then cover it with clear Contact paper or have it laminated.
   3. Make one copy of the sheet of instructions for students (Reproduction Page 85) and the answer key (Reproduction Page 86).
   4. Obtain small buttons or coins for use as markers, one for each player.
   5. Put all components of the game in a large plastic Zip-Lock bag.

   The instructions provided on Reproduction Page 85 set up the game in competitive fashion. Players are pitted against one another, racing against one another to reach the end. If you prefer not to encourage competition within the small groups, groups could be pitted against one another. Or all members of a small group could work together in a race against the clock to see whether they can move a single marker to the end before, say, twenty minutes has elapsed.

EXERCISE SENTENCES FOR THE GAME

1. *I really like them; their my friends.*
2. *She excepted our invitation to go to the game.*
3. *Don't ask me; its they're decision.*
4. *I was relieved to find that I past my math test.*
5. *We had very bad whether last week.*
6. *Don't worry; everything will be all right.*
7. *I walked right in to the wall.*
8. *She was very impolite; she didn't have any manors.*
9. *It was a beautiful site to see.*
10. *Sam forgot about his piano lessen.*
11. *In England we saw many beautiful feudal manners.*
12. *It's a locale store.*
13. *She threw the fruit away; it was a real waist.*
14. *I really liked the play, irregardless of what the critics said.*
15. *This rule is generally true; however, their are a few acceptions.*
16. *I all ready paid that bill.*
17. *May I sit down?*
18. *Whose their?*
19. *I don't no witch book you want.*
20. *Who do you wish to sea?*
21. *I recieved too lovly Christmas cards.*
22. *Your the best friend I've ever had.*
23. *Linda wrote the letter, stamped the envelope, ceiled, and maled it.*
24. *Were very disappointed with Sue's performance.*
25. *Liberty is a basic human rite.*
26. *Hours past while we weighted.*
27. *I gave her good advise.*
28. *I think that Bobby is taller then she.*
29. *She looked beautiful in her wedding gown as she walked down the isle.*
30. *He was a fine person; I believe his sole will go to heaven.*
31. *I studied the principals of geometry for more than three ours.*
32. *Their was no apparent effect.*
33. *The door handle was very lose; it must of fallen off.*
34. *The road was a dead end; it lead too a grassy field.*
35. *Its to hard to understand; let's forget it.*
36. *They were making to much noise; I tolled them to be quite.*
37. *The highway was long, narrow and strait.*
38 *Eugene O'Neill was a great playwrite.*
39. *Jennifer all ways ware tie-died jeans.*

40. *She had two go a way on vacation.*
41. *This year they're were fewer at the party then last.*
42. *We studied the ancient rights and rituals.*
43. *The principle suspended five students.*
44. *Everyone attended accept Jill.*
45. *Mr. Young was the soul survivor of the crash.*
46. *That's you're coat.*
47. *The coral straights are about a mile from the Canary Aisles.*
48. *Who's dog is that?*
49. *Forget it; its all in the passed.*
50. *Our house is being built on a new land cite.*
51. *Since Carrie died her hair black, she looks like a which.*
52. *She tried too advice me.*
53. *I am sole air to the company fortune.*
54. *I don't care weather you bring the pizza or the drinks.*
55. *She eats to much candy; she's gaining alot of wait.*
56. *I agree; your one-hundred percent rite.*
57. *It was a vary boaring experience.*
58. *She fell down the stares and broke her leg.*
59. *Lisa was speeding when the light changed; she slammed on the breaks*
60. *He burned the rug with the acid and lie.*
61. *The plain sored threw the sky as it made its assent.*
62. *The police told us too excess the damage.*
63. *The Carters adapted a three-month old baby.*
64. *He was robbed in a narrow, dark allay.*
65. *What you are doing is all together wrong.*
66. *She eluded to the classics on several occasions.*
67. *Don't altar your plans on are account.*
68. *You an Margaret look a like.*
69. *Little Elizabeth has a face like an angle.*
70. *Don't be sew ante-social.*
71. *The insurance agent apprised our house.*
72. *The diamonds are assured for one thousand dollars.*
73. *The family was not in attendents.*
74. *I baled you out of jail the last time.*
75. *Diane ate the hole bole of fruit.*
76. *The hunter shot but mist the bare.*
77. *Alice dyed Friday; they berried her too days latter.*
78. *We all celebrated her berthday.*
79. *The wind was fierce; it blue all night.*
80. *I served on the Bored of Education.*
81. *The dress had a pretty, embroidered boarder.*
82. *I was bourne in February.*
83. *The entire bridle party was dressed in blew.*
84. *We didn't have any cash, so the car sailsman build us a month latter.*

85. *The capitol of New York State is Albany.*
86. *There weren't any carats in the salad.*
87. *It was a vary fragrant cent.*
88. *I choose this option.*
89. *The chord snapped and the plant feel.*
90. *Leigh bought all knew cloths.*
91. *She confused the coma and the semicolon.*
92. *I complemented her on her great ideas.*
93. *She was very confidant.*
94. *She wasn't conscience of the problem.*
95. *The book was designed to expand the readers' conscientiousness.*
96. *I was late for the student counsel meeting.*
97. *John joined the Piece Core.*
98. *Every culture has its own set of traditions and custumms.*
99. *The water emptied into a little creak.*
100. *Her parents went on a luxury crews.*
101. *The hunter shoot three dear.*
102. *Cancer is a serious decease.*
103. *Her helplessness and dependents are irritating.*
104. *We had ice cream for desert.*
105. *Their was so much noise, that I was detracted.*
106. *The experts devised a good plan.*
107. *We had diner at five-thirty.*
108. *It was a two-fold situation; it had a dual purpose.*
109. *They decided to make Eddie due the work.*
110. *They emigrated to this country fifty years ago.*
111. *I don't no to what extant she agreed.*
112. *David was dizzy, pail, and feint.*
113. *The bus fair was increased alot.*
114. *Our Christmas tree was a northern fur.*
115. *You have a flare with words.*
116. *Max, our dog, has flees.*
117. *The receipt required eggs, flower, and milk.*
118. *The lunch line was to long, so we pushed foreword.*
119. *The meeting was conducted very formerly.*
120. *Darlene ranked forth in the beauty contest.*
121. *The police new that she was gilty by the sick look on her face.*
122. *The karate expert had a tight gripe on his opponent.*
123. *Snow, sleet, and hail feel for hours.*
124. *The small hair dodged off into the woods.*
125. *Dr. Barnard performed the first hart transplant.*
126. *The heal came off my knew shoes.*
127. *The music was so loud that I couldn't here the speaker.*
128. *Tomorrow is a wholly day.*
129. *The answer alludes me at the moment.*

130. *The statue represented an old Egyptian idel.*
131. *Our city boasts the leased number of accidents.*
132. *The thunder and lightening scarred Missy.*
133. *Michael implied for a lone.*
134. *Go threw the mane entrance.*
135. *Stake is my favorite meet.*
136. *The brave soldier received a special honorary metal.*
137. *The accident occured at midnight.*
138. *The tempature rose thirty degrees.*
139. *The old lady looked vary lonly.*
140. *After I gradate from high school I am hopping to go too collage.*
141. *Meeting the King was a great honer and privledge.*
142. *I hate spelling, puntuation, and grammer.*
143. *We made gravestone rubbings at the cemetary.*
144. *She had changed so much that I didn't reconize her.*
145. *Othello is one of Shakespeare's tradgedies.*
146. *Joan ownes fourty albums.*
147. *I'm definitly in favior of your suggestion.*
148. *I mean this vary sincerly.*
149. *Use your common scents.*
150. *She did a comprehensive, through job.*
151. *You are my freind; I beleive everything you say.*
152. *Allow me to congradulate you on your new appointment.*
153. *I tryed my best to be a good athelete.*
154. *Psyhcology and Phylosophy are two entirely seperate feilds.*
155. *I didn't do it on purpose; it was an incident.*
156. *What's your favorite pasttime?*
157. *The minature is very simular to the orignal.*
158. *What do you consider relevent?*
159. *I don't like fir coats; I perfer lether.*
160. *The cut looked soar; it didn't heel vary well.*
161. *He though the ball threw the window.*
162. *The captain saluted and boughed.*
163. *The sky was a pail blew.*
164. *Cite all references.*
165. *There were fewer car accidents this year than last.*
166. *The principal gave all the students a two-week vacation.*
167. *Of the two, you're the better dancer.*
168. *It's your party; do as you please.*
169. *Who's at the door?*
170. *Everything is all right.*
171. *May I give my opinion?*
172. *Everyone must listen; there are no exceptions.*
173. *I am very confident that everything will be fine.*
174. *The old man was losing his sight.*

175. *The cow escaped from the corral.*
176. *I can't draw a straight line.*
177. *There is less water in this container than in the other.*
178. *We were never formally introduced.*

INSTRUCTIONS FOR PLAYING THE SPELLING GAME

1. Approximately four persons can play this game.
2. Lay the game board on the floor or other flat surface such as a table or desk.
3. Give the answer key to one person (either a player or someone who wants to watch but not play). This person will consult the answer key when necessary to check an answer, and hence will be referred to as "the Judge." Warn the Judge not to let anyone see the answers.
4. Shuffle and stack all the sentence cards. Place them face down near the game board.
5. Roll dice or draw lots or guess a number to determine who goes first.
6. Place your markers in the space labelled "Start" on the game board.
7. The first player draws a sentence card from the top of the stack. The player reads it and determines whether or not all of the words are spelled according to acceptable standard English. Sentences may contain one or more errors.
8. If the player decides that there are no spelling errors in the sentence, he or she must show it to the other players to see whether they agree. If they don't agree, the Judge checks the answer key. If the Judge upholds the player's opinion, then the player may move ahead two spaces. If the player is wrong (that is, if the sentence does contain misspelled words), then he or she loses the next turn.
9. If the player decides that a word or words in the sentence are misspelled, he or she must identify each, correctly spell each, and explain the correction. If the Judge and other players agree with the player's correction(s), the player may move ahead the number of spaces equal to the number of misspelled words in the sentence. If the other players do not agree, then the group must discuss the question until they reach agreement. If they cannot agree, they must consult the Judge, whose answer, based on the key, overrules all other players. The Judge must explain the answer to the other players. If the player's answer is upheld by the Judge, then the player may move ahead as many spaces as there are misspelled words in the sentence; otherwise, the player may not move ahead or take his or her next turn.
10. The player whose marker reaches the "Finish" space first is the winner.

ANSWER KEY FOR SPELLING GAME

1. they're	(1)	21. received, two, lovely	(3)	41. there, than	(2)
2. accepted	(1)	22. you're	(1)	42. rites	(1)
3. it's, their	(2)	23. sealed, mailed	(2)	43. principal	(1)
4. passed	(1)	24. we're	(1)	44. except	(1)
5. weather	(1)	25. right	(1)	45. sole	(1)
6. alright	(1)	26. passed, waited	(2)	46. your	(1)
7. into	(1)	27. advice	(1)	47. straights, isles	(2)
8. manners	(1)	28. than	(1)	48. whose	(1)
9. sight	(1)	29. aisle	(1)	49. it's, past	(2)
10. lesson	(1)	30. soul	(1)	50. site	(1)
11. manors	(1)	31. principles, hours	(2)	51. dyed, witch	(2)
12. local	(1)	32. there	(1)	52. to, advise	(2)
13. waste	(1)	33. loose, (of) have	(2)	53. heir	(1)
14. regardless	(1)	34. led, to	(2)	54. whether	(1)
15. there, exceptions	(2)	35. it's, too	(2)	55. too, a lot, weight	(3)
16. already	(1)	36. too, told, quiet	(3)	56. you're, right	(2)
17. no errors	(2)	37. straight	(1)	57. very, boring	(2)
18. who's, there	(2)	38. playwright	(1)	58. stairs	(1)
19. know, which	(2)	39. always, wears, tie-dyed	(3)	59. brakes	(1)
20. whom, see	(2)	40. to, away	(2)	60. lye	(1)

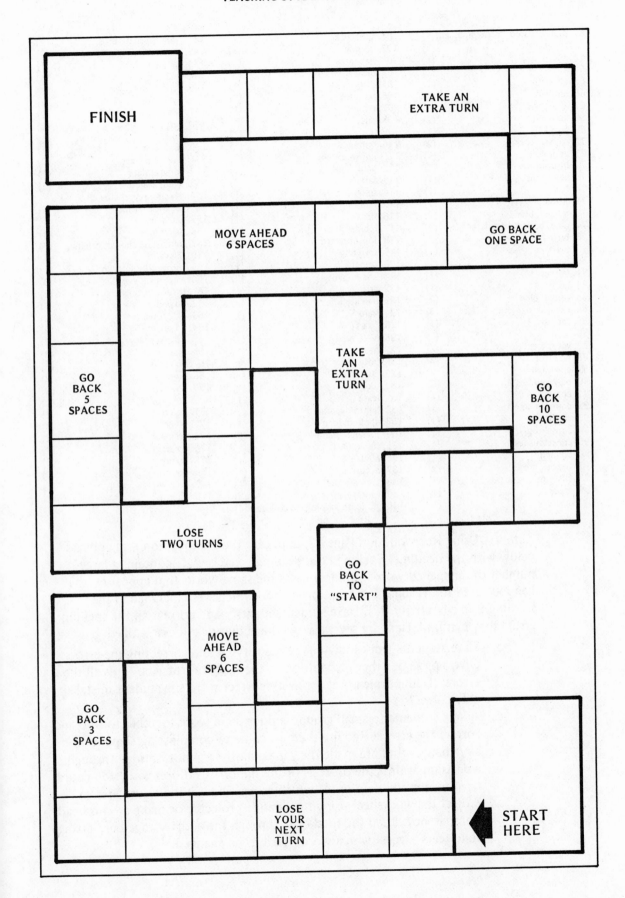

61. plane, soared, through, ascent (4)
62. to, access (2)
63. adopted (1)
64. alley (1)
65. altogether (1)
66. alluded (1)
67. alter, our (2)
68. and, alike (2)
69. angel (1)
70. so, anti-social (2)
71. appraised (1)
72. insured (1)
73. attendance (1)
74. bailed (1)
75. whole, bowl (2)
76. missed, bear (2)
77. died, buried, two, later (4)
78. birthday (1)
79. blew (1)
80. board (1)
81. border (1)
82. born (1)
83. bridal, blue (2)
84. car salesman, billed, later (3)
85. capital (1)
86. carrots (1)
87. very, scent (2)
88. no error (2)
89. cord, fell (2)
90. new, clothes (2)
91. comma (1)
92. complimented (1)
93. confident (1)
94. conscious (1)
95. consciousness (1)
96. council (1)
97. Peace Corps (2)
98. customs (1)
99. creek (1)
100. cruise (1)

101. shot, deer (2)
102. disease (1)
103. dependence (1)
104. dessert (1)
105. distracted (1)
106. no error (2)
107. dinner (1)
108. duel (1)
109. do (1)
110. immigrated (1)
111. know, extent (2)
112. pale, faint (2)
113. fare, a lot (2)
114. fir (1)
115. flair (1)
116. fleas (1)
117. recipe, flour (2)
118. too, forward (2)
119. formally (1)
120. fourth (1)
121. knew, guilty (2)
122. grip (1)
123. hale, fell (2)
124. hare (1)
125. heart (1)
126. heel, new (2)
127. hear (1)
128. holy (1)
129. eludes (1)
130. idol (1)
131. least (1)
132. lightning, scared (2)
133. applied, loan (2)
134. through, main (2)
135. steak, meat (2)
136. medal (1)
137. occurred (1)
138. temperature (1)
139. very, lonely (2)
140. graduate, hoping, to college (4)

141. honor, privilege (2)
142. punctuation, grammar (2)
143. cemetery (1)
144. recognize (1)
145. tragedies (1)
146. owns, forty (2)
147. definitely, favor (2)
148. very, sincerely (2)
149. sense (1)
150. thorough (1)
151. friend, believe (2)
152. congratulate (1)
153. tried, athlete (2)
154. psychology, philosophy, separate, fields (4)
155. accident (1)
156. pastime (1)
157. miniature, similar, original (3)
158. relevant (1)
159. fur, prefer, leather (3)
160. sore, heal, very (3)
161. threw, through (2)
162. bowed (1)
163. pale, blue (2)
164. no error (2)
165. no error (2)
166. no error (2)
167. no error (2)
168. no error (2)
169. no error (2)
170. no error (2)
171. no error (2)
172. no error (2)
173. no error (2)
174. no error (2)
175. no error (2)
176. no error (2)
177. no error (2)
178. no error (2)

3. *Activity.* Using Reproduction Page 87, duplicate the composition that appears below with the heading "Spelling Proofreading Exercise." It contains a large number of misspelled words—in most cases the same words that appear on the handout used for Teacher Presentation #1 and which were included in the Spelling Game (Activity #2). Have students identify and correct all the spelling errors they can find. Here are several ways the activity can be organized:

   a. Have students work individually identifying and correcting the errors. Give a prize or other recognition to the first student who finds all the errors. (Deduct one point for every correct word the student mistakenly corrects.)

   b. Assign students to small groups and let them work together to find and correct the errors. Require them to come to complete agreement on any changes that are made (i.e., the majority cannot railroad through a decision against the protests of the minority). If you wish, you could have groups compete to see which group finds all the errors first.

   c. Project the worksheet using the opaque projector or make an overhead transparency. Lead the total class through the activity together, letting volunteers suggest which words need to be changed.

SPELLING PROOFREADING EXERCISE

Recently I learned a very important lesson about <u>releiving</u> my own problems rather than expecting others to help me <u>bare</u> my troubles. I had been feeling pretty blue for some time. My dog, who had been with me <u>sinse</u> I was a little more then a baby, just <u>layed</u> down one evening, on the <u>bear</u> basement floor, and <u>dyed</u>. Of <u>coarse</u>, I <u>new</u> he had <u>lead</u> a good life, and he was <u>definately</u> not young, having lived six years, or about the same as <u>fourty two</u> years in the life of a <u>humane</u> being. Therefore, his death shouldn't have been considered a <u>tradgedy</u>. But it was, nonetheless, <u>a truely</u> sad <u>occassion</u>, and I couldn't seem to get over the <u>affect</u> of <u>loosing</u> such a good old faithful friend.

One day it <u>occured</u> to me that I had not really <u>tryed</u> to do anything about <u>overcomming</u> the <u>indefinate</u> <u>sence</u> of loneliness that was making me feel depressed all the time, ever <u>sinse</u> my dog <u>dyed</u>. I hadn't <u>truely</u> <u>tryed</u> to <u>except</u> the fact that the death had <u>occured</u>, <u>weather</u> I <u>choose</u> to <u>reconize</u> it or not, and the time had come, I knew, when I must use good <u>sence</u> and move on into new <u>activitys</u>, <u>seperating</u> myself from the <u>passed</u>.

I decided to follow the <u>principal</u> of replacement in training myself to a new and better attitude. I would replace the fun I <u>use</u> to have with Beau with other pleasures and <u>persuits</u>. (<u>Incidently</u>, this method is good <u>phsychology</u>, and I recommend it to anyone who has <u>alot</u> of problems <u>acheiving</u> <u>piece</u> of mind after <u>loosing</u> a pet.)

The first thing I did on the evening this idea finally <u>occured</u> to me was to check the <u>temparture</u> on the thermometer outside my window. Sure enough, it was a lovely warm 70 degrees, perfect gardening <u>whether</u>, and I knew I'd be <u>alright</u> planting flower seeds. I quickly <u>through</u> on my gardening <u>cloths</u> and went to the garage to get the tools I had <u>recieved</u> as a birthday gift. I also took <u>alot</u> of seeds I had <u>layed</u> away for the spring day when the <u>temperture</u> would be <u>alright</u> for planting.

Bearing these things with me to the back yard, I began to plant seeds along the <u>boundry</u> of our yard. I <u>choose</u> a place where the sun almost <u>allways</u> shone. I felt better at once, as soon as I began digging in the warm soil. Gardening has <u>allways</u> been a soothing <u>passtime</u> for me and <u>immediatly</u> it began to divert my mind from poor Beau's death.

I did feel a little guilty about going ahead with the flower <u>graden</u> without waiting for my little brother, but I <u>beleive</u> the older child should have some <u>privileges</u> which <u>definately</u> belong to him, so my <u>conscious</u> didn't hurt me <u>to</u> badly. My gardening soothed my spirit, and the whole experience <u>lead</u> me to a realization that life goes on, and one must move with it and not let any <u>tradegy</u>, <u>wether</u> major or <u>miner</u>, <u>effect</u> him <u>to</u> much.

4. *Evaluation.* Use the sentences from the Spelling Game (see Activity #2 above) to construct a quiz in which students must locate and correct misspelled words.

5. *Teacher Presentation.* Using Reproduction Page 88, duplicate and distribute to students the "Guide to Punctuation" below. Point out to students that this Guide summarizes the basic principles of punctuation, and that these rules will be the basis of all punctuation activities that follow. You may wish to go over the sheet with the class, providing additional explanation and examples.

GUIDE TO PUNCTUATION

THE COMMA (,)
The comma is used:
(1) To set off appositives (words that clarify or identify that which precedes or comes before it):

   Kristin, my younger sister, is going to Washington.

(2) To set off a direct address (words that tell to whom a remark is directed):

> *Listen, Diane, you'd better not be late again.*

(3) To set off a quotation:

> *"Don't hit the telephone pole," shrieked the driver education teacher, "or you'll go back to study hall forever."*

(4) After each word in a series:

> *The store was all out of peanuts, popcorn, and pretzels.*

(5) Following an introductory participial phrase:

> *Hearing the bell, I ran!*

(6) Following such words as yes, no, oh, well, perhaps, etc.:

> *Oh, what a beautiful dog.*

(7) Before the state in an address:

> *Albany, New York*

(8) Between the day of the month and the year:

> *June 24, 1950.*

(9) To set off such transitional expressions as however, therefore, conversely, and nevertheless:

> *We all failed the test. It was, therefore, discarded.*

THE COLON (:)

The colon is used:

(1) To introduce a famous quotation:

> *We can fully understand Cassius's philosophy when he says: "The fault, dear Brutus, is not in our stars, But in ourselves, that we are underlings."*

(2) To set up or prepare the reader for a list or a series:

> *The reasons for his dismissal include: tardiness, incompetence, dishonesty, and disrespect.*
>
> *Will the following people report to the office: Mary, Kevin, Bill, and Jo-Ann.*
>
> *The recipe calls for: butter, sugar, milk, and salt.*

THE SEMICOLON (;)

The semicolon is used:

(1) To separate two independent clauses when the conjunction has been omitted:

> *It rained all afternoon; we stayed in the house and watched television.*

(2) To separate items in a series that contains commas:

> *The dinner list included: Martin Norton, Ph.D.; Kelly Gaffney, M.D.; and Henry Owens, D.D.S.*

QUOTATION MARKS ("   ")

Quotation marks are used:

(1) To indicate titles of poems, essays, short stories, songs, and articles:

> *My favorite poem is "Dover Beach."*
>
> *Edgar Allen Poe's short story "The Masque of the Red Death" is frightening.*
>
> *The song title "Somebody Done Somebody Wrong Song" is the longest on the record.*
>
> *Do you like the poem "Ode to a Grecian Urn"?*

(2) To quote a person's direct comments:

> *"It's nice to see you," said Mrs. Benson.*
>
> *"Where have you been?" asked Mary. "I've been waiting for an hour."*

UNDERLINE (_____)

Underline:

(1) To indicate the titles of novels, plays, paintings, and magazines:

> *Picasso's <u>Guernica</u> is a famous painting.*

Daniel DeFoe's <u>Moll Flanders</u> is one of the first British novels.
Samuel Beckett's <u>Waiting for Godot</u> is one of the best modern plays.
Do you read <u>Time</u> magazine?

THE APOSTROPHE (')
Use the apostrophe:
(1) To indicate possession (Add an apostrophe and an "s" to most words to create the singular possessive form.):
> *That is Alice's purse.*
> *Here is Jane's letter.*
(2) To indicate possession of a plural word (Add an apostrophe for most words.):
> *She is one of hundreds who belong to the Teachers' Association.*
> *Check <u>The Readers' Guide to Periodical Literature</u>.*

In cases where the plural is not formed by adding an "s," an apostrophe and then an "s" should be added to form the possessive.

> *child (singular)*   *children (plural)*   *children's (plural possessive)*
> *woman (singular)*   *women (plural)*   *women's (plural possessive)*

Don't use apostrophes with possessive pronouns—theirs, ours, yours, mine, hers, his, its.
(3) To indicate the omission of a letter in a contraction:
> *I didn't go. (didn't = did not: the apostrophe takes the place of the "o" in "not")*
> *I wasn't at home. (wasn't = was not: the apostrophe takes the place of the "o" in "not")*

THE PERIOD (.)
The period is used:
(1) To end a complete sentence:
> *I cannot find my car keys.*
> *Tomorrow is Saturday.*
(2) To punctuate abbreviations:
> *Street is abbreviated "St."*
> *Mister is abbreviated "Mr."*
> *Governor is abbreviated "Gov."*

THE QUESTION MARK (?)
The question mark is used:
(1) As the end punctuation of an interrogative sentence (one that asks a question):
> *Where is the bank?*
> *What is your name?*
> *Who is that man over there?*
> *When are you leaving?*

6. *Activity.* Assign students to small groups of three or four students each and have them play the Punctuation Game. The game is built around forty sentences, thirty-four of which contain one or more errors in punctuation. The purpose is for students to identify and correct the punctuation errors, and thus improve their proofreading skills.

   The student draws two kinds of cards—those on which are printed the sentences described above and smaller cards bearing marks of punctuation. The object is to correctly match punctuation cards with sentence cards that require punctuation. After a player matches a sentence and the necessary punctuation cards, the card is discarded. Play continues until one player manages to discard all the cards in his or her hand and thus is the winner.

Since players must show the other players their cards when they attempt to discard them, and allow them to determine whether the sentence is correctly punctuated, all players get frequent practice proofreading for punctuation.

Prepare one set of materials for every three or four students in the class. For each set photocopy the forty sentences provided on Reproduction Page 89. Cut out each sentence and mount it on a 3" x 5" index card, using rubber cement or transparent tape. Shuffle the sentence cards so they are not in any specific order.

Then cut 37 3" x 5" index cards in half, so that from each you have created two smaller cards measuring 2½" x 3". On each of the smaller cards draw a large mark of punctuation and below it write the name of that mark of punctuation. Prepare the following numbers of cards:

ten periods
twenty commas
five question marks
eight sets of quotation marks
fifteen semicolons
ten exclamation points
five underlines

Then reproduce the instructions for playing the game (Reproduction Page 90) and the answer key (Reproduction Page 91). Insert all materials for a single game set into a large Zip-Lock bag to keep the components from getting lost.

The game can be used by a small group of students who have special difficulties with punctuation or need extra practice, or by students who finish other activities before the rest of the class. Or, by making six to eight sets, you can have the class divide into small groups and all play at the same time.

SENTENCE CARDS FOR PUNCTUATION GAME

1. *Mr. Martin who is our principal has been transferred.*
2. *We left on Sunday and arrived home the next day.*
3. *I bought records jeans and beads.*
4. *The test was difficult everyone failed.*
5. *Who wrote the poem The Road Not Taken.*
6. *The following people were late Bill Mary Bob Martin and Maureen.*
7. *Roads were slippery we therefore drove very carefully.*
8. *Where are you going.*
9. *The essays were interesting however there were many spelling errors.*
10. *Yes I agree.*
11. *The old ski lodge was torn down in August and a new one was built the next year.*
12. *Anne is a thoughtful friendly girl.*
13. *Robert Dobbs M.D. is her family doctor.*
14. *We visited Darwin White and Company Incorporated.*
15. *Mrs Waters Mr Moore and Ms. Woodruff are school board members.*
16. *When I finally received my driver's license I was very excited.*
17. *Disturbed by the thunder the dog howled all night.*
18. *Stop that right now she yelled or I'll spank you.*
19. *Out out brief candle whispered the young actor.*

20. *May I quote asked Mrs. Green*
21. *Oh you do look tired.*
22. *On February 23 1976 Sally leaves for Boston.*
23. *Allison was born in Maple Tree Falls Nebraska on May 9 1956.*
24. *The Mill on The Floss a sensitive poignant novel by George Eliot is a classic.*
25. *Seventeen is my favorite magazine my parents read Time.*
26. *Mrs. Conway said to check The Readers Guide to Periodical Literature.*
27. *He that hath the steerage of my course direct my sails read Larry who plays Hamlet.*
28. *What's so funny asked Cindy.*
29. *It's your house not theirs.*
30. *Go to the ladies department.*
31. *Carolyns friends are very nice.*
32. *James books are torn ripped and yellowed with age.*
33. *That car looks like the Smiths.*
34. *The students desks are dirty.*
35. *The childrens toys are broken.*
36. *The following people were not present: Mary Harvey, C.P.A.; Jason Barnes, M.D.*
37. *That's fine with me.*
38. *I bought flowers, candy, and clothes.*
39. *The book is a best-seller; everyone is reading it.*
40. *It is your decision, not mine.*

INSTRUCTIONS FOR PUNCTUATION GAME

1. The object of the game is to match cards bearing punctuation marks with sentences that require those marks in order to be punctuated correctly. The first player to get rid of all his or her cards by properly matching sentences with punctuation marks is the winner.
2. Three to five persons can play this game.
3. Choose one person to serve as the Judge and hand him or her the answer key. This person will consult the answer key to determine whether a player has made a correct match. If necessary, the Judge can also be a player.
4. Shuffle the sentence cards (large ones) and place them in a stack face down.
5. Shuffle the punctuation mark cards (small ones) and place them in a stack face down.
6. Beside each stack of cards, turn one card face up as the beginning of a discard pile.
7. Have one player serve as dealer and give each player two sentence cards and two punctuation mark cards without looking at them.
8. The player to the right of the dealer goes first. First, the player draws a card from *either* the sentence card stack or the punctuation mark card stack. Or, the player can take either the sentence card or punctuation mark card that has been placed face up on the discard pile. Whichever choice the player takes, he or she draws only one card. Then the player attempts to match sentence cards and punctuation mark cards in order to punctuate the sentences correctly. For example, if the player has a sentence card that needs a semi-colon and a comma in order to be correctly punctuated, and if there happens to be a semi-colon and a comma among his or her punctuation marks, the player can put the two punctuation marks with the sentence card and have a "match." If a player thinks he or she has a match, the player tells the group of a wish to discard those cards and they check to make sure the player has punctuated the sentence(s) correctly. If they all agree that the punctuation is right (and the Judge concurs after consulting the answer key), the player may discard the cards used for the "match" by placing them face up on the respective piles. If the player

has punctuated the sentence incorrectly, according to the other players and/or the Judge, then he or she cannot discard the cards and also loses the next turn.

9. Players can discard "matches" only when it is their turn. They do so *after* drawing one new card from one of the four piles.

10. Play continues until one player has discarded all his or her cards by matching.

11. If players use all the cards in the stacks of sentence cards or punctuation mark cards, they shuffle all but the top card in the discard pile and turn these face down to use as a new stack.

ANSWER KEY FOR PUNCTUATION GAME

1. Martin, principal,
2. no error
3. records, jeans, and beads
4. difficult;
5. "The Road Not Taken"?
6. late: Bill, Mary, Bob, Martin, and Maureen
7. slippery; ,therefore,
8. going?
9. ;however,
10. Yes,
11. August,
12. thoughtful,
13. Dobbs, M.D.,
14. Darwin, White, and Company, Incorporated
15. Mrs. Waters, Mr. Moore, and Ms. Woodruff
16. license,
17. thunder,
18. "Stop... now," yelled, "or... you."
19. "Out, out... candle."
20. "May... quote?"
21. Oh,
22. February 23, 1976, Sally
23. Maple Tree Falls, May 9,
24. The Mill on The Floss, a sensitive, Eliot,
25. Seventeen magazine; Time
26. The Readers' Guide to Periodical Literature
27. "He... sails." Larry,
28. "What's... funny?"
29. house,
30. ladies'
31. Carolyn's
32. Jame's torn, ripped,
33. Smiths'
34. students'
35. children's
36. no errors
37. no errors
38. no errors
39. no errors
40. no errors

7. *Activity.* Using Reproduction Page 92, duplicate the paragraph below, which on the Reproduction Page contains a large number of punctuation mistakes. This version of the exercise has the errors corrected; the one on Reproduction Page 92, of course, does not. Have students identify and correct all the punctuation errors they can find. If you wish to give the total class guided practice in proofreading for punctuation, you could project the paragraph using the opaque or overhead projector and call on volunteers to point out errors. Make sure to require students to explain *why* they think a correction is necessary.

Painting is a multifaceted, versatile, and diverse field. There are many different, distinctive types of painting, such as naturalistic, nonrepresentational, geometric, biomorphic, symbolic, and literal, etc. Good artists always consider the possibilities open to them. They carefully decide how to communicate their feelings, what colors to use, what style, technique and manner to employ. Competent, serious artists use their medium, explore its range and scope, and attempt to bring both their medium and their message into harmonious, lucid focus. It's the artist's job, according to many experts, to convey the message as expressively as possible. Many of the paintings that we laugh off and label simple, silly and childish are really the products of enormous effort, tenacious, unending hard work, and limitless, creative decision. Don't be like one of my neighbors who said, "That painting is crooked, and any two-year-old could do better." Next time you view a painting, give it a fair chance; consider its message, its purpose, its expressiveness. Don't just decide on face value whether or not it's good.

8. *Activity.* Make additional punctuation proofreading exercises for students by typing an essay on a spirit duplicating master, omitting all the marks of punctuation and having students add them where needed.

9. *Evaluation.* Use the items from the Punctuation Game to construct a quiz in which students must locate and correct punctuation errors.

10. *Teacher Presentation.* Review with the class the more common errors in usage and syntax—including subject-verb agreement, pronoun-antecedent agreement, the uses and degrees of adjectives and adverbs, parallel construction, double negatives, nonstandard idiomatic expressions, and the tenses of the following verbs: freeze, break, speak, swim, sing, shake, forecast, sprain, take, go, open, and give. Several instructional sessions on usage and syntax may be necessary for a thorough review. Or students can read the explanations that appear in textbooks such as those suggested at the end of this chapter.

11. *Activity.* Have students play the Usage Game. This game, played in small groups of three to five students, is identical to the Spelling Game (Activity #2) described previously, except it gives students practice in identifying and correcting errors in grammatical usage and syntax rather than spelling. Like the Spelling Game, it requires students to inspect sentences which may or may not contain errors. A player who correctly identifies the errors and explains them to the rest of the group is allowed to move his or her marker forward on the board. To prepare a set of the materials needed for the Usage Game, photocopy the sentences below, using Reproduction Page 93. Cut them out and mount each on a 3" x 5" index card. The same board as is used for the Spelling Game (Reproduction Page 84) can be used for the Usage Game. Instructions for playing the Usage Game are shown on page 140, and can be duplicated using Reproduction Page 94. Review the directions under Activity #2 above for preparing the materials and organizing the class to play the game. The answer key for the Usage Game appears on page 140, and can be duplicated using Reproduction Page 95.

SENTENCES FOR USAGE GAME

1. *The road is froze.*
2. *He don't want to stay any longer.*
3. *Sarah is the nicest of the two.*
4. *Each of you are expected to listen.*
5. *She must of went to the store with her brother.*
6. *I couldn't care less.*
7. *I don't remember never having seen that film.*
8. *He did it all himself.*
9. *There isn't no candy left.*
10. *Don't let no one see these exam papers.*
11. *Everyone made their own lunch.*
12. *Drive very careful.*
13. *She looked very nicely in her new dress.*
14. *Us students know a lot about our school.*

15. *I think that politics are interesting.*
16. *My scissors is broken.*
17. *Patience and honesty are fine virtues.*
18. *Bring them papers over here.*
19. *Ham and eggs are my favorite meal.*
20. *Field trips is more better than homework.*
21. *Mrs. Hayden is more nice than Mr. Gray.*
22. *The television is broke.*
23. *There isn't nothing more to say.*
24. *Them shoes is mine.*
25. *Buy three dozen of eggs.*
26. *We has all the time in the world.*
27. *We had just began when it started to rain.*
28. *We sung for two hours.*
29. *Leslie and me washed, dried, and polish the car.*
30. *Harold is old-fashion and prejudice.*
31. *When you finish wiped the dishes, you can leave.*
32. *This is between Mary and I.*
33. *Her and her brother are my cousins.*
34. *Alls you got to do is read the directions.*
35. *She must not of been very happy.*
36. *You are smarter than her.*
37. *They has got my folder.*
38. *She's the beautifullest person I ever meet.*
39. *I tried to be honest with he.*
40. *Communications are a new and exciting field.*
41. *We will run, jump, do some racing, jogging, and exercising.*
42. *He's more skinnier than me.*
43. *We swum all afternoon.*
44. *I was all shoken up by the accident.*
45. *The child snuck down the stairs quiet.*
46. *They had a real nice day.*
47. *We was home by nine o'clock.*
48. *Yesterday I went ice skating and come home exhausted.*
49. *The job, although interesting and exciting, weren't exactly what I wanted.*
50. *To who do you wish to speak?*
51. *I seen Jill downtown.*
52. *John, one of two hundred boys participating, are winning every event.*
53. *Mrs. Fine, which is my typing teacher, is retiring.*
54. *There is two kind of books—dull and interesting.*
55. *I read where she got sick.*
56. *Each of the five hundred team members are signed up.*
57. *Whom may I ask are you?*
58. *I wish to see Cathy and he.*
59. *The weatherman forecasted rain for tonight.*

60. *I was very tired when I finally sit down.*
61. *This is a occasion to remember.*
62. *Karen and me is friends.*
63. *You look very sickly.*
64. *That music sounds well.*
65. *Ask whoever you wish.*
66. *That pair of shoes are beautiful.*
67. *My pants is torn.*
68. *There is less apples in that bag.*
69. *You done everything real good.*
70. *There isn't any more potatoes.*
71. *Him and me went to the concert.*
72. *I am older than she.*
73. *This is between David and me.*
74. *This problem is among the two school boards.*
75. *Either Marty or Jeff are going to go to Yale.*
76. *Stealing these books are prohibited.*
77. *There isn't any quick answers.*
78. *The media are always objective.*
79. *I got into my car, fastened my seatbelt, checked my mirrors, locked the door, turned on the motor, and starting driving away.*
80. *They got a nice house.*
81. *Mary has often spoke of you.*
82. *Following training, the dog reverted back to his old ways.*
83. *Lisa sprung her ankle.*
84. *Annie had took all my cigarettes.*
85. *Lenny loaned he ten dollars.*
86. *That was the worstest game I ever seen.*
87. *The both of us went together.*
88. *My sister she is very irritating.*
89. *They did that there art work all by theirselves.*
90. *Joanne's childrens is real fresh.*
91. *That there girl is Kevin's sister.*
92. *We will leave the door opened.*
93. *By this time next week, we will have already went.*
94. *She must of gave me the keys.*
95. *She went with they to the movies.*
96. *One of my friends and I is going to New York.*
97. *Ceramics are my favorite hobby.*
98. *Mr. Mitchell and his wife, two of our best customers, is sick.*
99. *Neither Kristin nor Juanita are old enough to vote.*
100. *She came in, sat down, and starts talking.*
101. *I was suppose to write an essay.*
102. *I sat down and rest.*

INSTRUCTIONS FOR PLAYING THE USAGE GAME

1. Approximately four persons can play this game.
2. Lay the game board on the floor or other flat surface such as a table or desk.
3. Give the answer key to one person (either a player or someone who wants to watch but not play). This person will consult the answer key when necessary to check an answer, and hence will be referred to as "the Judge." Warn the Judge not to let anyone see the answers.
4. Shuffle and stack all the sentence cards. Place them face down near the game board.
5. Roll dice or draw lots or guess a number to determine who goes first.
6. Place your markers in the space labelled "Start" on the game board.
7. The first player draws a sentence card from the top of the stack. The player reads it and determines whether or not it contains any error(s) in standard English. Sentences may contain no, one, two or three errors.
8. If the player decides there are no usage errors in the sentence, he or she must show it to the other players to see whether they agree. If they don't agree, the Judge checks the answer key. If the Judge upholds the player's opinion, then the player may move ahead two spaces. If the player is wrong, that is, if the sentence does contain one or more usage errors, then he or she loses the next turn.
9. A player who decides that the sentence does contain a usage error must identify each error, correct it, and explain the correction to the other players. If the Judge and other players agree with the correction, the player may move ahead the number of spaces equal to the number of usage errors in the sentence. If the other players do not agree, then the group must discuss the issue until they reach agreement. If they cannot agree, they must consult the Judge. The Judge's answer, based on the key, overrules all other players. The Judge must explain the answer to the other players. If the player's answer is upheld by the Judge, then the player may move ahead as many spaces as there are usage errors in the sentence. If the player is wrong, he or she loses the next turn.
10. The player whose marker reaches the "Finish" space first is the winner.

ANSWER KEY FOR USAGE GAME

1. frozen	(1)	28. sang	(1)	53. who (not which)	(1)
2. doesn't	(1)	29. I, polished	(2)	54. are kinds	(2)
3. nicer	(1)	30. old-fashioned, prejudiced	(2)	55. that (not where)	(1)
4. is	(1)	31. wiping	(1)	56. Each.... is	(1)
5. must have gone	(2)	32. me (not I)	(1)	57. Who	(1)
6. no error	(2)	33. She	(1)	58. him	(1)
7. ever	(1)	34. All you have	(2)	59. forecast	(1)
8. himself	(1)	35. have (not of)	(1)	60. sat	(1)
9. any	(1)	36. she	(1)	61. an	(1)
10. anyone	(1)	37. have	(1)	62. I are	(2)
11. his (not their)	(1)	38. most beautiful person I ever met	(2)	63. sick	(1)
12. carefully	(1)			64. good	(1)
13. nice	(1)	39. him	(1)	65. whomever	(1)
14. We	(1)	40. is (not are)	(1)	66. is	(1)
15. politics is	(1)	41. run, jump, race, jog, and exercise.	(3)	67. are	(1)
16. scissors are	(1)			68. are fewer	(2)
17. no error	(2)	42. He's skinnier than I	(2)	69. did really well	(3)
18. those	(1)	43. swam	(1)	70. aren't	(1)
19. is	(1)	44. shaken up	(1)	71. He and I	(2)
20. are better	(2)	45. sneaked quietly	(2)	72. no error	(2)
21. nicer	(1)	46. really	(1)	73. no error	(2)
22. broken	(1)	47. were	(1)	74. between	(1)
23. anything	(1)	48. came	(1)	75. Either... is	(1)
24. Those... are	(2)	49. The job.... wasn't	(1)	76. Stealing... is	(1)
25. dozens	(1)	50. whom	(1)	77. aren't	(1)
26. have	(1)	51. I saw	(1)	78. no error	(2)
27. begun	(1)	52. John... is	(1)	79. drove	(1)

80. have	(1)	88. my sister is	(1)	95. them	(1)
81. spoken	(1)	89. did that (not that there)		96. are	(1)
82. reverted (not reverted back)	(1)	themselves	(2)	97. Ceramics is	(1)
83. sprained	(1)	90. children are really	(3)	98. are	(1)
84. had taken	(1)	91. That (not that there)	(1)	99. Neither... is	(1)
85. lent (not loaned) him	(2)	92. open	(1)	100. started	(1)
86. worst...saw	(2)	93. gone	(1)	101. supposed	(1)
87. Both (not the both)	(1)	94. must have given	(3)	102. rested	(1)

12. *Activity.* Using Reproduction Page 96, duplicate the composition below, "The Grammar Witch." The Reproduction Page contains a large number of errors in usage and syntax as well as a few in spelling and punctuation (for purposes of review). Have students identify and correct all the errors they can find. Here are several ways to organize the activity:

1. Have students work individually identifying and correcting the errors. Give recognition to the first student who finds all the errors. Deduct one point for every correct word the student mistakenly corrects.
2. Assign students to small groups and let them work together to find and correct the errors.
3. Use the worksheet for a total class lesson. Project it using an opaque or overhead projector, or give each student a copy, and lead the class through it.

The version of "The Grammar Witch" that appears here has been corrected; the version that appears on Reproduction Page 96, of course, has not.

"The Grammar Witch"

Once upon a time, a long time ago, in a green asbestos-shingled cottage by a deep, dark lake which they say had monsters in its depths, there was a lady who was known as the grammar witch. The number of people who were lost in her grammar ovens was never known for sure, but it must have been considerable, according to the local gossip about whose family had lost its third member and whose family had lost its fourth, fifth, sixth, etc.

She was one of those witches, also, who didn't care about others' misusing grammar as long as they tried, really tried, as hard as she. A lot of people don't feel that way; they think you're a social outcast whose need for grammar and usage lessons outweighs any good points which you might have. Either they or she is wrong, it's obvious, in their attitude.

Anyhow, this witch used to sit herself down by the lake as comfortably as can be, and watch for unwary victims whom she could entice into her grammar ovens. There were many weary travelers she caught on their way past her cottage, going home from work. She would lie in wait ten hours at a time; that's a long, tiring time to sit in one place. As a matter of fact, ten hours is too long to do any one thing, it seems to me. However, remember she was a witch, and they are not like the rest of us.

Well, she would lie there and wait and turn over in her mind all the grammar lessons she would teach to whomever she caught, no matter who they were. Either subjects or objects was her favorite lesson and she would teach them to absolutely anyone; she wasn't particular. Businessmen, for instance, along with a lot of employees, were her favorite victims. It was they who aroused in her a regular frenzy of teaching and inspired her to pedagogical extremes that were hers alone.

Be that as it may, since the victims she lured in and tried to teach were seldom fascinated by her efforts, she usually ended in a violent, towering rage and popped them, *screaming, writhing, and sobbing into her ovens, which always had clouds of smoke pouring from their chimneys.*

Now that may sound cruel, inhuman, and atrocious to you, but if so, you're not thinking enough about how hard all this was on the poor, frustrated, grammar witch. Think how she must have felt when whoever she was trying to teach just ignored her fine lessons and acted as if they thought their lives would be perfectly happy without knowing grammar. Isn't that disgusting?

One day in her ovens, a quite routine day, actually, there was a businessman whom she'd caught on his way home from work, a truck driver whose car had stalled near her cottage, a high school student who had forgotten to do his homework, and three pastry cooks whom she felt convinced she could never educate to the joys of grammar. Poor things. Their attitudes were not good; they were less willing than the high school student, although they were, to tell the truth, somewhat smarter than he. I would not like to be him. Would you? Oh, well.

Well, if you're wondering why this short, unhappy story of the grammar witch is, indeed, short, which is seldom the case with stories these days, let me remind you, dear students, that another day, another hour you might well have another story to read, carefully trying to catch all errors in grammar, and that other story will have spelling problems in it; so this story—or another like it—can't be too long. Isn't that right? Oh, well.

13. *Evaluation.* Construct a quiz using items from the Usage Game, page 137.

TOPIC III. LANGUAGE THAT GETS IN THE WAY

1. *Teacher Presentation.* All during elementary school, teachers encourage their students to develop ever more extensive vocabularies and to use ever more effective words in their writing. Most students progress in these skills in a satisfactory manner; however, a substantial number of students misinterpret these lessons and adopt the notion that in order to be good writers, they must use fancy, flowery language. They prefer a long word to a short one, an uncommon one to a common one, a pretty one to a plain one.

These students are often difficult to persuade that simple, direct language is preferable. They feel they have been taught that wordy, metaphorical constructions are more admirable and somehow more exciting than straight talk.

Explain to your class that styles of writing change as styles in hair and clothes do. Demonstrate this fact by passing out excerpts from writing created at different times in history, or by reading several samples aloud. (Suggestions: Thackeray, Pepys, or Dickens as contrasted to Twain—the voice of Huck Finn!— Stephen Crane, Theodore Dreiser, or contemporary writers like James Farrell, Bernard Malamud or Ernest Hemingway) Help your students see that writing has gotten simpler, more direct and, actually, easier to read and understand, as styles have changed through the years.

You might, for a rule of thumb in writing, put on the board George Orwell's often-quoted rules from his essay "Politics and the English Language":

1. Never use a metaphor, simile or other figure of speech which you are used to seeing in print.
2. Never use a long word where a short one will do.
3. If it is possible to cut a word, always cut it out.
4. Never use the passive where you can use the active.

5. Never use a foreign phrase, a scientific word or a jargon word if you can think of an everyday English equivalent.
6. Break any of these rules sooner than say anything barbarous.

2. *Activity.* Following is a listing of pairs of words or phrases. One item of each pair is a simple "everyday" expression, and the other is a less common usage, perhaps longer, more technical, more formal, or more pretentious. Using Reproduction Page 97, duplicate the list below. Give copies to your students and, working with the class as a whole, select those words which you and the class agree are more simple, direct and precise and, hence, more suitable for their writing.

face - countenance	carried - conveyed
said - uttered	truthfulness - veracity
head - cranium	talkative - verbose
leg - limb	poor - poverty stricken
feet - pedal extremities	eye - orb
toes - pedal digits	sun - solar body
hair - crowning glory	star - heavenly body
sky - heavens	man - gentleman
building - edifice	ate - consumed
car - vehicle	lie - prevaricate
die - pass away	chew - masticate
green - verdant	kiss - osculate
minister - man of the cloth	

3. *Activity.* On the other hand, your students will need to learn the important lesson that under-writing is just as undesirable as over-writing. Following is a list of paired expressions that you and your students can use to arrive at a listing of usages that are widely accepted in informal conversation but which are much less acceptable in writing. Using Reproduction Page 98, duplicate the following list and distribute it. Work with the total class or have students work individually, circling the item in each pair that is more appropriate to formal, written expression. Then have students see if they can give other examples of expressions that are a part of our spoken language, but which are not appropriate in writing except when deliberately used as nonstandard or colloquial.

snuck - sneaked
all shook up - all shaken up
I could care less - I could not care less
kid - child
guy - man or boy
phony - false
ripped off - stolen
rap - discuss
they fell out - they quarreled
had a fit - became upset
told her off - criticized her frankly
had a ball - had a good time
irregardless - regardless
fantastic - very satisfactory
fabulous - unbelievably satisfactory
broke up - ended the relationship
he's crazy - he's wrong
took the rap - took the blame
a jerk - someone I don't like
laid it on the line - spoke frankly
pulled the rug out from under someone - removed someone's support

4. *Activity.* Present to the class the following paragraph which is filled with pretentious, inflated diction. Ask them, working individually or in pairs, to remove the words they feel are out of place and replace them with more direct, precise words. When everyone has finished, have several revised paragraphs read aloud, so students can see how different or similar they are. Be sure to emphasize again how much more effective paragraphs are with simple, direct language which says precisely what it means.

Sample Paragraph

Her erudite asseverations are highly enigmatic. It certainly would behoove her to recapitulate and revise. Her rhetorical style, which is esoteric and hyperbolic, is an impediment to lucid communication. Her diction is neologistic and arbitrary. I am incredulous as to the discrepancy between her content and style.

5. *Activity.* Present to the class the following paragraph which is underwritten, containing many informal, nonstandard expressions that are not appropriate for written expression. Ask students, working individually or in pairs, to remove expressions they feel are out of place and to replace them with language more appropriate to writing. Remind them to make verb tenses consistent too. When everyone has finished, have several revised paragraphs read aloud, so the students can see how different or similar they are. Be sure to emphasize that slang and nonstandard usage are not inherently "wrong" but are merely inappropriate in formal writing situations such as most of the composition assignments students will encounter.

Sample Paragraph

Her smart ideas were confusing. It certainly would have been good if she thought it over and changed stuff. Her writing style, which nobody understands, is blown up and wrecks understanding. Her picking of words is new and made up. I don't believe the difference in what she feels and wants to say and what she really says.

6. *Activity.* Have students take paragraphs they have previously written and revise them to substitute flowery or pretentious diction and wordy constructions. They can then exchange these and see if other students can detect the unsuitable language in each other's writing and replace it with everyday language.

7. *Activity.* Repeat Activity #6, except focus on slang and nonstandard usage.

8. *Activity.* Assign students at random to small groups of four or five and challenge each group to make a list of all the stale, overused metaphorical expressions they can think of. It might be helpful for you to remind them that a metaphor says one thing to mean another, as when we say "Red" to mean Communist or "creep" to mean someone unattractive to us. Following is a list that you can use to "prime the pump" (a metaphor!) or fill in expressions they overlook. After they have worked for twenty or thirty minutes, have students share and compare their lists.

    stand up for what I believe
    dig him
    my hopes went down the drain
    uphill climb

grain of salt
struck a sour note
ran the show with an iron hand
I died laughing
no bed of roses
went ape over her
he came hat in hand
he cooled off toward her and gave her the gate
she got the axe
he's a real pile-driver
took off like a shot
in apple pie order
all broken up
went to pieces
shook up
had a fit
lost her marbles
fell flat on his face
tore through her speech
caused raised eyebrows
make waves
rock the boat
fall in line
take it easy
kill time
journey through life
give your heart away
his heart broke
shake a leg
cut it out
knock it off
dress fit to kill
a snail's pace

9. *Activity.* Assign students at random to small groups of four or five and challenge each group to make a list of all the stale, overused similes they can think of. Remind them that a simile compares one thing to another, using "as" or "like." If the simile is familiar to the writer, very likely it is stale and should not be used. Here are some examples to get students started:

hard as a rock
hard as nails
dead as a doornail
quick as a wink
run like the wind
sing like a bird
slow as molasses in January
hot as a firecracker
ugly as a mud fence
rough as a cob
slept like a log
snore like a buzz saw
greedy as a pig
ate like a horse
happy as a lark
light as a feather
cursed like a sailor

10. *Activity.* Using Reproduction Page 99, duplicate the following paragraphs that are resplendent with clichés. Distribute copies to the class. Have students work in pairs or independently to remove all the clichés and, where suitable, replace them with fresh and original language.

   A. *First and foremost, with your permission, I'd like to give you a rundown of facts and figures on George Johnson, our captain. He is a fine figure of a man, towering over most ordinary men at a height of 6'3". He is as strong as a bull and light on his feet as well, with bulging muscles and rugged features. Rough and ready and always spoiling for a fight, he never runs from trouble, but to be perfectly frank about it, runs after it fast and furiously. It will come as no surprise to you, then, to learn that trouble is his middle name, or that he often finds himself on the wrong side of the law. Nonetheless he has a gentle side to his nature as well, and is considered far and wide—when all is said and done—to be a pillar of the community.*

   B. *The next member of the team to claim our attention is none other than Bob Jones, the pride and joy of the fans and a mountain of a man with a heart of gold. He is a tiger during games, but off the field is as meek as a lamb, a paragon of manly virtues admired by old and young alike. He is generous to a fault and always ready to lend a helping hand to those less fortunate than himself. A cool customer when the game is up for grabs, he relaxes when it is in the bag and plays as hard off the field as he works on it.*

11. *Activity.* Below is a list of clichés. Working with the class, take the items in the list one at a time. Speak the first half of the cliché and see if someone in the class can call out the other half. If someone can, that is a sure sign that it is a cliché. For example, read "leaps and . . ." from the list. Pause for someone to supply the missing "bounds." If no one does, read the cliché to the class and go on to the next one. Alternate approach: reproduce the list, with the second half of the clichés missing and have students fill in the blanks working individually.

ups and (downs)	*wedded (bliss)*
flesh and (blood)	*rude (awakening)*
sink or (swim)	*fresh as (a daisy)*
tit for (tat)	*regular as (clockwork)*
sixes and (sevens)	*snug as (a bug in a rug)*
wrack and (ruin)	*lost in (thought)*
fits and (starts)	*up in (arms)*
rhyme or (reason)	*cool as (a cucumber)*
flesh and (blood)	*pleased as (punch)*
pride and (joy)	*dead as (a doornail)*
kith and (kin)	*malice (aforethought)*
nip and (tuck)	*standing (offer)*
leaps and (bounds)	*sneaking (suspicion)*
hale and (hearty)	*square (shooter)*
rough and (tumble)	*likeable (chap)*
hammer and (tongs)	*depths of (despair)*
fine and (dandy)	*all wool and (a yard wide)*
hard and (fast)	*at cross (purposes)*
straight and (narrow)	*in dire (straits)*
time and (tide)	*ulterior (motives)*
by and (large)	*fiendish (glee)*
wine, women and (song)	*trusty (revolver)*
morning, noon and (night)	*watery (grave)*
high, wide and (handsome)	*vicious (circle)*
free, white and (twenty-one)	*faithful (retainer)*
sadder and (wiser)	*crying (shame)*
humble (servant)	*diamond in the (rough)*

all due (modesty)
in the nick of (time)
clear as (crystal) (a bell)
quick as (a flash)
good as (my word)

motley (throng; crew)
humble (abode)
filthy (lucre)
coin of (the realm)

ASSESSING ACHIEVEMENT OF OBJECTIVES

To measure the extent to which students have mastered the skills taught in this unit, reproduce a student-written essay (or paragraph) that contains errors of all the types covered by the revision check list you have prepared for your students. Give a copy to each student and have them identify and correct each weakness. Grade students in terms of their thoroughness in identifying weaknesses and the appropriateness of their corrections.

RESOURCES FOR TEACHING PROOFREADING AND REVISION

Below is a selected list of resources useful for teaching the skills of proofreading, editing, and revision. They are classified as either audio-visual material (films, filmstrips, records, photo-sets, slide-tape programs, etc.) or books for students. Addresses of publishers can be found in the alphabetical list on pages 151–153. Prices, where given, are only approximate, since changes occur frequently.

Audio-Visual Materials

Brush up on Punctuation. Four filmstrips examine in detail the uses of and reasons for various marks of punctuation, focusing on the comma, semicolon, parenthesis, dash, colon, quotation marks, etc. Script included. Appropriate for average and advanced students. $45.95 with records, $52.95 with cassettes. Applause Productions.

Use of Pronouns. Four filmstrips describing the use of personal pronouns and nouns, pronoun case, compound personal pronouns, reflexives and inflexives. $32.95. Applause Productions.

The Use of Verbs. Six filmstrips discussing in detail: the use and misuse of tense; transitive and intransitive, linking, regular and irregular verbs; dangling participles; and subject/predicate agreement. Informative and helpful. Appropriate for all students. $32.95. Applause Productions.

Tracking Down Sentence Problems I. Four filmstrips designed to help students to improve their understanding of English. Includes practice exercises related to pronouns, agreement, and awkward shifts. $45.95 with two records, $55.95 with four cassettes. Applause Productions.

Tracking Down Sentence Problems II. Four filmstrips providing practice drills and exercises in locating and correcting such problems related to sentence structure as fragments, run-ons, dangling modifiers, and wordiness. Script included. $45.95 with two records, $55.95 with four cassettes. Applause Productions.

The Basics of Good Spelling. One record or cassette. Provides instruction and learning aids designed to teach the correct spelling of 400 frequently misspelled words. LP Record, $6.75, cassette, $7.95. Applause Productions.

Punctuation Problems. A title in the *Conquering Composition* Series. Contains four full-color filmstrips, four LP record sides or cassettes, and four scripts. Examines: end punctuation—use and misuse, rules, and methods of improvement; the comma—its functions and proper uses; the semicolon; parenthesis; dash; colon; and quotation marks. Interesting, appealing format. Suitable for all students. $42.00 with records; $48.00 with cassettes. Filmstrip House.

The Sense of a Sentence. A filmstrip which deals with sentence structure and use. Explains what a sentence is and why it is a necessary component in writing. Visually attractive, contemporary illustrations. $20.00. R.M.I. Educational Films, Inc.

Mechanics: Capitalization. One of seven parts

of the *Composition Skills* series. Contains forty transparencies in a plastic case ($52.65), practice pages, and duplicating masters ($.85 per set).

Mechanics: Punctuation. Forty-six transparencies in a plastic case ($62.00), practice pages, and duplicating masters ($.25 per set). Special teaching guide pages simplify teaching and planning and suggest ways to motivate and involve students. Fine for all students. Encyclopaedia Britannica Corp.

Books for Students

Writing Errors You Hate to Make and How to Avoid Them by Richard Uhlich. Examination of sentence fragments and run-ons, clauses, compound subjects, pronoun agreement, problems with antecedents, inverted work order, and suggestions on how to correct all of these technical, mechanical mistakes. Excellent workbook format that allows students to respond to many of the exercises right in the book. Ideal for all students. Teachers guide available. $.50 Paperbound, Xerox Corp.

A Student's First Aid to Writing by Theodore Grieder and Josephine Grieder. Covers a wide variety of difficulties related to mechanics—punctuation, clauses, case, sentence structure, faulty usage, spelling, and the total composition. Specific exercises provided for each of the thirteen chapters, with notes to the instructor, answer key, and review exercises. Combination text/workbook. May be used as a consumable product. (Space is provided for students to respond to the exercise right in the book.) Thorough and effective. Appropriate for more advanced students. $2.95. Littlefield, Adams and Co.

English Competence Handbook by Paul Kalkstein, Thomas J. Regan, and K. Kelly Wise. Provides instruction in the four fundamental comma and spelling rules. Usage and diction. Helpful as a supplementary text. Appropriate for more advanced students, Paperbound. Independent School Press.

Errors in English and Ways to Correct Them by Harry Shaw. Excellent, thorough discussion of correct usage (includes definitions of hundreds of words frequently misused), correct sentence structure, spelling, punctuation, mechanics, grammar, and sentence diagramming. Outstanding explanations and examples. An extremely valuable handbook for average and advanced students. Paperbound. $2.50. Barnes and Noble Books.

Punctuate It Right! by Harry Shaw. A thorough guide to the purposes of punctuation and mechanics. Detailed analysis of twenty-five different marks of punctuation and their uses—instructive models and samples provided throughout. Comprehensive glossaries and appendices concerning terms and application of mechanical principles related to punctuation. A valuable handbook for more advanced students. Paperbound. $1.95. Barnes and Noble Books.

Common Errors in English: And How to Avoid Them by Alexander M. Witherspoon. Contains substantial chapters on usage—general rules, colloquialisms and slang, grammatical relationships, and diction. Alphabetical list of frequently misused words and phrases points out correct usages. Includes a thorough chapter on spelling—rules, aids, special rules and exceptions, plurals, compound words, and rules related to suffixes and prefixes. Excellent list of the correct spelling of frequently misspelled words. Fine for all students. Paperbound. $2.95. Littlefield, Adams and Company.

About Punctuation. A brief, easy to understand guide to correct punctuation. Includes explanations and examples of the uses of the major marks of punctuation, and their relationships to conjunctions, phrases, clauses, series, and sentences. Excellent, simple and direct—covers every imaginable situation. Fine for all students, especially those with minor learning difficulties. Paperbound. $1.00. Channing L. Bete.

Check That Punctuation! by Harold Braker. Includes explanation of the uses of fourteen different marks of punctuation, including comma, semicolon, dash, and period. Provides helpful punctuation tests and a glossary of grammatical terms. Easy-to-follow format and instructive model and samples presented throughout. Appropriate for more advanced students. Paperbound. College Entrance Publications.

Practical English Handbook by Floyd C. Watkins, William B. Dillingham, and Edwin T. Martin. A comprehensive handbook examining tense, mood, agreement, usage, number, verb forms, punctuation, consistency (in six separate areas), case, mechanics, diction, style, and composition. Excellent examples and models provided throughout. A fine resource for average and advanced students. Teachers guide available. $5.25. Houghton Mifflin.

The Student Writer's Guide by Eliot D. Allan and Ethel B. Colbrunn. Thorough examination of agreement, usage, diction, case, tense, punctuation (including explanations and examples of twelve different marks of punctuation), mechanics, and manuscript form. Models and samples provided throughout. Exercises and assignments included. Combination text/workbook format. May be used as a consumable product. Paperbound. $4.00. Everett/Edwards Inc.

A Composition Handbook by William E. Merriss and David H. Griswold. Deals with sentence errors (run-ons and fragments), necessary and superfluous commas, quotation marks, capitals, letters, tense, agreement, case, diction and style. Exercises and practice assignments included. Designed for grades seven through twelve. Appropriate for older students with learning difficulties. Paperbound. Independent School Press.

Writing Handbook by Michael P. Kammer, S.J. and Charles W. Mulligan, S.J. A comprehensive handbook covering parts of speech, the sentence, syntax (subjects and predicates, agreement, verb use, case, phrases, and clauses), spelling, and diagramming. Numerous examples, lists, models and diagrams provided. Very thorough! Suitable for advanced students only. Paperbound. Loyola University Press.

Vitalized English by Mary Didas. Contains sections on usage, words frequently misspelled, mechanical problems associated with grammar, case, tenses, phrases and structure. Provides exercises and review assignments along with copies of recent New York State Regents Examination questions in English, and practice sections for college entrance tests. Useful to the advanced student. Paperbound. CEBCO Standard Publishing.

Experiments in Effective Writing by Victor E. Gould. Includes sections on syntax (the participle, gerund, infinitive, appositive, and working verb) and "Rhetoric of Productive Sentences" (the principles of direction of movement, texture, levels of specificity). Also examines semantics as a factor related to style. For advanced students only. Teacher's manual available. Paperbound. $2.10. Harcourt Brace Jovanovich.

Good Usage by Paul Mowbray Wheeler. Examination of clauses and sentences, fragments, the comma, omissions, parallelism, agreement (subject/predicate and pronoun/antecedent), case, verbs, idiomatic usage, and misplaced modifiers. Numerous exercises and practice assignments. Combination text/workbook format—may be used as a consumable product. Clear and direct. Suitable for average and advanced students. Paperbound. College Entrance Book Company.

Grammar Lives by Ronald T. Shepherd and John MacDonald. Covers the parts of speech (definitions and correct uses), common usage problems, sentence structure and combination (common difficulties with compound sentences, fragments, and run-ons), and sentence and paragraph patterns. Visually attractive, easy-to-follow format. Helpful diagrams, models and samples. Activities and exercises provided. Interesting and instructive. Appropriate for average and advanced students. Teacher's manual available. Paperbound. McDougal, Littell and Co.

Write It Right! by Gail Kredenser. Discusses diction, word consciousness, effectiveness, and expressive impact, dangling modifiers, idioms, grammatical difficulties, split construction, antecedents, and punctuation. Explanations provided in well-delineated outline framework along with examples. Clear and concise. Appropriate for average and advanced students. Paperbound. Barnes and Noble.

The Art of Styling Sentences: Twenty Patterns to Success by Marie L. Wadell, Robert M. Esch, and Roberta R. Walker. Employs the principle of modeling (also called patterning) to teach correct sentence structure. Twenty sentence patterns are illustrated, explained and presented for practice as students are taught the functions of these patterns. However, emphasis is on practical application of the rules. Also offers chapters on figurative language in sentences, excerpts from famous literary works illustrating the twenty sentence patterns. Notes to the instructor included. Appropriate for general classroom use or individual study, most suitable for more advanced students. Paperbound. $1.50. Barrons Educational Series, Inc.

Spelling Your Way to Success by Joseph Mersand and Francis Griffith. Provides systematic, incremental instruction toward independent spelling improvement. Teaches concrete skills and self-reliance; designed to discourage dictionary dependence. Includes lists of frequently misspelled words, exercises and progress tests designed to measure improvement. Fine for all students. Paperbound, $1.95; Hardcover, $4.75. Barron's Educational Series, Inc.

1001 Pitfalls in English Grammar by Vincent F. Hopper. Includes analysis of the most common errors in technical English—spelling, grammar, word choice, and punctuation. Especially helpful to bilingual students learning English as a second language. Contains numerous examples and practice assignments designed to clarify important problematic areas. Appropriate for all students. Paperbound. $2.95. Barron's Educational Series, Inc.

Card Guide to English Grammar, Punctuation, and Usage by Vincent F. Hopper. One four-page laminated card presents the fundamentals of grammar, usage and punctuation. Offers definitions of parts of speech, sentence parts, and subject and verb agreement. Provides examples of correct and incorrect uses of ten different marks of punctuation. Extensive guide to correct usage listing commonly misused words. Card is hole-punched and can be inserted into a two, three or five ring binder. Condensed, complete and clear. An excellent, handy reference for all students. Paperbound. $1.25. Barron's Educational Series, Inc.

Systematic Spelling edited by Myron R. Williams and Carl M. Saspar. A brief, informative book; presents eight approaches to correct spelling: pronunciation, principles of letter combinations with four rules, plurals, prefixes and suffixes, derivation, association, compounds, and possessives. Includes a list of 600 commonly misspelled words along with suggestions on how to learn to spell them correctly. Exercises and practice assignments throughout. Designed for grades seven to twelve. Fine for all students. Paperbound. $.80. Educators Publishing Service, Inc.

Spellbound by Elsie T. Rak. Remedial worktext designed for junior-senior high students reading far below grade level. Based on *Remedial Training* by Gillingham and the spelling workbooks of Mildred Plunkett. Developmental emphasis with step-by-step progression from simple to complex spelling principles. Thorough exercises (oral and written) provide practice and kinesthetic reinforcement. Excellent for students with learning problems. Teacher's manual available. Paperbound. $2.00. Educators Publishing Service, Inc.

Handbook of English: Reference and Study Guide-Spelling by Joseph R. Orgel. Volume two in a series which covers all aspects of standard English. Deals with prefixes, words, silent letters, pluralizations, homonyms, word derivations, and language development. Extensive word lists, exercises and prescribed strategies toward spelling improvement.

A fine resource for average and advanced students. Paperbound. $2.50. Educators Publishing Service, Inc.

Handbook of English: Reference and Study Guide—Punctuation by Joseph R. Orgel. Volume one in a series which covers all aspects of Standard English. Discusses correct and incorrect uses of punctuation. Detailed analysis and explanation of practice exercises and achievement tests which measure improvement and serve as reinforcement to instruction. Designed for high school and college students. Paperbound. $2.00. Educators Publishing Service, Inc.

A Concise Guide to Clear Writing (taken from *Clear Writing* by Marilyn B. Gilbert). Contains a list of helpful, necessary transitional words and linking phrases plus words and phrases which point out contrasts, results, time relationships and mood changes. Exceptional chart format which increases comprehension and facilitates understanding. Appropriate for advanced students. Paperbound. John Wiley and Sons, Inc.

Can/May, Caps, and Commas by Eric Broudy and A. M. Goldstein. Deals with both usage and mechanics. Includes glossary of standard English usage, and exercises that measure comprehension and improvement. Detailed examination of mechanics, capital letters, semicolons, and spelling with extensive final review section. Excellent, visually attractive, easy-to-follow format. Appropriate for average and advanced students. Paperbound. Silver Burdett.

Sentence Improvement by Malcolm Moore. This non-graded workbook is flexible and easily adapted for total classroom study. Teaches the basic principles of sentence structure and then examines problems related to style and usage. Excellent examples enrich the discussion of sentence patterns, clauses, phrases, and parallel structures. Exercises included. Paperbound. $1.65. Houghton Mifflin.

The Teaching of English Usage by Robert C. Pooley. A descriptive, situationally based approach to determining "correctness" in language usage. By teaching informal standard English, it avoids the rigidity of rules and do's and don'ts. Interesting approach. Designed for junior and senior high school students. Paperbound. $4.95. National Council of Teachers of English.

APPENDIX

A

Addresses of Producers of Resources

Addison-Wesley Publishing Company
Reading, Massachusetts 01867

Allyn and Bacon, Inc.
470 Atlantic Avenue
Boston, Massachusetts 02210

Amsco School Publications
315 Hudson Street
New York, New York 10013

Applause Productions
85 Longview Road
Port Washington, New York 11050

Arco Publishing Company
219 Park Avenue South
New York, New York 10003

Argus Communications
7440 Natchez Avenue
Niles, Illinois 60648

Bantam Books
666 Fifth Avenue
New York, New York 10019

Barnes and Noble
Division of Harper and Row, Publishers
10 East 53rd Street
New York, New York 10022

Barron's Education Series
113 Crossways Park Drive
Woodbury, New York 11797

Channing L. Bete Company
45 Federal Street
Greenfield, Massachusetts 01301

Cambridge Book Company
488 Madison Avenue
New York, New York 10022

CEBCO/Standard Publishing
104 Fifth Avenue
New York, New York 10011

Center for the Humanities
Two Holland Avenue
White Plains, New York 10603

Citation Press
906 Sylvan Avenue
Englewood Cliffs, New Jersey 07632

Clarke, Irwin and Company, Ltd.
791 St. Claire Avenue, W.
Toronto, Ontario M6C 1B8, Canada

College Entrance Publications
104 Fifth Avenue
New York, New York 10011

Dodd, Mead and Company
79 Madison Avenue
New York, New York 10016

Doubleday Multimedia
1371 Reynolds Avenue
P. O. Box 11607
Santa Ana, California 92702

Eaton Paper Company
Pittsfield, Massachusetts 01201

Educational Research Associates
Box 767
Amherst, Massachusetts 01002

Educators Publishing Service, Inc.
75 Moulton Street
Cambridge, Massachusetts 02138

Encyclopaedia Britannica Educational Corp.
425 N. Michigan Avenue
Chicago, Illinois 60611

Everett/Edwards, Inc.
Post Office Box 1060
Deland, Florida 32720

Eye-Gate
146-01 Archer Avenue
Jamaica, New York 11435

Filmstrip House
6633 West Howard Street
Niles, Illinois 60648

Folkways Records
701 Seventh Avenue
New York, New York 10036

Follett Publishing Co.
1010 W. Washington Blvd.
Chicago, Illinois 60607

Frederick Muller Ltd.
Victoria Works,
Edgware Road
London NW 2, 6 LE, England

Glencoe Press
8701 Wilshire Blvd.
Beverly Hills, California 90211

Globe Book Company
175 Fifth Avenue
New York, New York 10010

Greystone Films Inc.
Box 303, Kingsbridge Station
Riverdale, New York 10463

Guidance Associates
757 Third Avenue
New York, New York 10017

Harcourt Brace Jovanovich
757 Third Avenue
New York, New York 10017

Hart Publishing Company
15 West Fourth Street
New York, New York 10012

Hayden Book Co., Inc.
50 Essex Street
Rochelle Park, New Jersey 07662

D.C. Heath and Company
125 Spring Street
Lexington, Massachusetts

Holt, Rinehart & Winston
383 Madison Avenue
New York, New York 10017

Houghton Mifflin Co.
2 Park Street
Boston, Massachusetts 02107

Independent School Press
51 River Street
Wellesley Hills, Massachusetts 02181

Interact
P.O. Box 262
Lakeside, California 92040

Thomas Klise Company
P.O. Box 3418
Peoria, Illinois 61614

Laidlaw Brothers
Thatcher & Madison
River Forest, Illinois 60305

J.B. Lippincott Company
East Washington Square
Philadelphia, Pennsylvania 19105

Littlefield, Adams, & Co.
81 Adams Drive
Totowa, New Jersey 07512

London Association for the Teaching of English
Blackie & Son, Ltd.
5 Fitzhardinge Street
London, W.I., England

Loyola University Press
3441 North Ashland Avenue
Chicago, Illinois 60657

Macmillan Publishing Co., Inc.
866 Third Avenue
New York, New York 10022

McDougal, Littell & Co.
P.O. Box 1667
Evanston, Illinois 60204

Mentor Book Company
1301 Avenue of the Americas
New York, New York 10019

National Council of Teachers of English
1111 Kenyon Road
Urbana, Illinois 61801

New York State English Council
Alan Nelson, Executive Secretary
Union College Humanities Center
Schenectady, New York 12308

Oxford University Press
200 Madison Avenue
New York, New York 10016

Pendulum Press, Inc.
The Academic Building
Saw Mill Road
West Haven, Connecticut 06516

Prentice-Hall, Inc.
Educational Book Division
Englewood Cliffs, New Jersey 07632

Prentice-Hall Media
150 White Plains Road, Box 186
Tarrytown, New York 10591

Random House Inc.
201 E. 50th Street
New York, New York 10022

The Reading Lab, Inc.
55 Day Street
South Norwalk, Connecticut 06854

RMI Educational Films, Inc.
701 Westport Road
Kansas City, Missouri 64111

S-L Film Productions
P. O. Box 41108
Los Angeles, California 90041

Scholastic Book Services
904 Sylvan Avenue
Englewood Cliffs, New Jersey 07632

Scholastic Records
906 Sylvan Avenue
Englewood Cliffs, New Jersey 07632

Scott Education Division
104 Lower Westfield Road
Holyoke, Massachusetts 01040

Silver Burdett Company
Morristown, New Jersey 07960

Teachers College Press
1234 Amsterdam Avenue
New York, New York 10027

Teachers & Writers Collaborative
490 Hudson Street
New York, New York 10014

The University of Chicago Press
5801 Ellis Avenue
Chicago, Illinois 60637

J. Weston Walch, Publisher
Portland, Maine 04104

Westwood Educational Production
701 Westport Road
Kansas City, Missouri 64111

John Wiley & Sons, Inc.
605 Third Avenue
New York, New York 10016

H. W. Wilson Co.
950 University Avenue
Bronx, New York 10452

Xerox Educational Publications
Education Center
1250 Fairwood Avenue
Columbus, Ohio 43216

B

Reproduction Pages

The pages that follow have been provided to facilitate the reproducing of exercises, sample compositions, and materials needed for activities suggested in the preceding pages. Each page is perforated to make removal from this book easier. Once removed, a page can be used in several ways:

1. *For projection with an opaque projector.* No further preparation is necessary if the page is to be used with an opaque projector. Simply insert it in the projector and the page can be viewed by the entire class.
2. *For projection with an overhead projector.* The Reproduction Page must be converted to a transparency for use on an overhead projector. Overlay the Reproduction Page with a blank transparency and run both of them through a copying machine.
3. *For duplication with a spirit duplicator.* A master can be made from the Reproduction Page by overlaying it with a special heat sensitive spirit master and running both through a copying machine. The spirit master can then be used to reproduce 50 to 100 copies on paper.

NAME_____ SECTION_____

Sample Topic Sentences

We never got along well after that.

Household plants add much to the charm of any house.

A cat's diet should not be varied from day to day.

A brisk walk after dinner can have a number of beneficial effects.

Some girls wear so much make-up that it detracts from their charm instead of enhancing it.

Putting too much effort into getting high grades can prevent one from profiting fully from an education.

I would rather take an examination than write a paper as a means of being graded.

Physical education classes are a source of embarrassment to many students.

The average student—the one who makes mostly C's—is spared many problems in school.

The room had been thoroughly ransacked.

Her locker looked like the nest of a pack-rat.

The mailman on our route had good cause to fear dogs.

Many students truly enjoy going to school.

There are many satisfactions to be gained from making bread.

Students in the 1970's seem more apathetic toward social issues than they were in the '60's.

The bee is, indeed, a busy insect.

Green beans are easy to grow.

Only humankind does not order its days by the sun.

Lawn mowing need not be a boring task.

Breakfast is my favorite meal.

A good banana split is a work of art.

It was my fault more than his that we did not remain friends.

A boy can learn much from owning a dog.

I was never able to learn in her class.

It was a day made for kites.

I began to think the hour would never end.

She seemed to delight in making me feel foolish.

Their names suited their personalities.

Many students feel that they should strive to use fancy language when they write.

For the invalid, particularly, food should be made visually attractive as well as nutritious.

Even the experienced pilot needs to return to flying school periodically.

Wood furniture will soon be priced out of the market for all but the rich.

It is easier to learn from a teacher one likes.

Some lessons are harder to learn than others.

The students resented having to go outside to smoke.

I never could believe the principal was my pal, even though my spelling teacher said he was.

Of course, short hair does have its advantages.

Fences are not always barriers between people.

Schoolrooms are usually drab and uninteresting looking places, at least in high school.

One cannot stay well informed just by reading one newspaper.

All too often people will treat their best friends as they would not treat their worst enemies.

Good manners have never been near the top of my list of most significant human values.

It turned out to be a terrible day for me.

She seemed to enjoy being miserable.

His term paper was a real work of art.

There, perched on my window sill, was an insect which looked like nothing so much as a miniature tyrannosaurus rex.

In many ways he was different from the rest of the fellows in our crowd.

Most of us would have a hard time tracing the origin of our personal beliefs.

I somehow felt especially at ease in her class.

Most of us find it easier to tolerate faults in ourselves than in others.

NAME_____ SECTION_____

Good and Bad Topic Sentences

INSTRUCTIONS: Some of the topic sentences below are specific enough to be developed in detail in one paragraph. Others are too broad and general. Still others make two or more statements in one sentence and are therefore poor topic sentences. Indicate after each sentence whether it is <u>okay</u> or whether it is <u>bad—too broad</u> or whether it is <u>bad—two subjects.</u>

Both dogs and cats have some habits which make them difficult to keep as pets in a small apartment.

Dachshunds make fine watch dogs.

Drinking eight glasses of water a day promotes good health.

The earth's oceans may already be irreversibly polluted.

There are many reasons why scientists consider it a mathematical certainty that human life similar to our species exists somewhere in the universe.

Cockroaches are equipped to survive us all.

Politics have fallen into disrepute in our society.

It is not difficult to paint a house.

World War II did not result in the social dislocations in Germany that were so disastrous after World War I.

Revisionist historians are giving us a much different view of the American Revolution than the one most of us gained in elementary school.

A satisfactory definition of the term "pollution" must reach into many areas of our lives and environment.

Weather, we are told, has significant effects on emotional balance and social behavior.

The science of weather prediction has existed as long as there have been herdsmen and food gatherers.

Psychological maturity is demonstrated by a giving, sharing, producing orientation to life.

Stonehenge can be described as a huge calendar.

The rehabilitation of America's major cities will require a massive infusion of tax money.

Three of the players on our school's 1955 football team went on to illustrious careers as professional players, and two of these individuals later became successful politicians.

Our float trip ended in an adventure we had not foreseen and which we were ill equipped to handle.

The secret of a successful camping trip lies in the preparations made before leaving home.

Parenthood is not as easy a task as many young people would argue.

Adolescence is not so much a time as a function.

Students often complain about a class being boring without realizing that they themselves may share the responsibility for a class's failure to come alive.

Youngsters' patterns of behavior are established well before they enter school.

Many famous men have come from disturbed and unhappy families.

A walk over a western prairie at dawn reveals a richness of life forms and activities that rivals an awakening city.

The river, like a person, shows itself in ever-changing activities and moods.

NAME_____ SECTION_____

Means of Paragraph Development

INSTRUCTIONS: Indicate the method of developing each paragraph in the space following it. Choose from these main methods of paragraph development: explanation, facts, description, narrative, or examples.

A. It had never been a large high school as compared to many city high schools, and now it was shrinking. At its peak, the student body had never numbered more than 1500, and by 1975, when the World War II "baby boom" had pretty well expended itself, the entering freshman class was 200 students smaller than the freshman class of just five years before. In September 1974, the faculty numbered 113, and already there were signs of professional staff reduction. Three retiring teachers were not replaced, and the foreign language department, for one, lost one teacher who was not replaced. Both part-time assistant coaches went elsewhere. It was obviously a shrinking faculty. Specialists such as counselors, reading experts and teachers trained for working with learning dis-abilities numbered considerably fewer in 1975 than in 1970, and hardly a department did not suffer the loss of non-professional aides and clerks. The number of principals went from four to three in 1975, and the staff of librarians was reduced from four to two. The facilities did not change; the school looked as large as ever, but the truth was that in many important ways the school was becoming smaller. _____

B. By the time Winston was three years old, he had already used up three of his nine lives. When he was almost a year old, in June, he was hit by a car and badly shaken up. We found him lying on the back doorstep, eyes closed and obviously in a state of shock. He was breathing shallowly, but cried out strongly when we picked him up to carry him into the house. He must have been badly bruised, for he hardly moved for several days and cried whenever anyone inadvertently touched him carelessly. In time he did recover, a sadder and wiser cat who never went near the street again. His next near miss was a virus infection in the following October. Antibiotics got him well by Christmas, in time for him to be shot in the leg and stomach by a young man trying out his new Christmas present, a 22 rifle. This was Winston's worst trauma, and it took all of Dr. Benedict's devotion and skill to pull him through. He had wire stitches in his stomach and wore a splint for weeks, clumping around the house sounding like Old Pew, the peg-legged sailor in *Treasure Island.* In three months or so he was as good as new and he seems to be looking forward to his six remaining lives. _____

C. Some television commercials demonstrate such questionable values with regard to human behavior that one wonders just what lessons children are learning as they sit transfixed before the screen. Perhaps, from one famous commercial, they are learning that it is perfectly all right to over-eat and over-drink because a foaming tablet in a glass of water will take care of all harmful consequences. Or they may be watching a version of the oft-taught lesson that in order to be happy one must be loved by everyone and the way to be universally lovable is to use the best smelling mouth washes, deodorants, and tooth pastes. For an even more telling example of pernicious teaching, the boys may be gleaning wisdom from a series of commercials which teach them that the way to man-hood is through good masculine violence and group camaraderie with plenty of full-bodied beer thrown in. With TV broadcasting such lessons for many hours a day, one wonders if parental teaching stands much of a chance. _____

D. Off campus activities have become much more of an integral part of our high school. As recently as 1971, there were no activities away from the high school that were approved for students. All students were expected to be in class or in one of the approved building areas from 8:15 a.m. to 2:45 p.m. No exceptions to this rule were allowed. In 1972, however, the school established a special program on an experimental basis. Fifty students, this first year, were permitted to attend school for a minimum of three hours and work at a job in the community for at least three more hours daily. A teacher was hired to meet with these students as a class at the high school and supervise their job experiences by maintaining a close contact with their employers. This program was so successful in meeting the needs of some students that by 1975, three hundred youngsters were enrolled in the work-study schedule and two additional teachers had been hired to work with students and their employers. There is now an almost equal number of students working as volunteers and trainees at various community support agencies for a portion of each day. This program is called Community Involvement, and it is available only to seniors as an enrichment experience. It seems a far cry from the school which was confined to one building and offered only six classes a day. _____

E. The noises of the storm surrounded us. The rolls of thunder never ceased, sometimes deep and roaring and sometimes dimly growling as if from a great distance. Periodically, sharp and dramatic crashes of thunder shook the house, warning of nearby lightning and sending the dog whining under the sofa for safety. The gutters soon overflowed and great streams of water splashed noisily down the front windows, while in the rear of the house an avalanche of water from the roof spurted from a downspout obstructed by leaves and splattered with great force on the patio stones. We were surrounded by rivers, it seemed, and through it all the heavy spray driven by wind sounded like bullets pelting against the roof and walls. The house creaked and quivered, feeling the strength of the gale, but it was a strong, well constructed house, and inside it we felt, if not a sense of quiet, at least an absence of fear. _____

F. Some books read in childhood are truly unforgettable. Some of the characters, the places, the adventures experienced with so much excitement when one is quite young, stay in one's mind as long as memory lasts. Such a character is Long John Silver in Robert Louis Stevenson's *Treasure Island.* Who, once acquainted with this wily old pirate, could ever forget him as he stomps along the decks of his ship, as quick on his crutch as other men with two good legs? As for Heidi, the little girl who lived in the Swiss Alps, who, having once roamed those upland meadows with her, could ever forget her as she drove her goats to pasture or milked them at the end of the day? She remains forever a child in memory. Childhood's memories of "The Song of Roland" and the friendship between Roland and Oliver are untarnished by any later historical knowledge, and the Knights of the Round Table still ride, in a golden haze of vague romantic memories, King Arthur at their head, with Lancelot, ever faithful, at his right hand. Who would give up these perfect childhood memories? _____

G. Whenever I looked at him, I thought of Uriah Heep, the groveling, obsequious, sly character in *David Copperfield.* This was unfair of me, because I knew nothing about him to justify the comparison, but there was something about the way he used his eyes, small and set deep in folds of flesh, that made me distrust his every word and deed. He darted little looks at me, and at others, as well, when he thought we were not watching him, and when caught in the act, winked and smiled and rubbed his hands for all the world like old Uriah. He never looked anyone full in the face, never held his gaze locked with one's own, but looked sidelong, or raised his eyes furtively from seeming to peer at something else beyond or beside the one he really wished to observe. Even after a year's experience of him, I would have been hard put to say what color his eyes were, lurking under the scraggly, sandy brows. I thought perhaps they had no color of their own, but like him, would take on whatever shade would seem to fit the moment's need.

———————

H. Roger and Steve sallied forth to try out the white water of the upper St. Francis River for all the world like experienced canoers who knew what they were doing. Both were powerful swimmers and intelligent, athletic young men whose bodies were well trained and adequate for any reasonable challenge. Both had been canoeing for a year or two and had encountered no challenge to shake their confidence. They decided that they would challenge the St. Francis, one of Missouri's heftier stretches of white water, and find out what real canoeing is all about. They would, of course, take every sensible precaution. Nothing could possibly go wrong, they thought. Four days later, when they brought home their dented and misshapen canoe, they knew what could go wrong.

———————

I. Transplanting seedlings need not be a traumatic experience for either the seedling or the beginning gardener. Small plants, like small children, are remarkably hardy and resilient, and capable of withstanding all sorts of shocks to their systems. A very few simple procedures will help your plants come through transplanting successfully. You should only transplant your seedlings when it is cloudy or overcast or after the sun has set. Too much heat is hard for them to take when they are already undergoing strain. Strain is considerably reduced, also, if you take up each plant in a trowel-full of its own soil and set it down in a hole big enough to receive a cup or so of water and all the soil you have kept pressed around the plant's roots. When you have pressed the plant firmly into place and given it another watering, your job is done. You need not fret if the plant looks a little spindly and droopy; next morning, after a quiet night's rest in its new spot, your plant will look healthier and sturdier than ever. ———————

J. Sometimes the student who talks and argues endlessly in class discussions learns less than the student who sits quietly, saying little or even nothing, but listening to the contributions of others. The talkative student may simply feel a need to defend his or her viewpoints against all other views, regardless of whether he or she has previously done much study in arriving at these beliefs. Or the student may feel that speaking with seeming authority will cause everyone to regard him or her as intelligent and well informed. Such a person may have an unconscious need to seem superior to others, a need that expresses itself in verbal contentiousness and a refusal to respect the views of others. Whatever the reasons for this talkativeness, it is apparent that the person cannot be thinking all the time he or she is talking, and it may be that the more thoughtful, silent student is actually engaging in a more productive activity. Since he or she is not continually producing output during the discussion, the quieter student may well be receiving valuable input or at least be gaining insight into various viewpoints, while the constant talker and arguer will remain merely defensive of his or her own. ———————

NAME_____ SECTION_____

Choosing A Method of Developing A Topic Sentence

INSTRUCTIONS: In the space provided after each topic sentence, write the best method of development for that paragraph: analysis, explanation, facts, description, narrative, examples.

A number of students in the audience could have taught that particular lesson as well as the teacher. _____

American cars are often named after animals or birds. _____

Every football lineman has his particular duties. _____

Even in warm weather, mountain climbers have been known to die of a too sudden drop in body temperature. _____

There are three separate political groups in the United States. _____

From the beginning, that vacation was more work than play. _____

The halls were uniformly drab and dingy. _____

The beagle has become a favorite of dog fanciers and outsells all other dogs in the United States. _____

Students in our school seem to fall into two categories. _____

There are still many government figures whose names are not tainted by scandal or hint of corruption. _____

By the end of the season, the team had set five local records and three state records in various styles of swimming. _____

One should never wax a car without giving it a thorough washing first. _____

One night the haunted house had visitors who were not ghosts. _____

The bleachers were a kaleidoscope of shifting colors. _____

The Gateway Arch in St. Louis, Missouri, is an architectural and technical marvel. _____

On a few occasions a President's wife has seemed to gain more respect and admiration than the President himself. _____

Many a famous beauty has found that her physical attributes have won her more misery than joy. _____

His records for passes completed and yards gained on the ground exceeded those of all but two former players at his school. _____

Class discussion is an effective way for students to share knowledge and experience and, thus, to learn from one another. _____

Great athletes, unfortunately, have not always proved to be great gentlemen._____

Most of the space in a vegetable garden can be planted at least twice during the growing season. _____

Long John Silver resides in the memory of all who have read *Treasure Island.* _____

I remember very well the day a tornado struck our school. _____

Tourism is Hawaii's most profitable business. _____

Their Christmas tree looked as if it had been trimmed by an interior decorator rather than the family themselves. _____

My first blind date was an exercise in embarrassment and helplessness. _____

Lights play an important part in any theatrical production. _____

The dance was a great financial success in spite of high expenses. _____

It is a mistake to exclude students from curriculum planning. _____

NAME_____   SECTION_____

Planning A Paragraph Based on Details

INSTRUCTIONS: Find a unifying principle or theme in each list of details and write it in the space provided. Then formulate a topic sentence covering as many of the given details as possible. Write the topic sentence for each list of details in the space provided. Then draw a line through the details which do not fit your topic sentence and indicate in the blank which method of development would be most appropriate for your topic sentence.

A. frequent dusty detours
   signs and arrows re-directing traffic
   a red schoolhouse on a hill
   heavy equipment at work
   great piles of gravel
   garbage in a ditch
   cement mixers
   clouds of dust hovering over earth-moving machines
   birds flying overhead
   cows grazing peacefully in nearby fields
   workmen in colorful hard hats
   huge steam shovels gulping broken cement
   school children waiting for a bus

   Unifying Theme: _____

   Topic Sentence: _____

   _____

   _____

   Method of Development: _____

B. bleachers full of colorfully dressed spectators
   dust rising from parking fields nearby
   the plunk of hard-hit balls on the clay
   applause after a long volley
   chefs busy at work in the clubhouse kitchen
   ball chasers scurrying out of the way
   swaying shade trees on the golf course
   spontaneous groan from crowd at missed lob
   tournament brought in $93,471.32
   crisp calls of line judges
   brillance of white tennis costumes in the sun
   rising tension at each crucial point
   borders of scarlet geraniums edging the spectators' area

   Unifying Theme: _____

   Topic Sentence: _____

167

_____

_____

Method of Development: _____

C. he was so harsh with his son that he left home

his eating habits became irregular

he carried on a continuous argument with his daughter over her dress

he read the morning paper

one day he told his boss that he disapproved of his methods of management

he began drinking early in the day

he quit attending church

he read only best sellers

he picked arguments with his long-suffering wife

he refused to see his doctor or his psychiatrist

he voted in all elections, as usual

he was cruel to the dog, and even kicked him in the ribs one day

he withdrew from lodge activities

he had always enjoyed fishing

he was a Yale graduate

Unifying Theme: _____

Topic Sentence: _____

_____

_____

Method of Development: _____

D. The Flurry rally was scheduled for 2:00 p.m., March 3, 1923

4,000 people gathered at the site

seventy-nine people were arrested

there was a fire at 93rd Street

fourteen people were hospitalized

traffic was stalled for a six block area around the scene

the speaker was to have been J. Singleton Flurry

all but four of those arrested were released

two persons were kept in the hospital overnight

I don't like J. Singleton Flurry

if the demonstrators had stayed out of the way, maybe the police could have done a
   better job

the demonstrators opposing Flurry marched in the streets

people should not flock to the scene of a riot

the speaker's stand was demolished

fire hoses finally dispersed the last of the crowd

Unifying Theme: _____

Topic Sentence: _____

_____

Method of Development: _____

E. it will not rise adequately without kneading
   the dough will be lumpy
   the final product will be heavy and dense
   bread is the staff of life
   yeast needs to be worked into every particle of the dough
   kneading works air into the dough, guaranteeing lightness
   kneading provides even texture
   kneading spreads yeast evenly, so when it ferments, it will cause tiny bubbles of carbon
      dioxide throughout the dough
   kneading is fun
   carbon dioxide bubbles stretch gluten in flour, thus leavening the bread

   Unifying Theme: _____

   Topic Sentence: _____

   _____

   _____

   Method of Development: _____

F. Gauguin did some of his most sensational work when he was wasting away with disease
   Toulouse-Lautrec was badly crippled as a result of a riding accident in his youth
   Virginia Woolf suffered from precarious mental health and spent time in mental hospitals
   Beethoven suffered from progressive deafness which finally became complete
   Julius Caesar was an epileptic
   John Milton lost his eyesight years before he wrote _Paradise Lost_
   Franklin D. Roosevelt lost the use of his legs as a result of an attack of polio
   Van Gogh continued to paint even when he was committed to an asylum
   Sylvia Plath had periodic depressions which finally drove her to suicide
   Marilyn Monroe had a tragic life

   Unifying Theme: _____

   Topic Sentence: _____

   _____

   _____

   Method of Development: _____

NAME_____ SECTION_____

Putting Details in Order

INSTRUCTIONS: Read each topic sentence and the list of details which support it. Decide what type of order might be the best for the details and number them in order.

A. *Topic Sentence:* The lawn was a disgraceful mess.
    Details: weeds among flowers
            pile of dead branches to one side
            an old automobile chassis beside the porch
            instead of grass there were weeds and bare, worn places
            bushes unpruned
            cement on front walk broken and crumbling
            fence sagging on left side of yard
            fence broken entirely on right side

B. *Topic Sentence:* The conference went on all day.
    Details: opening speech at 9:00
            lunch at 12:00
            pre-conference breakfast at 7:30
            workshops at 2:00 and 4:00
            cocktail hour
            seminar at 10:30

C. *Topic Sentence:* He persuaded her to stay in class.
    Details: he felt she would learn a lot
            he told her it would get more interesting
            he thought she would enjoy the new people coming in
            he would flunk her if she dropped out

D. *Topic Sentence:* She decided not to try for early graduation.
    Details: would have to go to summer school
            none of her friends were graduating early
            her father opposed her graduating early
            she felt she was not yet ready for college
            there were still some courses at the high school she wanted to take

NAME_____ SECTION_____

Improving the Order of Details

INSTRUCTIONS: Read the paragraphs below. In the space provided after each, indicate a better method of ordering the details and then number the details accordingly.

A. When you are baking a cake, it is important to double-check the ingredients as you put each one in. Being wrong with just one tablespoon of salt can mean an inedible cake rather than one of which you may be proud. Your first task is to read the recipe thoroughly and make sure you have all ingredients on hand. The orderly habit of putting everything away after you have used it is also a good one to cultivate. Mix the ingredients in the order and in the manner instructed by your recipe. Be sure to turn your oven to the proper setting at the very beginning, so that by the time your batter is prepared, the oven is properly preheated. It is wise, also, to prepare your pan at the beginning, to avoid having to stop and do so at the last minute. If you follow your recipe carefully, there is no reason you cannot succeed every time you bake a cake.

_____

B. The history of the school was a chronicle of constant expansion and construction. An entire new wing of classrooms was added when the school was only five years old. The original building was finished in 1958 and had only nineteen classrooms. Completed in 1963, the new wing added six more classrooms as well as additional library space. The original library seated only fifty-eight students. The gymnasium was doubled in size by construction undertaken in 1971, making it possible for the girls to have their own facilities, and in 1972, the pool, which had been part of the construction plan of 1968, was completed after two years of work. The original library and gymnasium had been planned and built to allow for ease of enlargement. Plans for their expansion had been presented even prior to the 1968 addition, but unfortunately the district voted against such an improvement at that time. The school board was pleased that the district approved the new gymnasium and pool as well as the new wing.

_____

C. Some students felt that there had been any number of occasions when the administration might have closed down the smoking lounge before the event which finally caused them to take action. For instance, there was a week early in the school year when freshmen who had come from the two different junior high schools began expressing animosity for one another, and several fist fights broke out when the faculty supervisor was not watching. Even worse, perhaps, was the time in January when a group of so called "jocks" harrassed a group of chorus students and a real free-for-all broke out before order was restored. Fortunately, or so the student smokers felt, the girl who was paralyzed after being shoved down a flight of stairs outside the lounge was withdrawn from school by her parents, and the administration failed to connect her injury with the smoking lounge. Trash was scattered all over the area by student groups expressing displeasure with various actions by the principal, and the student committee charged with emptying ashtrays and policing the lounge quietly withdrew from business early in the year. Another example of student misuse of the lounge could be seen in the graffiti of all degrees of obscenity which quickly defaced the walls.

D. Mrs. Burnell's yard showed the hours she spent each week caring for it. The flower border which stretched across the entire lot at the head of the house was a triumph of the industrious gardener. Not a weed could be seen among the rows and clumps of yellow daisies and dahlias, multicolored pansies and cosmos, and flaming poppies. Just as vivid were the clumps of scarlet salvia by the sidewalk leading to the front door. On either side of the white cement walk, near the doorstep, were neatly clipped beds of English ivy. The picket fence which ran entirely around the property also supported occasional tendrils of ivy, as well as one scarlet climber rose to the right of the front gate. Other roses appeared occasionally down the left side of the yard, which itself looked like a lovingly protected putting green, with hardly a blade of grass standing out from its fellows. No crabgrass was tolerated here, and no dandelion ever profaned the perfect expanse of velvet green.

E. When I was eight years old, my family moved to a house very different from any home I had known before. When I was two, we had lived in an old farmhouse with a large yard and huge elm trees shading the area where I played. That had been a wonderful place for a child to play. I had a fine play place later, also, when I was seven and we had a suburban bungalow with an enclosed yard and garden. It was from this bungalow that my father moved us—my mother, brother and me—to a townhouse in downtown Buffalo. Here there were no lawns, only sidewalks and streets and asphalt parking areas. I missed having a place to play. Even when we had lived in Chicago, during my first years at school, we were near a park, so that I didn't mind not having a yard. But in Buffalo we were far from any park, and my brother and I were not allowed to go far from home by ourselves. My mother solved our problem, finally, by converting the unused room on the third floor of our house into a play room, and here my brother and I spent many happy hours during the three years we stayed in Buffalo.

NAME_____ SECTION_____

Identifying Connectors

INSTRUCTIONS: *Circle all the connecting devices you can identify in the following paragraph.*

The reason for the Philadelphia Eagles' success in the National Football League was new General Manager and Coach Joe Kuharick. Virtually all of the Eagles' weaknesses were filled either by his trades or by his signing of draft choices. For instance, Kuharick saw that the initial need was a pile-driving fullback to complement the break-away running of his speedy halfback, Tim Brown. Hence Earl Groe was acquired from the Green Bay Packers. However, trading was not Kuharick's only accomplishment. He also had the knack of switching players from position to position in order to produce a diversified offense and an aggressive defense. For example, when his star halfback Tim Brown was injured, rookie Jack Concannon was placed in his halfback position. This was an especially interesting maneuver since the use of Concannon, who was a star quarterback at Boston College, gave him not only an excellent running threat, but a continual passing threat as well. Likewise, on defense, players were shuttled in and out, especially at the linebacker position. In this instance Maxie Baugh and Dave Lloyd were alternated constantly, depending on whether the situation called for the quarterback to be rushed or not. Although these accomplishments were great, there was another thing that Kuharick did which was even greater. Because of the Eagles' last place finish each of the past two years, there was much dissension on the Eagles' team. Even the ownership changed hands. Kuharick instilled a new spirit into the team. Now the Eagles were playing to win, as a team, and each individual was not just out for himself. Joe Kuharick did a remarkable job in making a successful team out of one that was struggling in last place just one short year ago.

Joe Finkelstein
(12th grade student)

NAME _____ SECTION_____

Supplying Connectors

INSTRUCTIONS: The following paragraph lacks coherence because the writer did not use connectors where necessary. Supply the needed connectors by inserting them in the paragraph.

The continued success of the Red Legs gave rise to several unexpected and not wholly desirable consequences. The team as a whole began to show signs of over-confidence. Their play on the field became just a little sloppy. Their activities off the field began to include certain lapses of training discipline. There were instances of rudeness toward fans who wanted autographs. Four players became loud and boisterous on a commercial airlines flight. They were actually ejected from the plane at the next scheduled landing. The team's playing became less sloppy after the manager imposed a few stiff penalties. He made it clear that the mark of a true champion lay in the ability to handle success as well as failure. He made it clear that any player who behaved in a rude or overbearing manner would be suspended. The team settled down and began to behave more acceptably both on and off the field.

NAME _____ SECTION_____

Improving Coherence Through Consistent Subjects

INSTRUCTIONS: Rewrite the following paragraph, making it more coherent by using one subject throughout.

A. Advance planning is half the secret of a good party. A wise hostess will want to examine her guest list and plan the sort of party those particular guests will most enjoy. Some people like a non-alcoholic punch, while others will feel cheated unless the refreshments include alcoholic beverages of some kind. Food is also a matter the hostess should consider carefully ahead of time. Dieters will not appreciate an array of creamy, high calorie goodies, but neither will the happy eaters enjoy munching carrot sticks and celery. The food, in short, will need to be planned to fit all the guests. Entertainment is also a matter concerning which guests might have a wide range of preferences. Young people tend to want a loud background of rock music, while quiet semi-classical or show music is usually more pleasing to adults. Pencil and paper games delight some guests, particularly adults, but dancing or quiet conversation is the choice of others. All these questions must be solved ahead of time if you are to be sure of a successful party.

NAME_____ SECTION_____

Sample Revision of Paragraph A

B. The experienced hostess knows that advance planning is half the secret of a good party. She will want to study her guest list and plan the sort of party those particular guests will most enjoy. She will want to know ahead of time which of her guests might prefer a non-alcoholic punch and which would feel cheated if she did not serve some kind of alcoholic beverage. If she is planning to feed her guests, the hostess will carefully consider what foods will be most suitable for her dieting guests while at the same time she will plan something a bit more palatable than carrot sticks and celery for those guests who eat heartily regardless of calories. The skilled party giver is also aware that guests may well have a wide range of preferences in entertainment. If her guests are all young, she may choose a loud background of rock music for dancing or listening, but if she is entertaining adults, she may prepare a program of show records or light classical music. She will be prepared for the possibility that some guests might enjoy cards or pen and pencil games as well as the likelihood that others would enjoy simply conversing or, perhaps, dancing. She will, in short, be thoroughly prepared to give a very successful party.

NAME _____   SECTION_____

Improving Coherence Through Sticking to Subject

INSTRUCTIONS: Rewrite the following paragraph, making it more coherent by sticking with the subject introduced in the topic sentence.

C. The police officers who patrol the northeast district of the city must cope with problems more numerous and complex than those of any other section of the inner city. The population density is the highest in the city, even though the district itself is the smallest in terms of city blocks. The nineteen eight-story buildings in the Jefferson Street high-rise housing project partially account for the large number of people living in such a restricted ground area. The narrow streets, shallow building lots, and almost hidden alleyways and inner courtyards are so densely crowded with old tenement buildings, multi-family houses, shacks, and sheds that fleeing criminals easily find a haven. Traffic in heroin and cocaine is heavy in the northeast district, and many known criminals live in the area. Glittering pastel Cadillacs are often seen parked amid the litter of the filthy streets, and at any time of day or night the painted street girls may be seen sallying forth to make their way to the more prosperous areas to the south. Known underworld characters live and work next door to pimps and numbers racketeers in this most multi-racial and ecumenical of neighborhoods. Most of the churches which once served the community have boarded up their broken windows and moved to the suburbs, and the school survives only with the help of armed guards. Yet, amid all this social refuse live many helpless, frightened citizens who need and value the help of the police.

NAME_____ SECTION_____

Sample Revision of Paragraph C

D. The police officers who patrol the northeast district of the city must cope with problems more numerous and complex than those of any other section of the inner city. They must cope with a population density which is the highest in the city, even though the district itself is the smallest in terms of city blocks. In the center of their patrol area are the nineteen eight-story buildings of the Jefferson Street high-rise housing project, which partially accounts for the large number of people living in such a restricted area. In other parts of the district the police are forced to find their way through a warren of narrow streets, shallow building lots, and almost hidden alleyways and inner courtyards so densely crowded with old tenement buildings, multi-family houses, shacks, and sheds that the fleeing criminal can easily find a haven the police cannot penetrate. Here, also, the police are faced with the city's heaviest traffic in heroin and cocaine, and they must maintain surveillance over the many known criminals who live in the area. They observe with frustration the glittering pastel Cadillacs parked amid the litter of the filthy streets and watch the painted street girls sally forth at all hours of the day and night to take their wares to the more prosperous areas to the south. They try to keep order on the streets where known underworld characters live and work next door to pimps and numbers racketeers, and where they receive little help from any other source. They have watched church organizations which once served the community board up their broken windows and move away, and they give what help they can to the armed guards who patrol the school. Yet, amid all this social refuse live many helpless, frightened citizens who need and value the help of the police.

NAME_____ SECTION_____

Improving Coherence by Eliminating Passive Voice

INSTRUCTIONS: The paragraph below is incoherent because there are a number of verbs in the passive voice. Rewrite the paragraph, putting all verbs in the active form and providing a subject for each verb.

A. As our car was driven through the gate, it was swung shut behind us, and our car was driven on. As we approached the next gate, it also was opened at our command. Our car was eyed with suspicion, but no stones were thrown, and no epithets were shouted that could be heard in the car. We had been promised that the way would be cleared for us, and it must be acknowledged that the pledge was meticulously honored.

Sample Revision of Paragraph A

B. As Pedro drove our car through the gate, the keeper pulled it shut behind us and we drove on down the road. Soon we saw another gate ahead, but in spite of some trepidation, we were able to pass through immediately upon showing our official pass to the guard. We saw groups of sullen peasants eyeing us with suspicion; but we had received a pledge that the road to the border would be clear for us, and that pledge was meticulously honored.

NAME_____ SECTION_____

Eliminating Passive Voice

INSTRUCTIONS: The paragraph below is incoherent because there are frequent verbs in the passive voice. Rewrite the paragraph, changing all verbs to active voice as needed to improve coherence.

C. A garden should be planned very carefully before a single seed is planted. Plans must be made not only for all the space that is available but also for all the time provided by your growing season. Each vegetable must be selected not only because it is enjoyed by your family and recommended by nutritionists, but also because the time taken in growing from seed to table is not out of proportion to the number of vegetables which can be produced by each plant. For instance, zucchini squash takes only forty-five days from seed to table, and once the first squash appears, if every succeeding one is picked before it reaches a length of eight or so inches, more squash will be produced steadily until the vines are killed by frost. It can be seen, therefore, that the space occupied by each zucchini plant is utilized productively. A similar extended productivity can be expected from tomatoes, green peppers, Swiss chard, and broccoli, and these vegetables are, hence, prized by home gardeners. Root vegetables, on the other hand, such as carrots, parsnips or radishes, produce only one vegetable for every seed, and should be planted only when the gardener knows they are well liked by the family.

NAME_____ SECTION_____

Sample Revision of Paragraph C

D. Home gardeners should plan their gardens carefully before they plant a single seed. They must plan not only for the space available to them but also for the time the growing season provides. They should select each vegetable they will grow not only because their families like it and because it has nutritional value, but because the time it will take in growing from seed to ripeness is not out of proportion with the number of vegetables each plant will produce. For instance, gardeners should know that zucchini squash takes only forty-five days from seed to ripeness, and that once they pick the first squash the plant will continue to produce right up to frost, as long as they pick each squash before it exceeds approximately 8" in length. Thus, they will utilize space productively by planting zucchini. They should know that they can expect a similar kind of extended productivity from tomatoes, green peppers, Swiss chard and broccoli, but that root vegetables such as radishes, carrots, and parsnips produce only one vegetable for each seed. They will want to be sure their families are fond of such one-shot vegetables before they devote a great deal of limited garden space to them.

NAME _____ SECTION_____

Establishing A Consistent Point of View

INSTRUCTIONS: The paragraph below is incoherent because of many errors in point of view. The writer did not choose the person and number of the subject and stick to it faithfully throughout. Rewrite the paragraph, improving coherence by making the point of view consistent.

A. Students often dislike a teacher because they do not understand him or her. It is not uncommon, for instance, for a student to make a negative judgment of a teacher and consequently have a bad experience in his or her class as a result of a simple cultural difference to which, in all fairness, no blame should be attached. We tend to judge teachers by standards more stringent than those one applies to himself, and, as a result, to put up artificial barriers which prevent a pleasant and productive relationship from developing between yourself and the teacher. The student is the one who loses in such a situation, and sometimes our loss is a great one, indeed. You will do well to remind yourself that teachers—in addition to being teachers—are husbands, fathers (wives and mothers), wage earners, bill payers, voters, gardeners, and a host of other things. And we will profit from learning to regard them in the context of their total personhood.

NAME_____ SECTION_____

Sample Revision of Paragraph A

B. Students often dislike a teacher because they do not understand him or her. It is not uncommon, for instance, for students to make a negative judgment of a teacher and, consequently, to have a bad experience in his or her class as a result of a simple cultural difference to which, in all fairness, no blame should attach. Students tend to judge teachers by standards more stringent than those by which they judge themselves, and, as a result, to put up artificial barriers which prevent pleasant and productive relationships from developing between themselves and certain teachers. Students are the ones who lose in such situations, and sometimes their loss is a great one, indeed. They would do well to remind themselves that teachers—in addition to being teachers—are also husbands and fathers (wives and mothers), wage earners, bill payers, voters, gardeners, and a host of other things. And students will profit from learning to regard them in the context of their total personhood.

NAME_____ SECTION_____

Improving Coherence Through Point of View

INSTRUCTIONS: The paragraph below lacks coherence because of frequent shifts in point of view. Rewrite the paragraph, making the point of view consistent.

C. I have observed that careful young drivers strongly resent the endless criticism heaped on the youthful driver as a class. They feel, and rightly so, that there is every kind of young driver, just as there are all degrees of skill among older drivers, and it is unfair to tar all with the same brush. The young fellow of nineteen who has never so much as had a parking ticket should not be unthinkingly lumped with the relatively small number of careless speed demons who create unfavorable statistics with regard to the youthful driver. One can understand their feelings.

NAME_____ SECTION_____

Sample Revision of Paragraph C

D. I have observed that careful young drivers strongly resent the endless criticism heaped on youthful drivers as a class. They feel, and rightly so, that there are all kinds of young drivers just as there are all degrees of skill among older drivers, and it is unfair to tar all with the same brush. They believe that young fellows of nineteen who have never had so much as a parking ticket do not deserve to be lumped with the careless speed demons who create unfavorable statistics for their age group. I can understand their feelings.

NAME _____ SECTION _____

Eliminating Inconsistent Verb Tenses

INSTRUCTIONS: Rewrite the paragraph below, improving the coherence by correcting the inconsistencies in verb tense.

A. The children poured on to the beach from the landing boat in a confused and noisy stream. Struggling to find their way to safety and fearful that the boat will pull away before they are safely ashore, they push and shove against those in the front ranks, heedless of the additional danger this creates. John, who was sitting in the stern of the craft before it reached the shore, was one of the last children to disembark. He looks around frantically, searching for his little sister, Susan, whom he last saw on the dock before they were placed aboard the big ship. Where was she?

NAME_____ SECTION_____

Sample Revision of Paragraph A

B. The children poured onto the beach from the landing boat in a confused and noisy stream. Struggling to find their way to safety and fearful that the boat would pull away before they were safely ashore, they pushed and shoved against those in the front ranks, heedless of the additional danger this created. John, who had been sitting in the stern of the craft before it reached the shore, was one of the last children to disembark. He looked around frantically, searching for his little sister, Susan, whom he had last seen on the dock before they were placed aboard the big ship. Where was she?

NAME_____ SECTION_____

Improving Coherence Through Verb Tense Consistency

INSTRUCTIONS: Improve the coherence of the following paragraph by rewriting it, correcting any inconsistencies in verb tense.

C. The basement looked as if everything that had ever come into it was still there, stacked in random layers through which one moves at one's own risk. Beside the entrance door, on the left, is a leaning tower of crates, some containing whole sets of books which were obviously never even unpacked and some overflowing with an accumulation of daily newspapers whose dates, one can see, stretched far into the past. Nothing seems ever to be thrown out. From the ceiling beams, dimly discernible in the feeble light from my flashlight, hang various sizes of wheels and tires and other parts of what might once upon a time have been unicycles or bicycles. And stacked in unbelievable disorder throughout the whole area were crates, baskets, bins, and boxes holding heaven only knows what and interspersed with, leaning against, and falling upon such objects as statues, paintings, urns, ship models, rolled up carpets, and, far to the back, in regal splendor, a gigantic cigarstore Indian who surveys the accumulated flotsam through unswerving and opaque eyes.

Sample Revision of Paragraph C

D. The basement looked as if everything that had ever come into it was still there, stacked in random layers through which one moved at one's own risk. Beside the entrance door, on the left, was a leaning tower of crates, some containing whole sets of books which had obviously never even been unpacked and some overflowing with an accumulation of daily newspapers whose dates, one could see, stretched far into the past. Apparently nothing was ever thrown out. From the ceiling beams, dimly discernible in the feeble light from my flashlight, hung various sizes of wheels and tires and other parts of what might once have been unicycles or bicycles. And stacked in unbelievable disorder throughout the whole area were crates, baskets, bins, and boxes holding heaven only knew what and interspersed with, leaning against and falling upon such objects as statues, paintings, urns, ship models, rolled-up carpets, and, far to the back, brooding in regal splendor, a gigantic cigar store Indian who surveyed the accumulated flotsam through unswerving and opaque eyes.

NAME _____ SECTION _____

Increasing Coherence Through Subordination

INSTRUCTIONS: The paragraph below is incoherent because it contains nothing but a series of short, choppy sentences. Improve coherence by connecting the simple sentences into compound or complex sentences.

A. I was in the valley. I could not see the old church building. I climbed up on a nearby outcropping of rock. It reached thirty feet above the valley floor. I could see much farther. I could see trees in a bend. I could see trees in a curving line. They were following the river's bend. I could see a hill on the other side of the river. On it I could see the old church building. The steeple caught the sun's last rays. It was white against the darkening evening sky.

NAME_____ SECTION_____

Sample Revision of Paragraph A

B. From where I was on the floor of the valley, I could not see the old church building. However, observing a nearby outcropping of rock which reached a height of almost thirty feet, I climbed to its top and discovered that I could see much farther. In the distance, a graceful line of trees followed the river's bend, and on the other side of the river, on a low hill, I could see the old church, its steeple a brilliant white in the sun's last rays against the darkening evening sky.

NAME_____ SECTION_____

Improving Coherence By Subordinating

INSTRUCTIONS: *Improve the incoherent paragraph below by combining sentences, making some ideas subordinate to others.*

He ran up the front steps. He burst through the door. The door slammed noisily against the wall. He didn't stop to close the door. He raced through the rooms. He kept calling Peter's name. His voice was hoarse and frantic with fear. He wanted to find Peter. He was afraid of what he might find. He raced upstairs. He flung open doors to bedrooms and closets. He raced back downstairs. He went down into the basement. A noise, half scream, half groan, burst from him. I stood at the top of the steps. I was afraid to go down. I knew what he had found.

NAME_____ SECTION_____

Removing Incoherence Through Gaps in Thought

INSTRUCTIONS: Read the following paragraphs, noting the glaring gaps in thought which the writer has left. How do these gaps make it difficult for you to understand the writer's meaning?

A. I have always said that "come the holocaust," I would want to be somewhere in the country with my mother. My mother was a country woman, born on a small farm in Missouri near the end of the 19th century. She had many skills her city daughters know nothing of, and she possessed a rich fund of old-time lore. She knew how to do many things that would be important to survival. After all, she was poor all her life. She was also accustomed to fending for herself and solving her own problems. When I was a child there were few things she could not fix more skillfully than could my city-bred father.

B. The porch was a shambles. There had been a storm in our absence, and the neighbor's dog had gotten in through a broken window. Apparently there had been a strong wind which played havoc with potted plants and hanging flower baskets.

NAME_____ SECTION_____

Sample Revision of Paragraphs A and B

C. I have always said that "come the holocaust," when survival would be the only issue, I would want to be somewhere in the country with my mother. My mother was a country woman, born on a small farm in Missouri near the end of the 19th century. Like all farm women of that time, she had many skills her city daughters know nothing of, and she possessed a rich fund of old-time lore which could mean the difference between living or dying in a time when there would be no stores, doctors or hospitals, and little medicine. She knew how to find a spring, spear a fish, butcher and skin an animal, set a trap, make soap, and do many other things that would be important to survival. After all, she was poor all her childhood, and poverty forced her and her brothers and sisters to learn many lessons which her more affluent children never had occasion to learn. She was accustomed to fending for herself and solving her own problems, which is a kind of independence we city people often lose, finding it easier to call a plumber or an electrician. When I was a child, I remember, there were few things she could not fix more skillfully than could my city-bred father.

D. The porch was a shambles. There had been a storm in our absence, and the wind had blown in a window so that rainwater had drenched the rug and furniture, and the neighbor's dog had gotten in through a broken window and rooted through all the containers and left muddy tracks over everything. Apparently there had been a strong wind which played havoc with potted plants and hanging flower baskets. Broken planters lay in shattered pieces on the floor and potting soil formed a thick mud over all.

NAME_____ SECTION_____

Eliminating Gaps in Thought

INSTRUCTIONS: *Improve the following paragraphs by filling in the gaps in thought, thus improving the coherence of the paragraphs.*

A. I always wanted to go to Harvard. I went to the University of New Mexico. My folks moved to Washington, D.C. I finished my degree at Harvard.

B. Eleanor found her schedule to be more demanding than she had anticipated during her two years of working full time and also attending night school to finish her nursing degree. During that time she was promoted to a supervisory position at the hospital. A shortage of critical care nurses often laid on her the responsibility of filling in an extra shift. The hospital more and more frequently sent her to other cities to attend medical workshops and symposia. Her husband, at the same time, was completing his Master of Arts degree. She often felt she was holding her real life in abeyance until she should have her degree.

NAME_____ SECTION_____

Sample Revision of Paragraphs A and B

C. When I was a child I always wanted to go to Harvard. My great-grandfather had gone there, and as a small child I heard many tales of Harvard life. My grandfather attended Harvard also and spoke often of his years there. He brought his family to New Mexico in the 1890's and my father attended the University of New Mexico. Dreams of Harvard seemed out of the question when I was eighteen, so I enrolled at the University of New Mexico also. However, because my folks moved to Washington, D.C. during my junior year, I was able to finish my degree at Harvard and thus fulfill my childhood dream.

D. Eleanor found her schedule to be more demanding than she had anticipated during her two years of working full time and also attending night school to finish her nursing degree. Had she continued to work simply as a staff nurse, she would, perhaps, have been able to manage without too much strain, but during that time she was promoted to a supervisory position at the hospital and, as a consequence, her responsibilities and her hours devoted to the hospital were greatly increased. One particular hardship stemmed from the shortage of critical care nurses at that time, which frequently required that she, as supervisor, fill in an extra shift in the Intensive Care Unit as well as performing all her usual supervisory duties. In addition, the hospital, evidently recognizing her increasing value as an employee, more and more frequently sent her to other cities to attend medical workshops and symposia. These absences not only made it difficult for her to keep her course work current, but deprived her, as well, of time she would have liked to devote to her personal life. Her husband, during this same time, was completing his Master of Arts degree at a nearby college and was, himself, on such a busy schedule that Eleanor and he sometimes felt that they saw one another only in passing. Small wonder that she often felt she was holding her real life in abeyance until she should have her degree.

NAME_____ SECTION_____

Filling Gaps with Extender Sentences

A. As Jules Henry commented in his book *Culture Against Man,* ours is an advertising culture in which we must learn that much of what purports to be truth is, instead, partial or total falsehood. Even the small child must learn that all that is advertised is not so. And unfortunately, everyone's youth is filled with more such disillusionments. Yet, in spite of constant disappointments, we retain some residue of faith. We try, over and over, to gain the blessings promised. When we want to be slim, we buy the $8.95 books which promise to tell us how to reduce without inconvenience. And we are hurt and disappointed when we don't lose ten pounds a week as the "doctor" said we would. We continue to try to believe even when it is no longer possible.

B. As Jules Henry commented in his book *Culture Against Man,* ours is an advertising culture in which we must learn that much of what purports to be truth is, instead, partial or total falsehood. Even the small child must learn that all that is advertised is not so. The "delicious," "candy-like" toothpaste that he badgered Mom to buy may well turn out to taste more like spearmint flavored chalk. Unfortunately, everyone's youth is filled with such disillusionments. Why does the complexion cure not take away teenage blemishes as promised? Yet, in spite of constant disappointments, we retain some residue of faith. Surely, we think, "they" wouldn't make that ad up out of whole cloth. We try, over and over, to gain the blessings promised. We show faith and buy, even when we doubt. When we want to be slim, we buy the $8.95 book which promises to tell us how to reduce without inconvenience. We won't have to give up anything. And we are hurt and disappointed when we don't lose ten pounds a week as the "doctor" said we would. We continue to try to believe even when it is no longer possible. We are like the early saint who cried out in anguish, "I believe, I believe, O, help Thou my unbelief."

NAME_____ SECTION_____

Providing Extender Sentences

INSTRUCTIONS: Improve the coherence of the paragraph below by inserting in the blanks sentences which further specify and extend the sentences they follow.

Different breeds of dogs have different qualities that endear them to their owners.

_____

_____

_____

_____ . The owners of Irish setters

will rhapsodize at length about the aesthetic appeal of their aristocratic animal. _____

_____

_____

On the other hand, dachshund owners seem to take particular pleasure in their little fellows'

feisty personalities. _____

_____

_____

Owners of big, powerful breeds such as German shepherds or boxers take particular pride in

their dogs' strength, while at the same time obviously taking pleasure in their loyalty._____

_____

_____

Dog owners, like the rest of us, differ in their tastes and needs, and it is fortunate that such diversity exists among the breeds of dogs.

Restricting A Subject

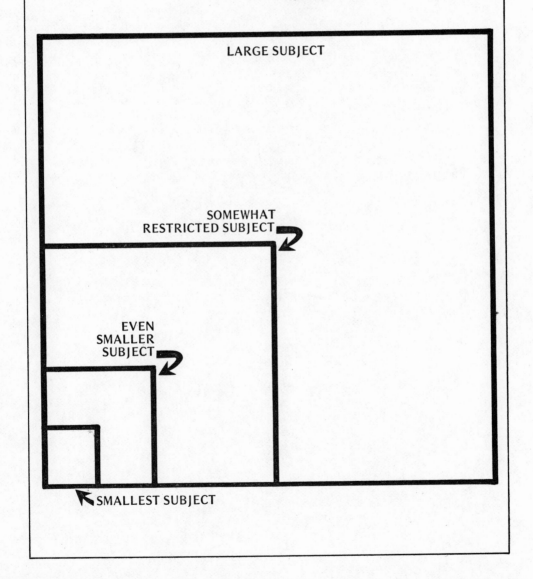

NAME _____ SECTION _____

Restricting the Global Topic

INSTRUCTIONS: Limit the following ideas which are general and global to a scope appropriate for a paper with only three or four developed paragraphs.

1. Health is important. _____

   _____

2. The topography of the continents has a pronounced effect on their weather patterns.

   _____

3. War, in the past, has been a reasonably effective means of settling international problems.

   _____

4. Malnutrition is found in all classes of people all over the world. _____

   _____

5. America is entering the postindustrial age. _____

   _____

6. Traffic deaths in the United States demonstrate the American urge to self-destruction.

   _____

7. It is possible for young people to take a conscious, significant part in assisting their own psychological growth. _____

   _____

8. Modern medicine has performed miracles in conquering diseases which once were scourges of humanity. _____

   _____

9. Great men have not always been successful fathers. _____

_____

10. In the United States, there is much more prestige to being youthful than to being old.

_____

11. In the history of wars is written the story of the human species' greatness and its

baseness. _____

_____

12. The "good old days" were not always so good. _____

_____

13. Many people act as if old age were something that could never happen to them. _____

_____

14. The automobile is one of the major causes of air pollution. _____

_____

NAME_____ SECTION_____

Enlarging the Limited Topic

INSTRUCTIONS: Enlarge the following ideas (which are limited enough to be topic sentences of paragraphs) to a scope which is appropriate for a paper of five to ten paragraphs.

1. A boy can learn much from owning a dog. _____
   _____

2. I lost a friendship by being thoughtless. _____
   _____

3. The water of the lake was a deep, dark blue. _____
   _____

4. I navigated the dark stairway cautiously. _____
   _____

5. The otter is the most playful of animals. _____
   _____

6. The whooping crane is one bird that apparently has been saved from extinction by timely conservation efforts. _____
   _____

7. The new member of Congress soon learns to give a little in order to get a little. _____
   _____

8. One should never betray a friend's confidence. _____
   _____

233

9. Ice cream has a good deal of nutritive value, even if it is fattening. _____

_____

10. Too much sun can cause skin cancer. _____

_____

11. Smoking by young people is increasing. _____

_____

12. Young people are pushed to choose careers before they are halfway through high school. _____

_____

13. Today, young people seem to learn their social values from their peers rather than their families. _____

_____

14. Some children in the early grades seem unduly eager to please their teachers. _____

_____

15. When making assignments, a teacher encourages students' growth by offering as many options as possible. _____

_____

NAME _____ SECTION _____

Determining Composition Size

INSTRUCTIONS: In the blank at the left of each subject, print the letter that corresponds to the size of composition it would take to develop that subject: a) a library, b) a shelf of books, c) a book, d) a chapter, e) a five- to ten-paragraph essay, f) a three-paragraph essay, g) one paragraph.

_____ 1. The apple is a remarkable fruit.

_____ 2. Drinking eight glasses of water a day is beneficial to health in a number of ways.

_____ 3. Achieving psychological maturity can also be called mastering the art of loving.

_____ 4. The history of the human race is revealed most truly in its art, architecture, literature, and music.

_____ 5. It does not matter if people are free, so long as they think they are.

_____ 6. The fall of Rome has been so instructive to people of all subsequent generations that if it had not occurred, it would have been invented.

_____ 7. Suicide has a long and respected history in Japan.

_____ 8. Tomatoes should not be planted in the same spot two years in a row.

_____ 9. Dogs are more expensive to feed than cats.

_____ 10. We will cherish our old people only when our society has changed so that people become loving and lovable.

_____ 11. There are still a number of prestigious careers for which a college education is not at all necessary.

_____ 12. Religion and humanity have coexisted from the beginning.

_____ 13. Fat people often lack self-esteem.

_____ 14. Obesity is a serious health problem in the United States.

_____ 15. It is possible to rear thin children and thus eradicate the problem of obesity.

_____ 16. Counting calories is the surest way for the nutrition-wise person to lose weight.

_____ 17. The functions and effects of cholesterol in the human blood comprise a complex and poorly understood subject.

_____ 18. We human beings have gained a great deal of knowledge about the workings of our bodies.

_____ 19. Obesity is hardly an asset to a happy social life.

_____ 20. The human soul has never been located, but it has been the subject of conjecture and study for thousands of years.

_____ 21. The early Christian church was indebted to many of the other so-called miracle religions for much of its form and substance.

_____ 22. "Progress" is a difficult term to define.

_____ 23. Modern art has developed in directions quite unrelated to the tastes and understandings of the public for whom it presumably was created.

_____ 24. The tiger in captivity can never be considered an entirely trustworthy animal.

_____ 25. Bear baiting, a popular spectacle in the London of Shakespeare's time, was a brutal sport.

_____ 26. The English bull dog was bred for bear baiting.

From Subject To Thesis

LARGE SUBJECT

SOMEWHAT RESTRICTED SUBJECT

EVEN SMALLER SUBJECT

THESIS

SMALLEST SUBJECT

Writer's point of view toward the subject

NAME _____ SECTION _____

Constructing a Thesis from a Restricted Subject

INSTRUCTIONS: The subjects below have already been restricted in size. For each, compose a thesis sentence that indicates a point of view toward that restricted subject.

winter in my community

deep sea fishing in Florida

my sophomore English class

experiences playing football in high school

learning to drive at school last year

thefts in the boys' locker room

snorkeling in clear water streams

The Cherokee Indians' trek to Oklahoma

being poor in this country

voting for the first time

making one's own clothes

a raft trip at the bottom of the Grand Canyon

changes in rock music

high school dress codes

old people in poor health

quiet, shy students

living in a high crime area

NAME _____ SECTION_____

Developing a Thesis by Relating Two Subjects

INSTRUCTIONS: An easy way to arrive at a thesis about a subject is to relate it to another subject. For example, the subject "loving families" can be related to the subject "crime" to produce the thesis "A loving family is a major preventive to crime." Using the following chart, name the second subject that has been related to the first subject to produce the thesis.

Subject	Thesis	Second Subject
loving families	A loving family is a major preventive to crime.	crime
football	Football teaches lessons of good citizenship and group awareness.	_____
football	Strategies of football are similar to military tactics.	_____
basketball	Basketball is more exciting than football for spectators.	_____
teen years	The teen years encompass some of the most important and consequential decisions a person will ever make.	_____
apples	An apple a day keeps the doctor away.	_____
grade chasing	Chasing the grade is not always the best way to get good grades.	_____
good human relations	Good human relations always thrive on open and honest communication.	_____
loyalty	People owe their highest loyalty to their own personal values, not to any person who would ask them to go against them.	_____
dress making	People who can make their own clothes will usually have better clothes for less money.	_____
Vitamin C	Taking high quantities of Vitamin C can help one avoid the common cold.	_____
careful driving	Motorists owe their passengers the courtesy of careful driving.	_____
good manners	All courtesy and so-called "good manners" are based on simple thoughtfulness.	_____
TV advertising	TV advertising makes it clear that there is something terribly undesirable and unattractive about growing old.	_____

NAME _____ SECTION_____

Constructing a Thesis by Relating One Subject to Another

INSTRUCTIONS: *Write a thesis that relates each of the following pairs of subjects.*

1. human beings - tornadoes _____
_____
_____

2. girls - basketball _____
_____
_____

3. cats - people_____
_____
_____

4. young men - women's liberation _____
_____
_____

5. sleep - teenagers_____
_____
_____

6. crime - unemployment_____
_____
_____

7. modern society - peace of mind _____
_____
_____

8. European public transit - Americans_____
_____
_____

9. spring - floating _____
_____
_____

NAME_____ SECTION_____

Determining the Subjects of Thesis Sentences

INSTRUCTIONS: The following thesis sentences have been composed by joining two subjects. Identify the two subjects in each sentence by drawing a line under each.

1. Regular applications of fertilizer are necessary to the maintenance of a good bluegrass lawn.

2. A gray and overcast day is a fine time to settle down with a good book.

3. Wicker furniture, with its light and airy design, is suitable for decorating a screened porch.

4. Breakfast should provide one-fourth or more of one's nutritional needs for the day.

5. Many plants, as well as animals, are on the growing list of endangered species.

6. Much of the white bread we purchase at the market has little food value beyond calories.

7. During the Sixties, hair became a symbol of cultural differences.

8. To many young people, the driver's license looks like a veritable ticket to freedom.

9. Every kitchen should have a singing bird to keep the cook cheerful.

10. People who keep cats for pets but who also like birds should attach bells to the cats' collars.

NAME _____ SECTION _____

Limiting the Sweeping Thesis

INSTRUCTIONS: Limit and qualify the sweeping thesis sentences below by, first, asking questions such as: all? everyone? always? everywhere? all kinds?, and, second, by rewriting the sentences in light of your answers.

1. Poverty is not as bad as it is thought to be.

2. Being rich is destructive to human character.

3. All politicians are just looking for a chance to get their hands into our pockets.

4. Surfing in Hawaii is something everyone can enjoy.

5. Hooking rugs is an excellent hobby.

6. Lawns should be mowed at least once a week if they are to be kept in good condition.

7. Music, after all, never hurt anyone.

8. The gravest problem facing manking today is inflation.

9. The ideal vacation includes sunshine, sports, a change of scenery and plenty of good food.

10. It is impossible to be well educated without some travel experience.

11. Everyone loves a frisky kitten.

12. It's a wonderful treat to have someone else do your work for you.

13. Young people enter senior high school with much fear and trepidation.

14. Seniors, in their arrogance, ignore the lowly underclassman.

15. Students find it hard to talk freely with teachers.

NAME _____ SECTION _____

Finding Weaknesses in Thesis Statements

INSTRUCTIONS: The following thesis statements are imprecise and misleading. Identify the weaknesses in each thesis sentence. Look for: words which could be taken more than one way or unqualified terms about which the reader might have questions. Then rewrite each thesis to make it more precise.

EXAMPLE: Catcher in the Rye is a dirty book and should be banned. **(dirty? entirely banned? everywhere? to all people?)**

1. Love makes the world go around. _____
   _____
   _____

2. Miami is a great place to go for holiday fun. _____
   _____
   _____

3. The free parts of the world are the only parts worth living in. _____
   _____
   _____

4. All good citizens of a democracy will welcome a chance to fight for liberty. _____
   _____
   _____

5. Patriotism demands that we respond to our country's needs. _____
   _____
   _____

6. A girl must behave like a lady if she wishes to be thought well bred. _____
   _____
   _____

7. The whole world loves a lover. _____
   _____
   _____

8. If one is not moving ahead, one is falling behind. _____
   _____
   _____

9. Most Americans are imbued with an old fashioned ambition to get ahead. _____
   _____
   _____

10. Americans have always been devoted to the land. _____
    _____
    _____

11. Loyalty is one of the noblest of human virtues. _____
    _____
    _____

12. A great portion of the world's population lives in poverty. _____
    _____
    _____

13. Every individual should devote at least a portion of his or her life to the pursuit of
    beauty. _____
    _____
    _____

14. According to an old adage, "Neatness and system are heaven's first laws, and cleanliness
    is next to godliness." _____
    _____
    _____

15. Professional football can do a lot for any major city._____
    _____
    _____

16. A country wishing to remain free must be prepared to do battle with those who would
    destroy its liberty. _____
    _____
    _____

NAME _____ SECTION _____

Unifying the Thesis Sentence

INSTRUCTIONS: The following list of sentences contains both unified and ununified thesis sentences. Identify the unified ones and correct the ununified ones by severing them, unifying them by finding a relationship between the various parts, or subordinating both parts to a higher generalization large enough to include them both.

1. All too often the father is not an important figure in the ghetto family and juvenile delinquency is a serious urban problem.

2. Like the extremes of poverty, an excess of wealth can be destructive of good human values.

3. Recent political events have revealed the dishonesty of many politicians and a movement should be started to identify the good, honest politicans in America.

4. If you learn a few labor saving devices, gardening need not be hard work, and it can also be profitable.

5. Cooking, like any creative work, is done best by those who enjoy it and can afford to buy the best ingredients.

6. While Americans are accustomed to a diet whose foundation is meat, more of the Earth's inhabitants eat a diet based on cereals.

7. New York is the biggest city in the United States, and San Francisco is the most cosmopolitan.

8. Dogs are always eager to please, and cats are independent.

9. In Denmark the cultural differences between the generations seem even greater than in the United States.

10. There were people who saw the Beatles as a Communist menace and were sure that long hair was a mark of moral degradation.

11. People who get up early know that dawn shows beautiful colors unlike those of the sky at sunset, when dramatic cloud formations catch everyone's attention and inspire poets, who in these days more often see the sunset than the sunrise.

NAME _____ SECTION_____

Evaluating Thesis Sentences

INSTRUCTIONS: Determine whether or not the thesis sentences below meet the criteria for good thesis sentences outlined by your teacher. Circle the numbers of those that meet the criteria, and revise those that do not.

1. I love apple pie.

2. The word "feline" refers to cats.

3. It seems to be true, as George Orwell said, that "all animals are equal but some are more equal than others."

4. A child can learn the lesson of responsibility from owning a dog.

5. Swimming has always been my favorite sport.

6. Many people between the ages of eight and eighteen play baseball.

7. Baseball fascinates as much by its possibilities for strategy as by its demonstration of athletic skills.

8. The trials of life tend to be overwhelming for many people.

9. A well reared cat is an endlessly entertaining pet.

10. There are not as many kings and queens in the world today as there were one hundred years ago.

11. Physical education classes are a feature of almost all American schools.

12. Football is an excellent sport.

13. There is a big difference between friendship and romance.

14. Young women today have an everwidening range of career opportunities open to them.

15. Movies are fine entertainment.

16. Not only are boys and girls sharing gym classes and home economics classes, but reallocation of educational funds and revision of traditional curricula are foreseen as consequences of the women's movement, and some educators are strongly opposed to the changes coming about.

NAME _____ SECTION_____

Dividing a Thesis into its Parts

INSTRUCTIONS: List the logical parts of each thesis sentence below. That is, list the aspects of the thesis which will have to be developed to cover the thesis entirely.

1. It is a mistake to provide a smoking lounge at any public high school.

2. In personal conversation we often use our own speaking for purposes other than to reveal ourselves or convey information.

3. Despite the absence of immediate victory, there are benefits derived from devoting oneself to a losing cause in which one sincerely believes.

4. It is difficult to identify any beneficial consequences of war which could not have been achieved by more peaceful means.

5. There are many lessons that young people could learn from old people if they lived more closely together.

6. Many Americans behave as if they considered themselves immune to the dire consequences of which they are warned by doctors, scientists, policemen, and safety experts.

7. Life becomes richer and more rewarding as we learn to break down the obstacles to free and open communication.

8. The history of the American Revolution as it is presented today is a far cry from the simple story of a battle for human liberty that most of us learned in grade school.

9. A civil war is one of the most horrifying of all human conflicts.

NAME _____ SECTION_____

Determining Order of Thesis Parts

INSTRUCTIONS: *Read each of the thesis sentences and parts listed below and determine the proper order of the parts, numbering them.*

1. *Thesis:* As a result of numerous disastrous experiences on blind dates, I am convinced that no right-minded young man should ever go on a date with a girl he doesn't already know.
    Parts: (numerous disastrous experiences)
    _____ a. Girl was so nervous she threw up in the car and cried all the way home.
    _____ b. Girl was 5'10" and made me feel like a pigmy.
    _____ c. Girl argued violently over everything I said, including the value of rock music, health food, politics, the sexual revolution, college education, communes and my way of dressing.
    _____ d. Girl wouldn't talk about anything.
    _____ e. Girl didn't know anything about sports.

2. *Thesis:* Lionel Farber's life was a demonstration in itself of how a criminal is created.
    Parts: (events in Farber's life)
    _____ a. His father, a convicted murderer, was executed.
    _____ b. His mother deserted the family when he was four.
    _____ c. He had a disfiguring birth mark on half his face.
    _____ d. He was brutalized by a neighborhood gang as a child.
    _____ e. He was unsuccessful in school.
    _____ f. His older brother, his model and a petty criminal, was his only friend and support.

3. *Thesis:* The new college freshman's first semester is a time when he or she is forced to make successful adjustments of many new demands.
    Parts: (new demands)
    _____ a. The freshman is forced to regulate his or her own life with no help.
    _____ b. Classes are harder, and teachers are more demanding.
    _____ c. The person is away from home and family, perhaps for the first time.
    _____ d. There is a roommate, a stranger the student must live with.
    _____ e. Unfamiliar environment is confusing.
    _____ f. He or she must choose companions and make friends.

4. *Thesis:* Persons who achieve reknown in one field often show great talent or competence in others.
    Parts: (multitalented people)
    _____ a. Albert Schweitzer: medical missionary, expert on Bach and organs
    _____ b. Albert Einstein: superb violinist, scientist

_____ c. Thomas Jefferson: inventor, statesman
_____ d. Eugene McCarthy: baseball player, poet, politician
_____ e. Winston Churchill: painter, statesman
_____ f. Ben Franklin: diplomat, printer, journalist, inventor

5. *Thesis:* Careful study has suggested certain circumstances which predispose a marriage to failure.

   Parts: (causes of failure in marriage)

   _____ a. Deep devotion to different religions by pair.
   _____ b. Coming from home broken by divorce.
   _____ c. Wide divergence in cultural or educational backgrounds.
   _____ d. Emotional immaturity of one or both people.
   _____ e. Short acquaintance before marriage.
   _____ f. Insufficient financial means.
   _____ g. Parental disapproval.

6. *Thesis:* The least experienced person can, with advance preparation, give a successful dinner party.

   Parts: (steps in preparation)

   _____ a. Plan arrangement of the table the day before.
   _____ b. Choose menu you already know how to cook.
   _____ c. Plan dishes that don't require last minute activities.
   _____ d. Polish silver well in advance.
   _____ e. Be sure table cloth and napkins are ironed the day before.
   _____ f. Plan in advance which serving dish will hold which item on the menu.
   _____ g. Choose records to provide congenial background music.

7. *Thesis:* A hospital is not the place to go for a rest.
   Parts: (unnerving elements of hospital life)

   _____ a. They wake you up to give you a sleeping pill.
   _____ b. After lunch, when you'd like a nap, it's visiting hours.
   _____ c. Constant stream of nurses, interns, etc.
   _____ d. Bathing you constantly.
   _____ e. Blood tests, samplings.
   _____ f. Nurses up at dawn.

NAME _____ SECTION_____

Dividing and Ordering the Thesis Sentence

INSTRUCTIONS: Divide the following thesis sentences into their parts. Then list the parts in logical order.

1. Good study habits go a long way toward producing good grades.

2. Some young people seem to know everything not to do to win friends.

3. Being an only child has certain advantages.

4. Even with the best intentions, many parents of adolescents alienate their children.

5. The high school principal must be an expert in many fields besides teaching.

6. Student honor codes are rarely successful in high schools.

7. Disciplinary measures in school should be aimed at teaching and helping students, rather than punishing them.

8. Much dating in high school is an exercise in ego building, rather than a matter of true friendship or love.

9. A long engagement period increases the likelihood of a successful marriage.

10. A good correspondent writes letters that are a pleasure to receive.

11. A particularly admirable kind of courage is demonstrated by the capacity to endure.

12. Many lessons one should learn during the years in school have little to do with academic knowledge.

NAME_____ SECTION_____

Test: Dividing and Ordering the Thesis

INSTRUCTIONS: Divide each of the thesis statements below into its logical parts and number the parts in a logical order.

1. The decision of what college to attend must be based on a number of considerations.

2. Our failures often teach us more than our successes.

3. The high school dropout creates many problems that will plague his or her future.

4. Based on all we know today, human society does not enjoy the prospect of a long and increasingly joyous future.

5. Punishment is seldom the most effective technique for teaching young people the guidelines for socially responsible behavior.

6. A valuable rule to live by is expressed in the question, what if everyone behaved as I am behaving.

NAME _____ SECTION _____

Transition Devices

It is the author's task to provide as much assistance as possible to the reader working his or her way through an essay. The author must be concerned with seeing to it that the reader does not get lost among the developmental details and fail to follow the idea sequence which has been prepared for him or her. That is, the author must strive to keep the reader informed about the organization of the paper. Perhaps the best way to keep the reader on the right path (aside from simple clarity and directness of language) is to provide "sign posts" wherever they might be helpful, much as the highway planner puts signs wherever there is a chance a driver might miss an important turn or overlook an intersection.

These signposts may take the form of deliberate transition sentences or even entire paragraphs at those points in the essay where the writer is concluding one section of the essay and moving to the next.

Such transitions may also be as simple as the addition of one word, such as the summing-up word "then" or the moving-on word "next." Or they may be an entire paragraph summing up the previous section and introducing the next. Whatever their form and length, the purpose of such signposts is simply to point the reader to the next part of the author's idea-structure and to assure the reader's easier comprehension of the essay.

One much used technique of achieving easy transitions through the structural frame-work of the essay is the use of leading questions. In the first part of her article "Let Us Speak to One Another," Ardis Whitman specifies at length the importance of communication in our lives. Reaching the second part of her essay, she asks, "Why, then, if communication is so important in our lives, are we unable to . . .?" and after discussing barriers which keep us from freely communicating, she goes on to ask, "But is there nothing we can do to improve the quality of our . . .?"

Following is a list of possible wordings for transitions:

1. It is evident, *then,* that the Gallic Wars proved Caesar's military genius.
2. *In spite of these* powerful arguments, there were still many dissenters.
3. Administrators, *however,* are not the only ones disturbed by this problem.
4. *Not only* must students solve these financial problems, *but* they are faced, *also,* with new and difficult academic challenges.
5. *Having seen* how the early Popes handled this problem, *let us* turn to the Popes of later centuries and see whether they were as successful.
6. We will go *either* to the movies *or* to the game.
7. *Having considered* the Renaissance, *let us now* move on to the Baroque period.
8. We decided, *finally,* to cancel the meeting.
9. No discussion of literature would be complete without mentioning Shakespeare.
10. *Granting that this viewpoint has some validity,* we still question its overall viability.

11. *In light of this evidence, then,* why is it that so many people continue to smoke?
12. *Let us turn, now,* to some other more positive issues.
13. *In concluding* this presentation of photography, let us discuss lighting.
14. Answers, *as we shall see,* are not easily formulated.
15. Hemingway is *not the only* author who deals with *this* theme.
16. *The third and last* example to be discussed involves the Supreme Court decision on euthanasia.
17. Let us consider, *on the other hand,* the benefits of vocational training.
18. The answers, *nevertheless,* remain to be seen.
19. Ice cream is fattening; yogurt, *conversely,* is low in calories.
20. We should mention, *in addition to the facts already presented,* that there were two witnesses.

NAME_____ SECTION_____

Transition Devices: Evaluation Activity

Part I Identifying Transitions

INSTRUCTIONS: In each group below you are given a sentence that you are to imagine is the last sentence in a paragraph, and two sentences from which to choose the first sentence of the next paragraph. Circle the letter of the sentence in each group that provides the smoothest transition. Underline the transitional or connecting devices.

1. A simple misunderstanding, then, can become a major stumbling block to communication between teenagers and parents.
   a) Embarrassment plays a considerable part in the lack of communication between generations.
   b) Embarrassment also plays a considerable part in this lack of communication between generations.

2. Reading a textbook assignment actively, therefore, is an excellent way to use your study time most effectively.
   a) Another effective study habit is that of raising the right questions as you read.
   b) You should learn to raise the right questions as you read.

3. Courses at the high school level are generally difficult, and students are often expected to work on their own.
   a) On the other hand, the junior high program is organized quite differently.
   b) The junior high program is organized quite differently.

4. But, in general, students who are interested in school take more active roles in school affairs than the apathetic students, for they run for offices, work hard on committees, help to make plans and formulate ideas, and interact with administrators and teachers.
   a) As a result of this more active role, interested students develop faster socially.
   b) Interested students often develop faster socially than students who are not interested in school.

5. We are not surprised, therefore, to learn that almost all teenagers are deeply interested in increasing their skills in human relations.
   a) Most young people are willing to work hard at any task which seems to contribute to group cohesiveness.
   b) One form this interest takes is a willingness on the part of most young people to work hard at any task which seems to contribute to group cohesiveness.

6. As a result of this experience, she never again cared to get on a horse.
   a) She turned her attention to bird watching, a safe pastime for one who loves the outdoors.
   b) She still loved the outdoors, however, and soon settled on birdwatching as an outdoor pastime somewhat safer than horseback riding.

7. With these instructions, she was finally able to finish step three with no further difficulty.
   a) Step four, however, was another problem entirely.
   b) Step four presented a problem.

8. After a great deal of hard work, she was able to turn in the completed paper on Thursday.
    a) Having managed to complete her English assignment for the week, she next turned her attention to her overdue biology reports.
    b) She turned her attention to her overdue biology reports.

9. We can see, then, that this method is relatively simple and requires little technical training.
    a) There are three other methods of which, unfortunately, this cannot be said.
    b) There are three difficult methods which require lengthy technical training.

10. She was, in short, the most beautiful girl he had ever seen.
    a) But it was not her physical beauty which drew him to her.
    b) He was not drawn to her because of her physical beauty.

Part II Writing Transitions

INSTRUCTIONS: In each group below you are given a sentence that you are to imagine is the last sentence in a paragraph, and another sentence which is the first sentence in the next paragraph. Rewrite the second sentence to provide a better transition between the paragraphs.

1. Thus, the American woman accepted the domination of her husband for many years, apparently without question or regret.
    Many American women will no longer accept domination passively.

    Better opening sentence for the second paragraph: _____
    _____
    _____
    _____

2. The materials were assembled and I was ready to begin work immediately.
    I attacked the Spanish translation, which I dreaded the most.

    Better opening sentence for second paragraph: _____
    _____
    _____
    _____

3. In fact, I was so far behind I was afraid I would not be able to finish the course.
    I had a deep interest in the next course in the sequence, so I caught up and finished the course on time.

    Better opening sentence for the second paragraph: _____
    _____
    _____
    _____

4. Having learned this hard lesson, I was never again tempted to take something that did not belong to me.
   It was hard for me to learn the lesson that I should always tell the truth.

   Better opening sentence for the second paragraph: _____

   _____

   _____

   _____

5. This particular incident contributed to the mutual hostility which finally led to the outbreak of fighting.
   An incident which brought two soldiers into personal conflict increased the tension on both sides.

   Better opening sentence for the second paragraph: _____

   _____

   _____

   _____

6. If all these considerations are taken into account ahead of time, it is clear that the actual arranging of the buffet will present no problems on the day of the dinner.
   Care must always be exercised in planning the guest list.

   Better opening sentence for the second paragraph: _____

   _____

   _____

   _____

NAME _____ SECTION_____

Four Common Types of Introductions

1. An *anecdotal introduction* relates an incident which demonstrates or exemplifies the author's thesis. It is usually quite brief, points clearly and directly to the thesis and easily culminates in a statement of the thesis. Its major advantage is in capturing the reader's interest both by its content and by its easy and informal style. This opening is more likely to be favored for articles written for popular consumption than for formal scholarly works. Here is an example of an anecdotal introduction:

   Thelma Gray and Lucy Tayler, both fifteen years old and known for their adventurous spirits, said goodbye to their mothers on a sunny morning in May, 1976, and set out for their bus stop at the corner. They were invited to a picnic and swimming party at a suburban park a few miles away. Clutching their bathing suits and bright beach towels, they hurried toward a fun-filled day with their friends. Thelma and Lucy, however, never reached that park and never saw their friends again. By nightfall their bodies had been found beside a seldom used road in an isolated area of the county near the park. Both had been bludgeoned to death. Police, reconstructing the young women's last day, determined that they were two more on a growing list of girls who had decided to hitch-hike and who had paid the ultimate price for their decision. Chief of Police Erwin T. Miller had tears in his eyes as he announced the cause of the teenagers' deaths and pleaded with other girls to heed police warnings against hitch-hiking. "People," he said, "who accept rides with strangers run the risk of losing their lives in the same tragic manner as these two poor girls."

2. The *outline introduction* includes a statement of the thesis along with the major parts to be covered in the essay. This introduction is not suitable for a brief essay, but may be very helpful to introduce a long essay on a difficult and complex subject. In such cases it is often helpful for the reader to know in advance exactly what aspects of a subject the author plans to develop and in what order. Thus, the reader is equipped with a "road-map" through the essay. Here is an example of the outline introduction:

   The American Civil War is often described as the bloodiest and most tragic experience in the nation's history. The very nature of civil war, with family members divided by differing loyalties and friend estranged from friend, is, of course, sufficient reason to regard such a war with particular horror. However, a study of the toll in human suffering in the war between the North and South requires close examination of the specific aspects of the conflict. This present study will attempt to show that immediate battlefield losses, serious as they were, represented only a minor portion of the human suffering caused by the war. An examination of actual direct casualties (dead and injured) for both North and South will comprise the opening section. Succeeding sections will examine in turn the prisoner of war camps of both North and South with their grossly inadequate living facilities, diet and medical provisions; military hospitals and other medical establishments, with emphasis on the primitive nature of facilities and technology; and legal and historical records of cases in which individuals of one side or the other were accused of wreaking atrocities on helpless persons in their power. The final section will deal with sufferings of civilian populations in areas where the two armies fought, foraged, and scorched the earth. The miseries of the American Civil War, we shall see, fell on soldier and citizen alike.

3. The *contrast introduction* is especially appropriate when your thesis contradicts or modifies a commonly held belief or assumption. It begins with several sentences explaining the commonly held opinion and then presents the thesis as the opposite of this belief or assumption. Here is an example of the contrast introduction:

> Most people assume that learning to ski is not extremely difficult. They imagine the process consists of little more than strapping on two long boards, pushing off at the top of a hill, and gliding gracefully and effortlessly to the bottom. However, learning to ski is more difficult than these people realize, and requires long hours of practice, extremely good physical condition, and a lot of determination.

4. The *funnel introduction* is very useful and common. The writer identifies the general subject area in the opening sentence, making some generalization aimed at arousing interest and, perhaps, establishing a bond of common awareness and knowledge with the reader. The author narrows the subject down step by step, sentence by sentence, to the specific aspect of the general subject and the specific viewpoint towards it that forms the thesis. In other words, the funnel introduction begins with a very broad general idea and continues with ideas that are more and more specific, until it arrives at the thesis sentence—the most specific idea in the introduction. Since it becomes more and more narrow from top to bottom, this kind of introduction is given the label "funnel." Here is an example of the funnel introduction:

> The life of a teenager in modern America is not always pleasant. He or she is faced with a multitude of conflicts and problems, many of which seem almost impossible to overcome. Most of these problems center around school, which is not surprising considering that the teenager devotes an average of eight hours a day to school and school-related activities. One of the primary problems created by school is the intense pressure for good grades.

NAME _____ SECTION _____

Identifying the Four Common Types of Introductions

INSTRUCTIONS: *Determine which method was used—anecdotal, outline, contrast, or funnel—in constructing each of the following introductions. Identify each paragraph by writing its correct type in the space provided.*

Paragraph I

Since of all the animals the human animal alone is capable of reasoning, it would seem to follow that above all animals human beings would be able to plan and execute a regimen for living that would result in vigorous health and a harmonious, productive life. That this is far from the case is evident to the most casual observer. The lowliest of animals, unaided by anything remotely resembling human intelligence, manage, more successfully than we, to eat what is good for them, sleep as much as their bodies require, exercise enough to stay agile and remain through life a functional part of nature's harmonious whole. Human beings get low marks in all these achievements. Our sophisticated intellect, far from being an aid to promotion of health, spurs us to destructive behavior in terms of food, drink, sleep, exercise, work, and play. An examination of human behavior with regard to these lifelong activities might well persuade one that good health is better promoted by animal instinct than by an intricate and miraculous brain.

Paragraph type _____

Paragraph II

Friendship is an art which requires more than common skill and commitment. It requires, in its highest form, knowledge of the mysteries of human motivation and a willingness to accept one's friends in terms of their own inner conceptions of themselves instead of by their all too often imperfect external expressions of self. This kind of knowledge and this capacity for acceptance are not easily gained, and are most often the consequences of long experience and practice. For young people, therefore, who are at the beginning of their practice of friendship, a simpler capacity must suffice. This can be found, I believe, in the deliberate development of the quality of loyalty. Of all the components which are important to a rich, long lasting friendship, loyalty is the most essential.

Paragraph type _____

Paragraph III

I wanted, more than anything, to be invited to join a sorority when I entered high school. I was sure that to be left out of this magic circle of popular girls would mean the absolute end of my hopes for teenage happiness and social success. Imagine my excitement, therefore, when I received invitations to rush parties from three different clubs. And imagine the frenzy of preparations I entered into, the endless efforts to insure the acceptability of my face, figure, hair, clothes, small talk, and table manners. I was to be whatever each club wanted me to be, perfect in all respects and equally pleasing to all. As it happens, I did join a sorority but not, it soon became apparent, because I was perfect in all respects. On the contrary, my making over began the day I joined. In time the magic circle became a restricting cage and I longed to exercise my own standards and search for my own goals. Many a young girl, I suggest, learns as I did that the important task of becoming one's best self is seldom served by unthinking efforts to become what others want you to be.

Paragraph type _____

Paragraph IV

From the beginning of history myths have abounded in which some magical elixir of youth or good health or long life has been hoped for, searched for, and, as some tales would have it, discovered and lost again. Such natural phenomena as geysers or sulphur springs have been thought to produce miraculously restorative waters, and people have traveled long distances to drink foul tasting potions in the hopes of regaining health or retaining youthful vigor. Even today, we are not far removed from our grandparents' faith in the "tonic" sold by the traveling medicine show. We buy billions of dollars worth of highly advertised, medically questionable elixirs of one kind or another and at the same time undervalue and ignore the true fountain of life which pours out its gifts in almost endless supply all around us. Water, the most accessible of all drinks, is also the most essential to human health, and yet, it is a rare person, indeed, who drinks as much water as he or she should. Every adult, according to current medical knowledge, should drink at least eight full glasses of water a day for maximum support of health.

Paragraph type _____

Paragraph V

A successful wedding, even a relatively small one, is generally the result of careful planning. There are, in fact, so many considerations to be kept in mind that it is common for the bride-to-be to hire a bridal consultant. Many girls, however, cannot afford such a consultant or, even if they can, prefer to do their own planning. Such an independent young woman might find helpful the following brief but complete collection of traditional and innovative ideas for planning a wedding. Her entire delightful task is covered, beginning with ideas for announcement of the engagement and written invitations to the wedding, and continuing through choices of wedding clothes; selection of attendants and conventions pertaining to their participation and the bride's obligations to them; choice of location, whether religious or social; decorations, including suggestions for color schemes, uses of flowers, candles and other lighting; personal flowers for the bride as well as the two mothers, any grandmothers and the various attendants; options available as to the ceremony itself, including readings and music; and the reception following the ceremony, be it large or small. Armed with such complete and helpful advance information, the least experienced young woman can take pleasure in planning her own wedding.

Paragraph type _____

Paragraph VI

Choosing a puppy to be a family pet is a happy and exciting occasion, but one which requires serious advance consideration. Many circumstances relate to the making of the proper choice, and the consequences of ignoring any of them could be expensive, inconvenient, and disappointing. The prospective owners should make a careful study of the suitability of the pet to the environment it will be living in, both as a puppy and as a full grown dog. They should learn about the dispositions and habits of the various breeds they are considering, with special concern, first, for the welfare of the children in the family and, second, for the feelings and safety of neighbors and others who might visit the house. They must be aware of the demands that proper care of their puppy will make on their time, energy, and funds and they must be sure that their selection is compatible with their actual situation. Thus, informed and knowledgable, the family should be ready to choose a pet which can add to the happiness of the household for many years.

Paragraph type _____

Paragraph VII

Great-grandmother Margaret, as she expected to be called, was my father's grandmother, and although she had lived with us as long as I could remember, my affection for her was tempered by a large measure of nervous respect. She was too distant, too dignified, for me to feel entirely at ease in her company. When she disappeared from our house one night without any explanation, I took for granted that she would be back, and when she did not return I began to wonder if others in the family might disappear also. I timidly questioned my mother, who assured me that no one else in the family would leave and that even great-grandmother Margaret had not really left, but was still watching over us from up in Heaven. This failed to reassure me. For some weeks I felt as if a stern, ghostly eye were, indeed, watching me, and it was a long time before I was free of a vague feeling of anxiety. The memory of this experience leads me to believe that small children should be carefully prepared for the experience of a death in the family and that when a death actually occurs, they should receive careful and reassuring explanations.

Paragraph type _____

NAME _____ SECTION _____

Constructing Funnel Introductions

INSTRUCTIONS: *Imagine that in each of the pairs of sentences below the generalization is the first sentence in an introductory paragraph and the thesis is the last sentence in that introduction. For each pair write a funnel introduction by connecting these two sentences with two or more other sentences that will lead the reader gradually from the large generalization to the more specific thesis sentence.*

1. *Generalization:* If there is one truism in our society which receives almost universal acceptance, it is the one which expresses our belief that experience is the best teacher.
    Thesis: Increasingly, we are putting our older people out to pasture and depriving ourselves of contributions they could be making.

2. *Generalization:* Puppy love is the rather condescending name adults give to the romantic feelings of very young people.
    Thesis: Parents should be aware that the feelings of young people involved in a first love affair may well be as intense as any they will ever experience.

3. *Generalization:* Nature is a great healer.
    Thesis: We must fight the constant efforts of powerful industrial forces to encroach on our great wilderness sanctuaries.

4. *Generalization:* No person will be truly educated without reading constantly for pleasure.
    Thesis: The best way for parents to be sure their child is a reader is to be readers themselves.

5. *Generalization:* Values are learned primarily in the home.
    Thesis: Parental example is the most powerful teacher of values.

6. *Generalization:* The first year away at college is both an adventure and a challenge.
    Thesis: The college freshman's first task is to learn to organize his or her time.

7. *Generalization:* Mother Nature is our best teacher.
    Thesis: People could improve their health if they would listen more attentively to the signals their bodies provide for them.

8. *Generalization:* The times are changing.
    Thesis: Within two decades some regulation on the manufacture and use of automobiles will be recognized as essential.

9. *Generalization:* Loneliness is the most painful of human emotions.
    Thesis: For emotional health an individual should engage in three different kinds of human relationships: intimate, casual and nurturant.

10. *Generalization:* Many people feel a need to be different from others, to stand out from the crowd.
    Thesis: True individualism need not preclude a comfortable acceptance of most group styles, customs and conventions.

NAME _____ SECTION _____

Testing Funnel Introductions for Coherence

INSTRUCTIONS: Test the following funnel introductions for coherence and consistent direction from the opening generalizations to the thesis sentence. (Check for large gaps in flow of ideas between sentences.)

I. Americans have always claimed to be devoted to quality education for all youngsters. Many school districts are currently caught in the fiscal squeeze, with costs rising rapidly and property taxes proving inadequate as a source of revenue. More and more parents claim that the schools are not doing a good job of preparing students to make their way in society, while educators suggest that parents are failing to do their part in influencing their children to behave acceptably in an educational setting. In the light of such an impasse, it is not surprising that parents are often unwilling to vote for increased costs to themselves for their children's schooling. When class sizes get too large, quality education involved becomes impossible.

II. Young people are taking an increasing interest in planning their own education. Students feel that they know best what they should be studying and should, therefore, be allowed a dominant role in establishing course requirements and evaluative criteria as well as actual lesson plans. In theory one can hardly quarrel with this viewpoint, but in practice several considerations must be kept firmly in mind if such student participation is to be fruitful.

III. Some people seem to have a natural gift for friendship. They are thoughtful; they remember birthdays and other important occasions. They seem to have an unusual ability to sense the feelings of others and to avoid trespassing on the private moods of their friends. After all, one doesn't always want to be with others or reveal what one is feeling, even to a friend. Sometimes one simply wants to be left alone. A person may not be upset or depressed, but may just feel a need for solitude. Solitude is essential to us all in some degree, and everyone should try to spend some quiet time alone each day.

IV. Clothes make the man, or so the saying goes. But what do they make him, one might well ask. His necktie must make him uncomfortable and his coat must make him hot, particularly if he remains faithful to it in summer time. His shirt collar and cuffs must make him feel stifled, his vest must make him feel padded, and his belt must make him feel like a package tied around the middle. The rebellion against such clothing as the right way, the only way to array oneself to face the world is not surprising; in fact, to many it seems long overdue. More and more men are gaining the courage to flout traditional standards for masculine dress and are daring to wear comfortable and colorful clothes to even the most formal business occasions. They are also beginning to wear their hair at casual lengths that please their sons and dismay their barbers. Men have gradually gotten used to hair styles that horrified them ten years ago. They would have been hard put to explain their horror in rational terms, but it was quite evident that their responses were to hair as a symbol rather than to hair as something real.

NAME_____ SECTION_____

Constructing Anecdotal Introductions

INSTRUCTIONS: Construct an anecdotal introductory paragraph for each of the thesis sentences given below. Be sure that you begin the introduction with the anecdote and lead into the thesis at the end. You may wish to change the wording of the thesis slightly to make it better fit your introduction.

1. The best camping trips are those that follow careful planning.

2. Tourists should remember that bears in state parks are not always as friendly as they seem.

3. What seems like a very small fib can have disastrous consequences.

4. There is no denying the fact that mothers often do know best.

5. A lesson worth learning is that sometimes a lesson cannot be taught; one must learn it for oneself.

6. Simple courtesy makes life more pleasant for everyone.

7. Parents should be aware that the example that they set speaks more loudly to their children than any words they say.

8. If parents will listen carefully, they will find that their children have much to teach them.

NAME_____ SECTION_____

Writing An Outline Introduction

INSTRUCTIONS: Write an introduction (outline type) for the following outline on the uses of airplanes in World Wars I and II.

Thesis: World War I provided only a glimpse of the contribution the airplane would make in such later wars as World War II.

I. Planes used for actual combat
   A. Fighter planes
      1. Numbers of planes, makes, etc.
         a. World War I
         b. World War II
      2. Missions accomplished and results
         a. World War I
         b. World War II
      3. Quality of aircraft as compared to enemy aircraft quality
         a. World War I
         b. World War II
      4. Assessment of value to war effort
         a. World War I
         b. World War II
   B. Bombers
      (same subdivisions as above)

II. Transport Planes
   A. Personnel Transport
      1. Planes available
         a. World War I
         b. World War II
      2. Men carried, numbers, where, when, success
         a. World War I
         b. World War II
      3. Assessment of importance to war effort
         a. World War I
         b. World War II
   B. Transportation of equipment
      (same subdivisions as above)

III. Reconnaissance planes

    A. Long range
        1. World War I
        2. World War II
    B. Combat support
        1. World War I
        2. World War II
    C. Spy planes
        1. World War I
        2. World War II

IV. Aircraft industry in America
    A. World War I
    B. World War II

NAME _____   SECTION _____

Constructing Contrast Introductions

INSTRUCTIONS: For each of the thesis sentences below, construct an introductory paragraph of the contrast type by beginning the introductory paragraph with a popular misconception that the thesis contradicts.

1. Ballet dancing requires that performers be in top physical condition.

2. Accepting praise gracefully requires skill.

3. On many occasions, honesty is not the best policy.

4. If one is always cautious, one misses some of life's greatest joys.

5. Harry Truman was perhaps America's most effective President of recent times.

NAME_____ SECTION_____

Constructing An Introduction

INSTRUCTIONS: Choose one of the thesis statements below and construct an effective introductory paragraph based on it.

1. One learns, as years go by, that there is always another day; there is always a new chapter beginning as the old one ends.

2. Young love is at least as serious and meaningful as the love of older persons.

3. One must develop his or her own ways of achieving peace of mind.

4. In the long run, your best friend is the one who is honest with you.

5. The development of missiles and rockets in both Russia and America rested on work done in Germany before and during World War II.

6. Both South and North stand convicted of poor treatment of prisoners during the War between the States.

7. The most significant war prizes of World War II were the minds of captured German scientists.

8. Where the white man went on his explorations, he took not only white culture and religion, but also white diseases and white weapons.

NAME_____ SECTION_____

Writing Conclusions

1. The conclusion can be a summary of the main points made in the essay—a reminder of the thesis and the arguments that the writer has used to support it. A summary conclusion is usually most suitable for long and complex essays—often those for which it is also helpful to provide the outline introduction.

2. The conclusion can be an "upside-down funnel." That is, it can begin with a restatement of the thesis and then enlarge the idea with statements that become more and more general to show the setting which gives the idea significance.

3. For shorter essays, a separate conclusion is not always needed. It is possible to include in the last supporting paragraph an extended clincher sentence in which you echo the thesis sentence and/or make some sort of significant final statement.

4. Since concluding paragraphs often sound tacked on, make special attempts to link the conclusion to the paragraph that precedes it by repeating an appropriate key word or idea and by utilizing the other connecting devices discussed previously.

Sample Conclusions

I. When the evidence is all in, then, the arguments against hitchhiking are overpowering. People who do not heed them take a grave risk. Indeed, Thelma Gray and Lucy Taylor might be alive today if they had realized that the stranger's invitation to ride was in reality an invitation to tragedy.

II. So much, then for humankind's superiority! It looks as if the animals have us beat on every aspect of health. When it comes to sleeping, eating, drinking, exercising, and maintaining activity throughout life, we might as well be mindless. Certainly we act as if we are.

III. Young people who develop these qualities and who learn to be truly loyal to friends will never find themselves friendless. They will have learned the skill most important to the art of friendship.

IV. Now the family is ready to start looking for that perfect puppy, the one who will bring pleasure to the entire household for many years. Good luck!

V. Many of the fears of childhood are, perhaps, unavoidable. The world, after all, is a big and fearful place, and there is much the child can learn only from experiencing it. However, the destructive fear which sometimes accompanies the early experience of death can be avoided or, at least, minimized if parents are sufficiently alert to their child's emotional needs. Properly prepared by loving and sensitive parents, there is no reason why a child's first knowledge of death cannot be a constructive, psychologically maturing experience.

NAME _____ SECTION _____

Essay Checklist

INSTRUCTIONS: *The following are the logical steps that a writer should take in writing an essay. As you complete each step, check it off and proceed to the next.*

_____ 1. Choose a topic you know well.

_____ 2. Narrow the topic down to a subject limited enough to be developed in detail in an essay of the length you plan to write.

_____ 3. Write a thesis sentence that indicates your point of view in relation to the restricted subject.

_____ 4. Check to make sure your thesis sentence contains only one idea.

_____ 5. Check to make sure your thesis sentence contains no words that may be interpreted in more than one way.

_____ 6. Analyze the thesis to determine what are the parts that must be developed in order to cover the thesis entirely. Write down the parts in list form.

_____ 7. Decide on the best order for the parts of the thesis.

_____ 8. Begin to write the essay, one paragraph at a time, starting with the introduction.

_____ 9. For each *developed* paragraph, construct a topic sentence and make an outline of the specific details before starting to write it.

_____ 10. Write a conclusion.

_____ 11. Check to make sure you have provided transitions as needed to guide the reader through the paper.

_____ 12. Proofread the rough draft to make sure it contains no errors in usage or spelling.

_____ 13. Copy the essay over and submit it to the teacher or distribute it to other students to read.

Chart of Dewey Decimal System

100 Who am I?
PHILOSOPHY
AND PSYCHOLOGY
(We think about ourselves)

200 Who made me?
RELIGION
(We think about God)

300 Who is the person in the next cave?
SOCIAL SCIENCES
(We think about other people)

400 How can I make that person understand me?
PHILOLOGY (Language)
(We learn to communicate with others through words)

500 How can I understand nature and the world about me?
SCIENCE
(We learn to understand nature on the land, in the sea, and in the sky)

600 How can I use what I know about nature?
APPLIED SCIENCE
AND USEFUL ARTS
(Primitive people learned about fire and how to make weapons. People through the ages learned about the wheel, about medicine, planting crops, cooking food, building bridges, and how to make all the things we use)

700 How can I enjoy my leisure time?
FINE ARTS
AND RECREATION
(By this time, primitive people had more time to do the things they enjoyed. They learned how to paint pictures and to create music. They also learned how to dance and to play games)

800 How can I give my children a record of people's heroic deeds?
LITERATURE
(People became storytellers. They created sagas, fables, epics, poetry, and plays about their ancestors and the people they knew. Later, people put these into writing for others to read)

900 How can I leave a record for people of the future?
HISTORY, GEOGRAPHY
AND BIOGRAPHY
(So people began to write about events that had occurred everywhere, and about people who had participated in these events)

000 GENERAL WORKS
The numbers up to 100 are used for bibliographics, books about books, and for books which contain information on many subjects. All reference books have *R* before the number.

NAME_____ SECTION_____

Sample Entries from the *Readers' Guide*

AIR pollution
How smog hurts your eyes. il Sci Digest 58:18 S '65
UCLA meteorologist sees civilization suffocating. Sci N L 88:136 Ag 28 '65
ANIMALS
Nature note; animal kingdom. Sci N L 88:155 S 4 '65
Training
In defense of bird brains. R. J. Herrnstein. il Atlan 216:101-4 S '65
ANTI-POVERTY program, 1964-
Politics and the poverty war; a look around the country. il U S News 59:61-3 S 6 '65
Poverty's neglected battlefront: legal aid. J. Witcover. Sat R 48:29-30 S 11 '65
See also
Los Angeles—Anti-poverty program
APPLICATIONS for positions
Tips for first-time job hunters. il Changing T 19:33-4 Jl '65
ARGO, Virgil N.
Mechanics of a turnover. Natur Hist 74: 26-9 bibliog(p74) Ag '65
AUDEN, Wystan Hugh
Epithalamium for Peter Mudford & Rita Auden; poem. New Yorker 41:34 Jl 31 '65
about
Poet's voice in the crowd. R. D. Spector. Sat R 48:29 Ag 7 '65
AURTHUR, Robert Alan
TV: the 21" bore. Nation 201:227-31 S 20 '65
AUTOMOBILES
Automobile in American life; symposium. il Atlan 216:73-108+ Jl '65; Discussion. 216: 52+ S '65
Testing
How good are American cars? J. R. Bond. Atlan 216:121-4 Jl '65; Same abr. Read Digest 87:174-6 S '65

BABIES. See Infants
BEN BELLA, Ahmed
Atlantic report. Atlan 216:14+ S '65
BERLIN (West Berlin)
Berlin: the cultural capital. Holiday 38:102 S '65
BERLIN wall, 1961-
Wall: three years later. E. von Kuegelgen. Nat R 17:764-5 S 7 '65
BICYCLES
Look what's happening to bicycles. A. Wall. il Pop Sci 187:108-11+ Ag '65
BIGGEST watermelon anybody ever saw; story. See Saroyan, W.
BLAKEY, G. Robert
Crisis in crime control. America 113:238-40 S 4 '65
BOND, John R.
How good are American cars? Atlan 216:121-4 Jl '65; Same abr. Read Digest 87:174-6 S '65
BURNS, James MacGregor
Shadow presidency. Nation 201:115-18 S 6 '65

CAMPING
Family approach to regional planning; Rocky Mountain National Park. D. S. Moore. Nat Parks Mag 39:19 S '65
Mexico
What's it like to camp in Mexico? Sunset 135: 50+ S '65
CARROLL, James D.
Forgotten amendment. Nation 201:121-2 S 6 '65
CHEKHOV, Anton Pavlovich
Cherry orchard. Criticism
Nation 201:87-8 Ag 16 '65
CHEN, Theodore H. E.
New citizens for a new society. bibliog f Cur Hist 49:155-63 S '65
CHERRY orchard; drama. See Chekhov, A. P.
CHICKEN-god; story. See Evtushenko, Y.
COLLEGE, Choice of
Which college is best? J. A. Perkins. il Sat R 48:71-2+ S 11 '65
COMPUTERS
What computers can't do. L. Eisenberg. il Harper 231:96-9 Ag '65

CRIME and criminals
United States
Crisis in crime control. G. R. Blakey. America 113:238-40 S 4 '65
See also
Criminal statistics
CRIMINAL statistics
Safest large city. il Am City 80:160+ Ag '65
CROWS
I love those ornery rascals. R. Starnes. Field & S 70:16+ S '65

DANCING
How I became a dancer. M. Graham. il Sat R 48:54 Ag 28 '65
DEAD SEA scrolls
Dead Sea scrolls: a new historical approach, by C. Roth. Review
Sat R 48:22-3 S 4 '65. T. H. Gaster
DE CARVALHO, George
Everything's up to date in Kuwait. Life 59: 96-8+ S 17 '65
DINOSAURS
Were dinosaurs a failure? A. Smith. il Sci Digest 58:86-9 S '65
DISNEY, Walt
Day with Disney. F. Whitaker. il por Am Artist 29:44-8+ S '65
DRAMAS
Criticisms, plots, etc.
Single works
See name of author for full entry
Cherry orchard. A. P. Chekhov
Homecoming. H. Pinter
Inadmissible evidence. J. Osborne
Odd couple. N. Simon

ECLIPSES, Solar
Further notes on the eclipse. il Sky & Tel 30:150 S '65
EDUCATION
China (People's Republic)
New citizens for a new society. T. H. E. Chen. bibliog f il Cur Hist 49:155-63 S '65
Russia
Soviet education's unsolved problems. H. J. Noah. il Sat R 48:54-6+ Ag 21 '65
United States
Faddishness in education. M. Smith. Sat R 48:53 Ag 21 '65
See also
Education of women—United States
EDUCATION of women
United States
Come back to the work force, mother! L. Velie. Read Digest 87:201-2+ S '65
ENGLISH language
Dictionary of modern English usage, by H. W. Fowler. Review
Life 59:6+ Ag 20 '65. G. Frazier
Terms and phrases
How not to write, what not to say. L. Kronenberger. Atlan 216:97-100 S '65
ERIE, LAKE
Hideous Hudson River: Lake Erie is dirty, too. America 113:148 Ag 14 '65
EVTUSHENKO, Evgenii Aleksandrovich
Chicken-god; story; tr. by D. Mann. Harper 231:64-8 Ag '65

FM. See Radio frequency modulation
FALL, Bernard B.
If Ho Chi Minh's army moves south in force—. N Y Times Mag p7+ S 5 '65
FLEMING, D. F.
Can Pax Americana succeed? Ann Am Acad 360:127-38 Jl '65
FRAZIER, George
Fowler's love affair with the language. Life 59:6+ Ag 20 '65

NAME _____ SECTION _____

Worksheet on the *Readers' Guide*

1. Make a list of the magazines subscribed to by your library.

2. Find the meanings for the following abbreviations:

abr	D	m	sup
Ag	ed	Mr	v
Ap	F	My	w
bibliog	il	N	+
bi-m	Ja	no	Sr Schol
bi-w	Je	O	Pop Sci
cond	Jl	S	Good H

3. Explain what is meant by a "See also" reference.

4. Explain each of the items in the following subject entry:

   Automobiles
       Automobile in American life, J.R. Bond. il.
       Read Digest 87:201-2+ S '65

   Automobiles -

   Automobile in American Life -

   J. R. Bond -

   il -

   Read Digest -

   87 -

   201-2+ -

   S -

   '65 -

5. Using the *Readers' Guide,* find and list the entry for one article on each of the following subjects:

   Eclipses -

   College students -

   White House -

6. For each of the above articles, write down the information needed to find the magazine.

NAME_____   SECTION_____

Quiz on the *Readers' Guide*

INSTRUCTIONS: Study the above Readers' Guide *entries and answer the following questions.*

1. Define an author entry. _____
_____

2. Give the example from the above list. _____
_____

3. If you were to change it to a subject entry, what would the subject be?_____
_____

4. Define a subject entry. _____
_____

5. Give an example from the above list. _____
_____

6. If you were to change it to an author entry, what would the heading be?_____
_____

7. Which entry has several magazines?_____
_____

8. Define a cross reference. _____
_____

9. Give an example from the above list. _____
_____

10. All but one magazine is from the same month. What is the title of that magazine?_____
_____

11. Which article is continued on other pages in the magazine? _____
_____

12. Which magazine article has pictures in it?_____
_____

13. List which magazines are published more than once a month. _____
_____

14. Give the author of an article on moving picture censorship. _____
_____

NAME _____   SECTION _____

The Card Catalog

The card catalog contains cards listing information about every book in the library, fiction and non-fiction alike.

The basic information includes the following: (See card below.)
  A. call number - 921
  B. subject - football
  C. author's name - Lou Greenwood
  D. author's birthday (and date of death if deceased) - 1923 - (1923–1974)
  E. title of the book - *Fourth and Goal*
  F. publisher - Prentice Books
  G. copyright date - 1960
  H. number of pages - 244
  I. illustrations (if any) - illus.
  J. other information which may include maps, annotation, tracing line, Library of Congress number, Dewey Decimal classification, and others.

For each book included, there are three types of cards in the card catalog. They are the subject card, author card and title card. All contain the same information but are listed and placed according to one of the three headings: subject, author or title.

```
921
  G  FOOTBALL
     Greenwood, Lou 1923–
     Fourth and Goal.
     Prentice Books 1960
     244p.  illus
```

The card catalog is set up alphabetically with drawer labels such as CEL-CRO, RYT-SAM, and VAL-YOU.

Call numbers of books of fiction consist of the letter "F" and the first letter of the author's last name. Story collections may be found with the letters SC in place of the author's initial.

```
921
  G  FOOTBALL
     Greenwood, Lou 1923–
```

```
921
  G   Greenwood, Lou 1923–
      Fourth and Goal
```

```
921
  G   Fourth and Goal
      Greenwood, Lou 1923–
```

NAME_____ SECTION_____

Worksheet on the Card Catalog

1. Name the three types of listings found for each book in the card catalog.

2. List at least eight types of information found on a card in the card catalog.

3. Using whatever information you need from the following list, make a card catalog entry on the card below.

   A book explains the workings of an automobile exhaust system. The author, Ronald Lewis, calls his book *By-products of Combustion.* In it he has diagrams and charts to explain his main points. Pictures of different types of systems help the reader to understand the principles of exhaust systems. Holt and Company were glad to publish this book, which costs $5.95. This is not expensive for a modern (1976) 375-page book. Mr. Lewis said that he was glad he waited until he was 50 before he had the book published, since he learned a lot of things while he worked on his son's cars.

4. Identify the area of the library one would look to find the following books. If the book is fiction, explain the letters given. If the book is non-fiction, give the Dewey Decimal classification where it is found.

   a) F.   c) F.   e) 655.36
       SC   L   L
   b) 944   d) 095
       C   W

   a)
   b)
   c)
   d)
   e)

NAME_____ SECTION_____

Quiz on Finding Information in the Library

1. List the categories of the DDS and assign them their correct numbers.

2. Place each of the following books in its most likely DDS category:
   A. *Catholicism, Then and Now*
   B. *Japan, A Nation on the Rise*
   C. *Fruitbearing Trees of North America*
   D. *Waterskiing for Beginners*
   E. *Poems of Rod McKuen*

3. Match the following:
   A. Glossary   _____ 1. Includes name of book, author and publisher
   B. Index   _____ 2. List of terms (vocabulary) found in text
   C. Title Page   _____ 3. Alphabetical list of sources used in writing the book
   D. Bibliography   _____ 4. Introduction to book
   E. Preface   _____ 5. Alphabetical list of subjects and their pages

4. List a reference book where one would most likely find the following:
   A. Synonym for "illegal"
   B. Author of a poem
   C. Rivers in Ohio
   D. Birthdate of Groucho Marx
   E. Population of Chicago

5. Identify each part of the following *Readers' Guide* entry:
   The Ranger's Lone Ranger, Paul Eisner, il Sp. Illus., 44:86–8 Je, 7, 1975

6. Answer the following questions about the catalog card
   on the right.
   A. What is its DDS classification?
   B. What does 1923 represent?
   C. What kind of card is this: Author, title, or subject?
   D. What is "Doubleday?"
   E. Are there pictures in the book?

   ```
   876.7

    S  Scott, Walter 1832-1923
       Lady of the Lake
       Doubleday 1965
       313p illus
   ```

NAME _____ SECTION_____

Quiz on Finding Information in the Library

I. PUT (T) OR (F) IN THE BLANK AT THE RIGHT OF EACH STATEMENT.

1. The index to the *World Almanac* is in the front. _____

2. A book about automobiles would be found in the 600's ("Applied Science"). _____

3. If a book is reprinted using the same material as before, it is called a revised edition. _____

4. The table of contents is arranged in alphabetical order. _____

5. The *Readers' Guide* is an index to magazines. _____

6. The colonial period in United States history is listed in the "g" drawer of the card catalog. _____

7. A bibliography is a list of books. _____

8. *Collier's* is a junior encyclopedia. _____

9. Webster's secondary school dictionary will give all possible meanings of a word. _____

10. *Current Biography* is a logical place to look for a picture of Bing Crosby. _____

11. It is not necessary to know the title of a magazine article to look up the article in the *Readers' Guide.* _____

12. The title card for the book *Dr. Tom Dooley* would be found after the subject DOGS in the card catalog. _____

13. A biography of Abraham Lincoln is in *Who's Who in America.* _____

14. The library receives only two copies of the *Readers' Guide* each year. _____

15. Supplementary material in a book is called the appendix. _____

16. Richard's *Atlas of New York State* is a logical place to look for material about New York State Indians. _____

17. Factual books about sports are in the 700's, a range where books on music and art are also found. _____

18. Biographies of individuals are arranged according to the initial of the author's last name. _____

19. The story collection is marked SC and is found after the 800's on the shelves. _____

20. The Dewey Decimal System divides books into ten classes. _____

21. Cross references are used in the *Readers' Guide,* the card catalog and encyclopedias. _____

22. *A Night to Remember* is listed in the "A" drawer of the card catalog. _____

23. Non-fiction books are arranged according to their subject matter. _____

24. A class number is the same as the Dewey Decimal number. _____

25. The copyright date is usually found on the back of the title page. _____

26. In the card catalog a subject heading is written either in capitals or in red. _____

27. All reference books in the library may be borrowed overnight. _____
28. Books on folklore are numbered 398. _____
29. When I request back copies of magazines, each magazine should be listed separately on a 3x5 card. _____
30. Two cents a day is charged for overdue books and $.25 a day for overdue reference books. _____
31. A biography of Christopher Columbus is found in *Webster's Biographical Dictionary*. _____
32. Acknowledgments in a book tell where you may look for more information. _____
33. If I lose my library pass card, I may borrow a card from someone else. _____
34. I can look up a magazine article in the *Readers' Guide* under its title. _____
35. If I do not know the meaning of the abbreviations in the *Readers' Guide,* I should ask the librarian. _____
36. Books written to help you learn French are in the 400's. _____
37. All books in circulation may be renewed indefinitely. _____
38. Statistics on many different subjects will be found in the *World Almanac.* _____
39. A copyright protects authors' rights to have income from their books. _____
40. The logical place to look for pamphlets is the vertical file. _____

II. **BELOW ARE SIX DRAWERS OF THE CARD CATALOG. GIVE THE NUMBER OF THE DRAWER IN WHICH YOU WOULD FIND THE FOLLOWING ITEMS.**

A	Ba-Bi	Bj-By	C	L-M	T-Z
1	2	3	4	5	6

no. of drawer

10,000 Jokes, Toasts, and Stories _____

The Witch of Blackbird Pond _____

BASKETBALL - FICTION _____

After the Civil War _____

BOATS AND BOATING _____

CARTOONS AND CARICATURES _____

Those 163 days _____

Mays, Willie _____

MYSTERY AND DETECTIVE STORIES _____

A Time to Stand _____

III. BELOW ARE FOUR CARDS FROM THE CATALOG. USING THESE, ANSWER EACH OF THE QUESTIONS THAT FOLLOW.

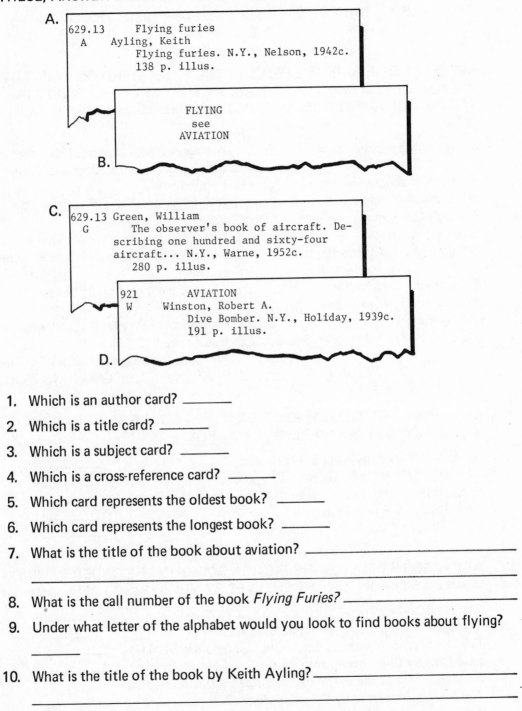

A.
```
629.13      Flying furies
  A     Ayling, Keith
              Flying furies. N.Y., Nelson, 1942c.
          138 p. illus.
```

```
          FLYING
            see
          AVIATION
```
B.

C.
```
629.13 Green, William
   G        The observer's book of aircraft. De-
        scribing one hundred and sixty-four
        aircraft... N.Y., Warne, 1952c.
          280 p. illus.
```

```
921         AVIATION
  W     Winston, Robert A.
          Dive Bomber. N.Y., Holiday, 1939c.
          191 p. illus.
```
D.

1. Which is an author card? _____

2. Which is a title card? _____

3. Which is a subject card? _____

4. Which is a cross-reference card? _____

5. Which card represents the oldest book? _____

6. Which card represents the longest book? _____

7. What is the title of the book about aviation? _____

_____

8. What is the call number of the book *Flying Furies?* _____

9. Under what letter of the alphabet would you look to find books about flying?

_____

10. What is the title of the book by Keith Ayling? _____

_____

11. Who wrote the book titled *The Observer's Book of Aircraft?* _____

_____

IV.   ARRANGE THE FOLLOWING CALL NUMBERS OF BOOKS IN CORRECT ORDER
BY NUMBERING THEM FROM 1 TO 8.

359	070.4	822	359	822.08	921	822.3	500
L	F	I	S	C	A	B	C

V.   REFERENCE: BEFORE THE ITEMS IN THE RIGHT-HAND COLUMN, PUT THE
NUMBER OF THE REFERENCE TOOL AT THE LEFT WHICH YOU WOULD USE
TO FIND THE ANSWER. (SOME NUMBERS WILL BE USED MORE THAN
ONCE.)

1.   *Richard's Atlas of New
     York State*
2.   *Current Biography*
3.   *World Almanac*
4.   *Card Catalog*
5.   *Readers' Guide*
6.   *Encyclopaedia Britannica*
7.   *Who's Who in America*
8.   *Goode's World Atlas*
9.   *Webster's Biographical
     Dictionary*

_____ A magazine article about U.S. space efforts.
_____ Biographical information about John F.
Kennedy
_____ A description of the life of the Iroquois
Indians
_____ Name of a book about skin diving
_____ Names of the members of the President's
cabinet
_____ All possible meanings of the word
"induction"
_____ Biography of Charles A. Lindbergh
_____ Map of the U.S.S.R.
_____ The author of the book *Day of Infamy*
_____ Biography of John Glenn (with a picture)

VI.   SHOW HOW THE FOLLOWING BIOGRAPHIES WOULD BE ARRANGED ON
THE SHELVES BY NUMBERING THEM FROM 1-5.

Sir Walter Raleigh by Nina Baker Brown   _____
The Wright Brothers by Quentin Reynolds   _____
Ethan Allen and the Green Mountain Boys by Slater Brown   _____
Lou Gehrig by Frank Graham   _____
Bing Crosby's Own Story: Call Me Lucky   _____

VII.   ARRANGE THE FOLLOWING FICTION BOOKS IN THE ORDER IN WHICH THEY
WOULD BE PLACED ON THE SHELVES BY NUMBERING THEM FROM 1-10.

Captain Blood by Rafael Sabatini   _____
The Swiss Family Robinson by Johann Wyss   _____
Twenty Thousand Leagues Under the Sea by Jules Verne   _____
Jane Eyre by Charlotte Bronte   _____
We Were There at the Battle of the Bulge by David Sheperd   _____
The Scarlet Pimpernel by Baroness Orczy   _____
Adventures of Sherlock Holmes by A. Conan Doyle   _____
Drums along the Mohawk by Walter Edmonds   _____
Masked Prowler by John George   _____
The Old Man and the Sea by Ernest Hemingway   _____

VIII. TELL WHAT INFORMATION IS FOUND IN ANY SEVEN OF THE FOLLOWING PARTS OF THE BOOK.

Copyright date _____

Preface _____

Title Page _____

Index _____

Table of Contents _____

Introduction _____

Appendix _____

Bibliography _____

IX. IN THE ANSWERS TO THE QUESTIONS BELOW, NO BOOK MAY BE USED TWICE.

A. NAME THREE PLACES IN OUR LIBRARY WHERE YOU WOULD LOOK FOR INFORMATION ON THE MAN WHO IS NOW PRESIDENT OF THE UNITED STATES.

1. _____   2. _____

3. _____

B. NAME TWO PLACES WHERE YOU WOULD LOOK FOR MATERIAL ON ATOMIC ENERGY.

1. _____   2. _____

NAME _____ SECTION _____

Ten Steps For Writing A Research Report

1. *Select a topic.* Choose something you care about. Spending time and effort on a topic of no interest to you leads to poor results.

2. *Narrow the topic.* Find smaller subjects within the major topic, making certain that the subtopics can be handled well in a relatively small paper.

3. *Formulate a thesis statement.* Reduce the narrowed topic area to a statement that can be proven, or that can be argued with pros and cons.

4. *Gather information.* Use the card catalog, *Readers' Guide,* and encyclopedias, as well as any other available source. As each source is used, record it in a working bibliography (a numbered list of sources which includes the bibliographical information of each source).

5. *Take notes:* Use an orderly process to record information deemed pertinent to proving the thesis sentence. This is most effectively done on note cards, with each one numbered to show its place in the sequence and lettered to show the source used, as recorded in the working bibliography. Note cards should include quotes, paraphrases and summations in addition to general knowledge the student may find.

6. *Outline.* Arrange the notes into the best order for proving the thesis sentence. If little work is done on the outline then more work will be required in writing the paper. Conversely, a thorough outline will make writing the paper a relatively simple task.

7. *Write the first draft.* Following the outline and using the note cards, write the first draft of your paper.

8. *Proofread.* Go over the first draft to find errors and be certain thoughts are presented in the best possible way. This is also the time to make sure that quotes, paraphrases and footnotes are in order.

9. *Write the final paper.* Using the corrected first draft, consider the revisions, changes and set-up of the footnotes, and write the final paper.

10. *Proofread the final draft.* Read the final copy carefully to make absolutely certain there are no errors in mechanics, form or expression. The final copy includes a title page, the paper itself, and a bibliography.

NAME _____ SECTION _____

Ideas for Research Papers

a musician
a poet
an inventor
a sports hero
an author
a movie star
a political leader
water skiing
snow skiing
hobbies
travels
movies
marriage
family life
boating safety
flying
archery
lacrosse
horse racing
witches
superstitions
hypnotism
ESP
violence
dreams
the White House
architecture
ceramics
wild animals
blindness
space travel
trees
oceans
snakes
spiders
student rights
giving blood
18 year old vote
ants
whales
rare animals
logic

water pollution
insecticides
pioneers
assassinations
antiques
women's rights
electronics
guns
hunting
major weapons
working women
women's liberation
men's liberation
inflation
coin collecting
art
music
cooking
insects
farming
photography
human-made Satellites
propaganda techniques
capitalism
busing
suicide
juvenile delinquency
alcohol
tobacco
marijuana
hard drugs
population explosion
food shortages
dancing
heart transplants
ghettos
religions: Jewish
religions: Catholic
religions: Protestant
religions: eastern
forts
storms

China
Japan
competition
miracles
crime
origins of English
UFO's
comic books
American Indians
the Amish
helicopters
unions
the police
patriotism
national defense
self-defense
Socialism
Communism
teenage driving
the United Nations
masonry
bicycles
democracy
hockey
education
Watergate
forest preservation
dinosaurs
the Middle East
Russia
wars
roller derby
ice skating
recycling
human rights
stamp collecting
the stock market
scouting
dogs
horses
poetry
fairy tales

plants	weather problems	energy shortage
clothing styles	canals	cars
national parks	Greek philosophy	shoes
air pollution	mail carriers	frogs
coins and money	circus	holidays
newspapers	Eskimos	etiquette
motorcycles	TV Shows	pets
blood pressure	lumber business	realism
occupations	dating	epilepsy
retardation	exercise	part-time jobs
coaches		

Sample Note Cards

The government is doing several things to help control automobile pollution. Laws requiring the installation of pollution control equipment on all models have done much to decrease emission pollution. These standards are to be even more stringent in the years ahead.

Passage from Article

Note Cards Recording These Ideas

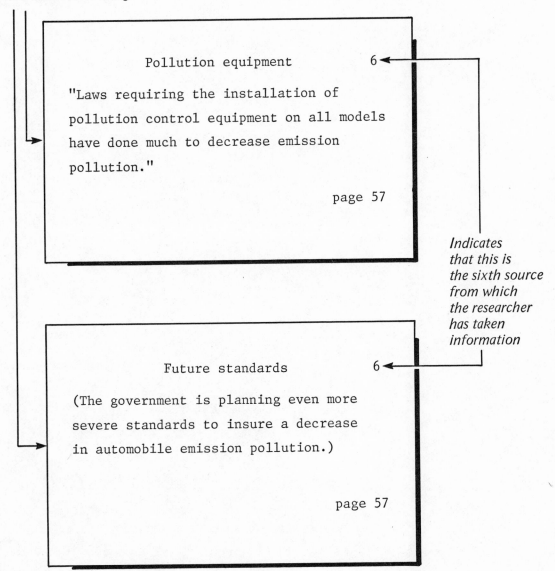

Indicates
that this is
the sixth source
from which
the researcher
has taken
information

NAME_____   SECTION_____

Worksheet on Notetaking

Less direct but still effective control came about when gas was in small supply and the number of miles driven was greatly reduced.

Mileage standards are being emphasized through publicizing EPA highway standards. Also the nation's car manufacturers are being encouraged to design and build cars which can deliver 40 mpg or better.

Ray Simon has said, "All Americans must make a strong effort to change their driving habits." With this kind of support from Washington, it seems reasonable to believe that automobile pollution will become less and less a factor in America's fight to clean up its air.

NAME_____ SECTION_____

The Bibliography

A bibliography is an alphabetized list of all information sources (books, magazines, ency-clopedias, pamphlets, interviews, etc.) used by an individual in writing an article, book, or paper.

The information that will ultimately go into the bibliography is obtained from each source as it is used. This information is usually written on 3 x 5 index cards. A separate card is kept for each source of information and is numbered to correspond to the number on the note cards from that source. Thus, each card represents one source, even though many pieces of information were obtained from that single source.

The following is a sample bibliography card for a book, the sixth source consulted by this researcher:

Type of source: book   6   ←——Number of
Author's name: Curtiss, John L.   source
Title: *After the Fact*
Place of publication: New York, New York
Publisher's name: Randolph Williams Co.
Copyright date: 1963

Once the researcher has recorded this information on the bibliography card, he or she can return the book to the library, can prepare the bibliography using only the bibliography cards, and can write the paper using only the notes on the note cards. Hence, the researcher does not have to keep all the works consulted on hand until the paper is finished.

FORMS FOR OTHER TYPES OF SOURCES:

Magazine: Type (magazine)
              Author's name
              Article title (in quotation marks)
              Magazine title (underlined)
              Volume number and page (separated by colon)
              Date

Encyclopedia: Type (encyclopedia)
              Author's name (if article is signed)
              Topic (in quotation marks)
              Title of encyclopedia (underlined)
              Year of edition
              Copyright date
              Volume and number
              Page

Newspaper: Type (newspaper)
                    Author (if given)
                    Title of article (in quotation marks)
                    Name of newspaper
                    Date
                    Page number

Interview: Type (interview)
                    Name of person interviewed
                    Date of interview
                    Place of interview

NAME _____ SECTION _____

Worksheet on Bibliography Cards

1. Book: *The Outsiders*
   author: S. E. Hinton
   page 47

   publisher — Bantam
   place — Boston
   date — 1962

2. Book: *Sister Carrie*
   author: Theodore Dreiser
   page 132

   publisher — Charles E. Merrill
   place — Columbus, Ohio
   date — 1969

3. Book: *The Word*
   author — Irving Wallace
   page 308

   publisher — Simon and Schuster
   place — New York
   date — 1972

4. Magazine: *Newsweek*
   article — "The Space Probe"
   pages 47-49

   date — May 14, 1968
   volume — 178
   author — Ralph Neely

5. Magazine: *Time*
   article — "A Future That Is Up for Grabs"
   pages 27-31

   date — November 20, 1972
   volume — 100
   author — none

6. Magazine: *Today's Education*
   article — "The Picture of America"
   pages 28-30

   date — November 1972
   volume — 61
   author — Charles B. Johnson, Jr.

7. Encyclopedia: *Colliers*
   author — Winston Bragg
   subject — whales
   page — 476

   publisher — Crowell Co. of Boston
   volume — 22
   printed — 1954

NAME_____ SECTION_____

Outlining Worksheet

1. Sort out the following items and fit them into the form listed below:
    Title — What I like about my hometown
    Main headings — location, school, facilities, people
    Unsorted list — friendly, near a large city, superior library, on a river, well trained
    teachers, parks, charitable, balanced curriculum, in the mountains,
    modern classrooms, recreation center, theaters

    Title —

    I.
        A.
        B.
        C.
    II.
        A.
        B.
        C.
        D.
    III.
        A.
        B.
        C.
    IV.
        A.
        B.

2. Now, without any heading outline for a guide, sort out the following and put them in a
    reasonable outline form.

    Bull dog   As Seeing Eye dog
    Irish setter   English setter
    Golden retriever   Sheep dog
    Kinds of dogs   German shepherd
    Poodles   Sport dogs
    Working dogs   House dogs
    Labrador retriever   Cocker spaniel
    As police dog   As guard dogs
    Retrievers   Setters

NAME _____ SECTION _____

Note Card Worksheet

Cars Manufactured 3 "Each day in Detroit, more than 18,000 cars come off the assembly line." pg. 84	**Equipment cuts 30%** 3 (If every car made was equipped with the devices already invented and tested, pollution from the automobile could be cut by at least 30%.) pg. 16
Future standards 1 (The government is planning even more severe standards to insure a decrease in automobile emission pollution.) pg. 57	**Conclusion** 4 "If these measures are taken, if this advice is followed, America will begin to rid itself of air pollution from the automobile." pg. 114
New equipment 4 (Invention of new equipment like pcv and catalytic converter is a large step forward.) pg. 111	**Tires, gas, etc.** 2 (Radial tires, nonleaded gas and smaller cars all aid in the drive to decrease the problem of automobile pollution.) pg. 117

1 Simon quote " 'All Americans must make a strong effort to change their driving habits.' " pg. 57	**4** Auto pollution #1 "Of all the threats to clean air that our country faces, automobile pollution has earned the right to be our number one priority." pg. 12

NAME _____ SECTION _____

Cars I Would Not Want to Own

John Richardson
(10th grade student)

There are over a quarter of a million automobiles sold in the United States each year. Many types are available; foreign cars and American cars, convertables and sedans, big cars and little cars. This variety is the result of the wide range of tastes of the driving population. There is three kinds of cars which doesn't suit my taste at all, and which I would never own. One type is impractical, another is little and ugly, and a third is poorly made.

An example of an impractical car is the Excalibur SS, perhaps you have never seen one of these cars. It bears a strong resemblance to the Dusenberg of years ago or to an old MG, early 1951 or 1952. One of the things I don't like about it are that it only comes in a convertable model. That's fine in the summer or on a sunny day, but when it rains or when winter comes, its rather impractical. Winter is perhaps the roughest though. Mainly because the car is not even equipped with a heater. And the softtop has plastic side windows and a plastic rear window that leaks and yellows in the sun and becomes briddle with age. This car is fitted with a 327 cubic inch engine from the Corvette Stingray. The car does not weigh more than 2000 pounds, compared to the Corvette, which weighs approximately 3200 pounds this year. With over 350 horsepower and so little weight, the Excalibur is very dangerous, you can't come near controlling shortcommings with a $10,000 price tag, you have a very impractical car.

A car that I wouldn't want is one of those ugly little foreign "bugs" you see everywhere. The Volkswagen is a good example, this simply isn't my idea of a car with good looks. In addition, its to small for safety. If you were hit in the side by a large car or by a truck, you'd be finished. You also can't ride for great distances in comfort, because the engine is to noisy and the interior is cramped. Another shortcomming is that Volkswagen's are to common. I don't want a car that every mothers son has, and if you look around any large parking lot in this city, you are bound to see at least ten Volkswagen's. Besides being so common, this car is to underpowered for freeway driving. Its almost impossible to pass a car on the expressway at sixty miles per hour, if there is a stiff crosswind blowing, you would think you were on a roller coaster. This is both unpleasant and unsafe.

The third type of car that I wouldn't like to own is one that is cheaply made. Ford Mustangs fall into this class—my family owned one once, and before we got rid of it the muffler fell off at least five times. By the time we sold it six months later, there was rattles in every corner. Meanwhile, the paint had started peeling off, to say nothing of the first layer of chrome on the bumpers. To top it off, whenever the driver made a hard left turn, the door on the passenger's side would fly open. My uncle own a Cougar, and it doesn't have these problems.

NAME _____ SECTION _____

Look-Alikes/Sound-Alikes

1. accent — ascent — assent
2. accept — except
3. access — excess
4. adapt — adept — adopt
5. advice — advise
6. affect — effect
7. allay — alley — alleys — allies — ally
8. already — all ready
9. altogether — all together
10. allude — elude
11. altar — alter
12. always — all ways
13. an — and
14. angel — angle
15. ante — anti- auntie
16. appraise — apprise
17. are — or — our — ore
18. assure — insure
19. attendance — attendants
20. bail — bale
21. ball — bole — boll — bowl
22. baring — barring — bearing
23. bear — bare
24. beat — beet
25. berry — bury
26. berth — birth
27. biding — bidding
28. blew — blue
29. boar — bore
30. board — bored
31. boarder — border
32. born — borne
33. brake — break
34. bread — bred
35. breadth — breath — breathe
36. brewed — brood
37. bridal — bridle
38. build — billed
39. Calvary — cavalry
40. capital — capitol
41. carat — caret — carrot
42. casual — causal
43. ceiling — sealing
44. cent — scent — sent
45. choose — chose
46. chord — cord
47. cite — sight — site
48. clothes — cloths
49. coarse — course
50. coma — comma
51. complement — compliment .
52. confidant — confident
53. conscience — conscious
54. conscientiousness — consciousness
55. consul — council — counsel
56. coral — corral
57. core — corps — corpse
58. costume — custom
59. creak — creek
60. crews — cruise
61. dairy — diary
62. days — daze
63. dear — deer
64. decease — disease
65. decent — descent — dissent
66. dependence — dependents
67. desert — desert — dessert
68. detract — distract
69. device — devise
70. die — dye
71. dining — dinning
72. dual — duel
73. due — do
74. emigrate — immigrate
75. envelop — envelope
76. ever — every
77. exalt — exult
78. extant — extent — extinct
79. faint — feint
80. fair — fare
81. fir — fur
82. flair — flare
83. flea — flee
84. flour — flower

85. forbear — forebear
86. foreward — forward
87. formally — formerly
88. forth — fourth
89. gilt — guilt
90. grip — gripe
91. hail — hale
92. hair — hare
93. hart — heart
94. heal — heel
95. hear — here
96. hoard — horde
97. hole — whole
98. holy — wholly
99. hoping — hopping
100. human — humane
101. idle — idol
102. its — it's
103. knew — new
104. later — latter
105. lead — lead — led
106. least — lest — leased
107. lessen — lesson
108. lie — lye
109. lightening — lightning
110. loan — lone
111. loose — lose — loss
112. mail — male
113. main — mane
114. manner — manor
115. maybe — may be
116. meat — meet
117. medal — meddle — metal — mettle
118. minor — miner
119. moral — morale
120. morning — mourning

121. of — off
122. on — one — won
123. pail — pale
124. pain — pane
125. pair — pare — pear
126. passed — past
127. peace — piece
128. pedal — peddle — petal
129. personal — personnel
130. pray — prey
131. precede — proceed
132. principal — principle
133. quiet — quite
134. right — rite — write
135. sail — sale
136. shear — sheer
137. shone — shown
138. sole — soul
139. stair — stare
140. stationary — stationery
141. steal — steel
142. tail — tale
143. then — than
144. their — there — they're
145. therefor — therefore
146. though — through — threw — thorough
147. to — too — two
148. tolled — told
149. vain — vane — vein
150. vice — vise
151. waist — waste
152. weather — whether
153. were — we're — where
154. whose — sho's
155. yolk — yoke
156. your — You're — yore

NAME _____ SECTION _____

Spelling Demons

there — their — they're
its — it's
to — too — two
forty
definite — definitely
occurred — occurrence
loneliness — lonely
receive, conceive, etc.
believe, relieve, etc.
thorough
friend
psychology
philosophy
cite — site — sight
height — weight — freight
congratulations
flow — flowed
fly — flew
tie — tied
fry — fried — try — tried
occasion
incidentally — accidentally

professor — profession
principle — principal
immediately
accept — except
led — lead
effect — affect
similar
truly — duly
whole — wholly
fire — fiery
maintenance
athlete
confidence
relevant
privilege
grammar
background
college
supposedly
undoubtedly
sense — since — scents
consider

overcoming — coming
recognize
passed — past
recommend
piece — peace
always
pastime
lose — loose
chose — choose
temperature
miniature
whether — weather
tragedy
than — then
separate
cloths — clothes
conscious
conscience
boundary
a lot
cemetery

NAME_____   SECTION_____

Sentence Cards for Spelling Game

1. I really like them; their my friends.
2. She excepted our invitation to go to the game.
3. Don't ask me; its they're decision.
4. I was relieved to find that I past my math test.
5. We had very bad whether last week.
6. Don't worry; everything will be all right.
7. I walked right in to the wall.
8. She was very impolite; she didn't have any manors.
9. It was a beautiful site to see.
10. Sam forgot about his piano lessen.
11. In England we saw many beautiful feudal manners.
12. It's a locale store.
13. She threw the fruit away; it was a real waist.
14. I really liked the play, irregardless of what the critics said.
15. This rule is generally true; however, their are a few acceptions.
16. I all ready paid that bill.
17. May I sit down?
18. Whose their?
19. I don't no witch book you want.
20. Who do you wish to sea?
21. I recieved too lovly Christmas cards.
22. Your the best friend I've ever had.
23. Linda wrote the letter, stamped the envelope, ceiled, and maled it.
24. Were very disappointed with Sue's performance.
25. Liberty is a basic human rite.
26. Hours past while we weighted.

27. I gave her good advise.
28. I think that Bobby is taller then she.
29. She looked beautiful in her wedding gown as she walked down the isle.
30. He was a fine person; I believe his sole will go to heaven.
31. I studied the principals of geometry for more than three ours.
32. Their was no apparent effect.
33. The door handle was very lose; it must of fallen off.
34. The road was a dead end; it lead too a grassy field.
35. Its to hard to understand; let's forget it.
36. They were making to much noise; I tolled them to be quite.
37. The highway was long, narrow and strait.
38. Eugene O'Neill was a great playwrite.
39. Jennifer all ways ware tie-died jeans.
40. She had two go a way on vacation.
41. This year they're were fewer at the party then last.
42. We studied the ancient rights and rituals.
43. The principle suspended five students.
44. Everyone attended accept Jill.
45. Mr. Young was the soul survivor of the crash.
46. That's you're coat.
47. The coral straights are about a mile from the Canary Aisles.
48. Who's dog is that?
49. Forget it; its all in the passed.
50. Our house is being built on a new cite.

51. Since Carrie died her hair black, she looks like a which.
52. She tried too advice me.
53. I am sole air to the company fortune.
54. I don't care weather you bring the pizza or the drinks.
55. She eats to much candy; she's gaining alot of wait.
56. I agree; your one-hundred percent rite.
57. It was a vary boaring experience.
58. She fell down the stares and broke her leg.
59. Lisa was speeding when the light changed; she slammed on the breaks.
60. He burned the rug with the acid and lie.
61. The plain sored threw the sky as it made its assent.
62. The police told us too excess the damage.
63. The Carters adapted a three-month old baby.
64. He was robbed in a narrow, dark allay.
65. What you are doing is all together wrong.
66. She eluded to the classics on several occasions.
67. Don't altar your plans on are account.
68. You an Margaret look a like.
69. Little Elizabeth has a face like an angle.
70. Don't be sew ante-social.
71. The insurance agent apprised our house.
72. The diamonds are assured for one thousand dollars.
73. The family was not in attendance.
74. I baled you out of jail the last time.

75. Diane ate the hole bole of fruit.
76. The hunter shot but mist the bare.
77. Alice dyed Friday; they berried her too days latter.
78. We all celebrated her berthday.
79. The wind was fierce; it blue all night.
80. I served on the Bored of Education.
81. The dress had a pretty, em-broidered border.
82. I was bourne in February.
83. The entire bridle party was dressed in blew.
84. We didn't have any cash, so the car sailsman build us a month latter.
85. The capitol of New York State is Albany.
86. There weren't any carats in the salad.
87. It was a vary fragrant cent.
88. I choose this option.
89. The chord snapped and the plant feel.
90. Leigh bought all knew cloths.
91. She confused the coma and the semicolon.
92. I complemented her on her great ideas.
93. She was very confidant.
94. She wasn't conscience of the problem.
95. The book was designed to expand the readers' conscientiousness.
96. I was late for the student counsel meeting.
97. John joined the Piece Core.
98. Every culture has its own set of traditions and customs.
99. The water emptied into a little creek.
100. Her parents went on a luxury crews.
101. The hunter shoot three dear.

102. Cancer is a serious decease.
103. Her helplessness and depen-dents are irritating.
104. We had ice cream for desert.
105. Their was so much noise, that I was detracted.
106. The experts devised a good plan.
107. We had diner at five-thirty.
108. It was a two-fold situation; it had a duel purpose.
109. They decided to make Eddie due the work.
110. They emigrated to this country fifty years ago.
111. I don't no to what extant she agreed.
112. David was dizzy, pail, and feint.
113. The bus fair was increased alot.
114. Our Christmas tree was a northern fur.
115. You have a flare with words.
116. Max, our dog, has flees.
117. The receipt required eggs, flower, and milk.
118. The lunch line was to long, so we pushed foreword.
119. The meeting was conducted very formerly.
120. Darlene ranked forth in the beauty contest.
121. The police new that she was gilty by the sick look on her face.
122. The karate expert had a tight gripe on his opponent.
123. Snow, sleet, and hail feel for hours.
124. The small hair dodged off into the woods.
125. Dr. Barnard performed the first hart transplant.
126. The heal came off my knew shoes.
127. The music was so loud that I couldn't here the speaker.

128. Tomorrow is a wholly day.
129. The answer alludes me at the present.
130. The statue represented an old Egyptian idel.
131. Our city boasts the leased number of accidents.
132. The thunder and lightening scarred Missy.
133. Michael implied for a lone.
134. Go threw the mane entrance.
135. Stake is my favorite meet.
136. The brave soldier received a special honorary metal.
137. The accident occured at midnight.
138. The tempature rose thirty degrees.
139. The old lady looked vary lonly.
140. After I gradate from high school I am hopping to go too collage.
141. Meeting the King was a great honer and privledge.
142. I hate spelling, puntu-ation, and grammar.
143. We made gravestone rubbings at the cemetary.
144. She had changed so much that I didn't reconize her.
145. *Othello* is one of Shake-speare's tradgedies.
146. Joan ownes fourty albums.
147. I'm definitly in favor of your suggestion.
148. I mean this vary sincerly.
149. Use your common scents.
150. She did a comprehensive, through job.
151. You are my freind; I be-leive everything you say.
152. Allow me to congradulate you on your new ap-pointment.
153. I tryed my best to be a good athelete.

154. Psychology and Phylosophy are two entirely seperate feilds.
155. I didn't do it on purpose; it was an incident.
156. What's your favorite past-time?
157. The minature is very simular to the orignal.
158. What do you consider relevent?
159. I don't like fir coats; I perfer lether.
160. The cut looked soar; it didn't heel vary well.

161. He though the ball threw the window.
162. The captain saluted and boughed.
163. The sky was a pail blew.
164. Cite all references.
165. There were fewer car accidents this year than last.
166. The principal gave all the students a two-week vacation.
167. Of the two, you're the better dancer.
168. It's your party; do as you please.

169. Who's at the door?
170. Everything is all right.
171. May I give my opinion?
172. Everyone must listen; there are no exceptions.
173. I am very confident that everything will be fine.
174. The old man was losing his sight.
175. The cow escaped from the corral.
176. I can't draw a straight line.
177. There is less water in this container than in the other.
178. We were never formally introduced.

NAME _____ SECTION _____

Game Board

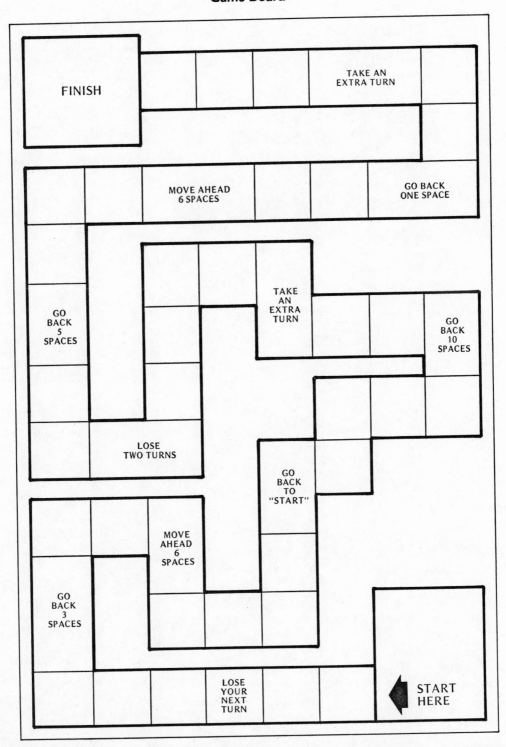

FINISH

TAKE AN
EXTRA TURN

MOVE AHEAD
6 SPACES

GO BACK
ONE SPACE

GO
BACK
5
SPACES

TAKE
AN
EXTRA
TURN

GO
BACK
10
SPACES

LOSE
TWO TURNS

GO
BACK
TO
"START"

MOVE
AHEAD
6
SPACES

GO
BACK
3
SPACES

LOSE
YOUR
NEXT
TURN

START
HERE

NAME _____ SECTION _____

Instructions For Playing The Spelling Game

1. Approximately four persons can play this game.

2. Lay the game board on the floor or other flat surface such as a table or desk.

3. Give the answer key to one person (either a player or someone who wants to watch but not play). This person will consult the answer key when necessary to check an answer, and hence will be referred to as "the Judge." Warn the Judge not to let anyone see the answers.

4. Shuffle and stack all the sentence cards. Place them face down near the game board.

5. Roll dice or draw lots or guess a number to determine who goes first.

6. Place your markers in the space labelled "Start" on the game board.

7. The first player draws a sentence card from the top of the stack. The player reads it and determines whether or not all of the words are spelled according to acceptable standard English. Sentences may contain one or more errors.

8. If the player decides that there are no spelling errors in the sentence, he or she must show it to the other players to see whether they agree. If they don't agree, the Judge checks the answer key. If the Judge upholds the player's opinion, then the player may move ahead two spaces. If the player is wrong (that is, if the sentence does contain misspelled words), then he or she loses the next turn.

9. If the player decides that a word or words in the sentence are misspelled, he or she must identify each, correctly spell each, and explain the correction. If the Judge and other players agree with the player's correction(s), the player may move ahead the number of spaces equal to the number of misspelled words in the sentence. If the other players do not agree, then the group must discuss the question until they reach agreement. If they cannot agree, they must consult the Judge, whose answer, based on the key, overrules all other players. The Judge must explain the answer to the other players. If the player's answer is upheld by the Judge, then the player may move ahead as many spaces as there are misspelled words in the sentence; otherwise, the player may not move ahead or take his or her next turn.

10. The player whose marker reaches the "Finish" space first is the winner.

NAME_____   SECTION_____

Answer Key for Spelling Game

#	Answer	
1.	they're	(1)
2.	accepted	(1)
3.	it's, their	(2)
4.	passed	(1)
5.	weather	(1)
6.	all right	(1)
7.	into	(1)
8.	manners	(1)
9.	sight	(1)
10.	lesson	(1)
11.	manors	(1)
12.	local	(1)
13.	waste	(1)
14.	regardless	(1)
15.	there, exceptions	(2)
16.	already	(1)
17.	no errors	(2)
18.	who's there	(2)
19.	know, which	(2)
20.	whom, see	(2)
21.	received, two, lovely	(3)
22.	you're	(1)
23.	sealed, mailed	(2)
24.	we're	(1)
25.	right	(1)
26.	passed, waited	(2)
27.	advice	(1)
28.	than	(1)
29.	aisle	(1)
30.	soul	(1)
31.	principles, hours	(2)
32.	there	(1)
33.	loose, have (not of)	(2)
34.	led, to	(2)
35.	it's, too	(2)
36.	too, told, quiet	(3)
37.	straight	(1)
38.	playwright	(1)
39.	always, wears, tie-dyed	(3)
40.	to, away	(2)
41.	there, than	(2)
42.	rites	(1)
43.	principal	(1)
44.	except	(1)
45.	sole	(1)
46.	your	(1)
47.	straits, isles	(2)
48.	whose	(1)
49.	it's, past	(2)
50.	site	(1)
51.	dyed, witch	(2)
52.	to, advise	(2)
53.	heir	(1)
54.	whether	(1)
55.	too, a lot, weight	(3)
56.	you're, right	(2)
57.	very, boring	(2)
58.	stairs	(1)
59.	brakes	(1)
60.	lye	(1)
61.	plane, soared, through, ascent	(4)
62.	to, access	(2)
63.	adopted	(1)
64.	alley	(1)
65.	altogether	(1)
66.	alluded	(1)
67.	alter, our	(2)
68.	and, alike	(2)
69.	angel	(1)
70.	so, antisocial	(2)
71.	appraised	(1)
72.	insured	(1)
73.	attendance	(1)
74.	bailed	(1)
75.	whole, bowl	(2)
76.	missed, bear	(2)
77.	died, buried, two, later	(4)
78.	birthday	(1)
79.	blew	(1)
80.	Board	(1)
81.	border	(1)
82.	born	(1)
83.	bridal, blue	(2)

84.	car salesman, billed, later	(3)	
85.	capital	(1)	
86.	carrots	(1)	
87.	very, scent	(2)	
88.	no error	(2)	
89.	cord, fell	(2)	
90.	new, clothes	(2)	
91.	comma	(1)	
92.	complimented	(1)	
93.	confident	(1)	
94.	conscious	(1)	
95.	consciousness	(1)	
96.	council	(1)	
97.	Peace Corps	(2)	
98.	customs	(1)	
99.	creek	(1)	
100.	cruise	(1)	
101.	shot, deer	(2)	
102.	disease	(1)	
103.	dependence	(1)	
104.	dessert	(1)	
105.	distracted	(1)	
106.	no error	(2)	
107.	dinner	(1)	
108.	dual	(1)	
109.	do	(1)	
110.	immigrated	(1)	
111.	know, extent	(2)	
112.	pale, faint	(2)	
113.	fare, a lot	(2)	
114.	fir	(1)	
115.	flair	(1)	
116.	fleas	(1)	
117.	recipe, flour	(2)	
118.	too, forward	(2)	
119.	formally	(1)	
120.	fourth	(1)	
121.	knew, guilty	(2)	
122.	grip	(1)	
123.	hale, fell	(2)	
124.	hare	(1)	
125.	heart	(1)	
126.	heel, new	(2)	
127.	hear	(1)	
128.	holy	(1)	

129.	eludes	(1)
130.	idol	(1)
131.	least	(1)
132.	lightning, scared	(2)
133.	applied, loan	(2)
134.	through, main	(2)
135.	steak, meat	(2)
136.	medal	(1)
137.	occurred	(1)
138.	temperature	(1)
139.	very, lonely	(2)
140.	graduate, hoping, to, college	(4)
141.	honor, privilege	(2)
142.	punctuation, grammar	(2)
143.	cemetery	(1)
144.	recognize	(1)
145.	tragedies	(1)
146.	owns, forty	(2)
147.	definitely, favor	(2)
148.	very, sincerely	(2)
149.	sense	(1)
150.	thorough	(1)
151.	friend, believe	(2)
152.	congratulate	(1)
153.	tried, athlete	(2)
154.	psychology, philosophy, separate, fields	(4)
155.	accident	(1)
156.	pastime	(1)
157.	miniature, similar, original	(3)
158.	relevant	(1)
159.	fur, prefer, leather	(3)
160.	sore, heal, very	(3)
161.	threw, through	(2)
162.	bowed	(1)
163.	pale, blue	(2)
164.	no error	(2)
165.	no error	(2)
166.	no error	(2)
167.	no error	(2)
168.	no error	(2)
169.	no error	(2)
170.	no error	(2)
171.	no error	(2)

172.	no error	(2)	176.	no error	(2)
173.	no error	(2)	177.	no error	(2)
174.	no error	(2)	178.	no error	(2)
175.	no error	(2)			

NAME_____ SECTION_____

Spelling Proofreading Exercise

INSTRUCTIONS: Underline each word misspelled and write it correctly and legibly above the line.

Recently I learned a very important lesson about releiving my own problems rather than expecting others to help me bare my troubles. I had been feeling pretty blue for some time, My dog, who had been with me sinse I was a little more then a baby, just layed down one evening, on the bear basement floor, and dyed. Of coarse, I new he had lead a good life, and he was definately not young, having lived six years, or about the same as fourty two years in the life of a humane being. Therefore, his death shouldn't have been considered a tradgedy. But it was, nonetheless, a truely sad occassion, and I couldn't seem to get over the affect of loosing such a good old faithful friend.

One day it occured to me that I had not really tryed to do anything about overcomming the indefinate sence of loneliness that was making me feel depressed all the time, ever sinse my dog dyed. I hadn't truely tryed to except the fact that the death had occured, weather I choose to reconize it or not, and the time had come, I knew, when I must use good sence and move on into new activitys, seperating myself from the passed.

I decided to follow the principal of replacement in training myself to a new and better attitude. I would replace the fun I use to have with Beau with other pleasures and persuits. (Incidently, this method is good phsychology, and I recommend it to anyone who has alot of problems acheiving piece of mind after loosing a pet.)

The first thing I did on the evening this idea finally occured to me was to check the temparture on the thermometer outside my window. Sure enough, it was a lovely warm 70 degrees, perfect gardening whether, and I knew I'd be alright planting flower seeds. I quickly through on my gardening cloths and went to the garage to get the tools I had recieved as a birthday gift. I also took alot of seeds I had layed away for the spring day when the temperture would be alright for planting.

Bearing these things with me to the back yard, I began to plant seeds along the boundry of our yard. I choose a place where the sun almost allways shone. I felt better at once, as soon as I began digging in the warm soil. Gardening has allways been a soothing passtime for me and immediatly it began to divert my mind from poor Beau's death.

I did feel a little guilty about going ahead with the flower garden without waiting for my little brother, but I beleive the older child should have some priveleges which definately belong to him, so my conscious didn't hurt me to badly. My gardening soothed my spirit, and the whole experience lead me to a realization that life goes on, and one must move with it and not let any tradegy, wether major or miner, effect him to much.

NAME_____ SECTION_____

The Comma (,)

The comma is used:

1. To set off appositives (words that clarify or identify that which precedes or comes before it):

   Kristin, my younger sister, is going to Washington.

2. To set off a direct address (words that tell to whom a remark is directed):

   Listen, Diane, you'd better not be late again.

3. To set off a quotation:

   "Don't hit the telephone pole," shrieked the driver education teacher, "or you'll go back to study hall forever."

4. After each word in a series:

   The store was all out of peanuts, popcorn, and pretzels.

5. Following an introductory participial phrase:

   Hearing the bell, I ran!

6. Following such words as yes, no, oh, well, perhaps, etc.:

   Oh, what a beautiful dog.

7. Before the state in an address:

   Albany, New York

8. Between the day of the month and the year:

   June 24, 1950.

9. To set off such transitional expressions as however, therefore, conversely, and nevertheless:

   We all failed the test. It was, therefore, discarded.

The Colon (:)

The colon is used:

1. To introduce a famous quotation:

   We can fully understand Cassius's philosophy when he says:
   "The fault, dear Brutus, is not in our stars,
   But in ourselves, that we are underlings."

2. To set up or prepare the reader for a list or a series:

   The reasons for his dismissal include: tardiness, incompetence, dishonesty, and disrespect.

   Will the following people report to the office: Mary, Kevin, Bill, and Jo-Ann.

   The recipe calls for: butter, sugar, milk, and salt.

The Semicolon (;)

The semicolon is used:

1. To separate two independent clauses when the conjunction has been omitted:

    It rained all afternoon; we stayed in the house and watched television.

2. To separate items in a series that contains commas:

    The dinner list included: Martin Norton, Ph.D.; Kelly Gaffney, M.D.; and Henry Owens, D.D.S.

Quotation Marks (" ")

Quotation marks are used:

1. To indicate titles of poems, essays, short stories, songs, and articles:

    My favorite poem is "Dover Beach."

    Edgar Allen Poe's short story "The Masque of the Red Death" is frightening.

    The song title "Somebody Done Somebody Wrong Song" is the longest on the record.

    Do you like the poem "Ode to a Grecian Urn"?

2. To quote a person's direct comments:

    "It's nice to see you," said Mrs. Benson.

    "Where have you been?" asked Mary. "I've been waiting for an hour."

Underline (_____)

Underline:

1. To indicate the titles of novels, plays, paintings, and magazines:

    Picasso's Guernica is a famous painting.

    Daniel Defoe's Moll Flanders is one of the first British novels.

    Samuel Beckett's Waiting for Godot is one of the best modern plays.

    Do you read Time magazine?

The Apostrophe (')

Use the apostrophe:

1. To indicate possession. (Add an apostrophe and an "s" to most words to create the singular possessive form.):

    That is Alice's purse.

    Here is Jan's letter.

2. To indicate possession of a plural word. (Add an apostrophe for most words.):

    She is one of hundreds who belong to the Teachers' Association.

    Check The Readers' Guide to Periodical Literature.

In cases where the plural is not formed by adding an "s," an apostrophe and then an s should be added to form the possessive.

child (singular)   children (plural)   children's (plural possessive)
woman (singular)   women (plural)   women's (plural possessive)

Don't use apostrophes with possessive pronouns—theirs, ours, yours, mine, hers, his, its.

3. To indicate the omission of a letter in a contraction:

I didn't go. (didn't—did not: the apostrophe takes the place of the "o" in "not")

I wasn't at home. (wasn't — was not; the apostrophe takes the place of the "o" in "not")

The Period (.)

The period is used:

(1) To end a complete sentence:

I cannot find my car keys.

Tomorrow is Saturday.

(2) To punctuate abbreviations:

"Street" is abbreviated "St."

"Mister" is abbreviated "Mr."

"Missus" is abbreviated "Mrs."

"Governor" is abbreviated "Gov."

The Question Mark (?)

The question mark is used:

(1) As the end punctuation of an interrogative sentence (one that asks a question):

Where is the bank?

What is your name?

Who is that man over there?

When are you leaving?

NAME_____   SECTION_____

Sentence Cards for Punctuation Game

1. Mr. Martin who is our principal has been transferred.

2. We left on Sunday and arrived home the next day.

3. I bought records jeans and beads.

4. The test was difficult everyone failed.

5. Who wrote the poem The Road Not Taken.

6. The following people were late Bill Mary Bob Martin and Maureen.

7. Roads were slippery we therefore drove very carefully.

8. Where are you going.

9. The essays were interesting however there were many spelling errors.

10. Yes I agree.

11. The old ski lodge was torn down in August and a new one was built the next year.

12. Anne is a thoughtful friendly girl.

13. Robert Dobbs M.D. is her family doctor.

14. We visited Darwin White and Company Incorporated.

15. Mrs Waters Mr Moore and Ms Woodruff are school board members.

16. When I finally received my driver's license I was very excited.

17. Disturbed by the thunder the dog howled all night.

18. Stop that right now she yelled or I'll spank you.

19. Out out brief candle whispered the young actor.

20. May I quote asked Mrs. Green.

21. Oh you do look tired.

22. On February 23 1976 Sally leaves for Boston.

23. Allison was born in Maple Tree Falls Nebraska on May 9 1956.

24. The Mill on The Floss a sensitive poignant novel by George Eliot is a classic.

25. Seventeen is my favorite magazine my parents read Time.

26. Mrs. Conway said to check The Readers Guide to Periodical Literature.

27. He that hath the steerage of my course direct my sails read Larry who plays Hamlet.

28. What's so funny asked Cindy.

29. It's your house not theirs.

30. Go to the ladies department.

31. Carolyns friends are very nice.

32. James books are torn ripped and yellowed with age.

33. That car looks like the Smiths.

34. The students desks are dirty.

35. The childrens toys are broken.

36. The following people were not present: Mary Harvey, C.P.A.; Jason Barnes, M.D.

37. That's fine with me.

38. I bought flowers, candy, and clothes.

39. The book is a best-seller; everyone is reading it.

40. It is your decision, not mine.

Instructions for Punctuation Game

1. The object of the game is to match cards bearing punctuation marks with sentences that require those marks in order to be punctuated correctly. The first player to get rid of all his or her cards by properly matching sentences with punctuation marks is the winner.

2. Three to five persons can play this game.

3. Choose one person to serve as the Judge and hand him or her the answer key. This person will consult the answer key to determine whether a player has made a correct match. If necessary, the Judge can also be a player.

4. Shuffle the sentence cards (large ones) and place them in a stack face down.

5. Shuffle the punctuation marks cards (small ones) and place them in a stack face down.

6. Beside each stack of cards, turn one card face up as the beginning of a discard pile.

7. Have one player serve as dealer and give each player two sentence cards and two punctuation mark cards without looking at them.

8. The player to the right of the dealer goes first. First, the player draws a card from *either* the sentence card stack or the punctuation mark card stack. Or, the player can take either the sentence card or punctuation mark card that has been placed face up on the discard pile. Whichever choice the player takes, he or she draws only one card. Then the player attempts to match Sentence Cards and Punctuation Mark Cards in order to punctuate the sentences correctly. For example, if the player has a Sentence Card that needs a semi-colon and a comma in order to be correctly punctuated, and if there happens to be a semi-colon and a comma among his or her Punctuation Marks, the player can put the two Punctuation Marks with the Sentence Card and have a "match." If a player thinks he or she has a match, the player tells the group of a wish to discard those cards and they check to make sure the player has punctuated the sentence(s) correctly. If they all agree that the punctuation is right (and the Judge concurs after consulting the answer key), the player may discard the cards used for the "match" by placing them face up on the respective piles. If the player has punctuated the sentence incorrectly, according to the other players and/or the Judge, then he or she cannot discard the cards and also loses the next turn.

9. Players can discard "matches" only when it is their turn. They do so *after* drawing one new card from one of the four piles.

10. Play continues until one player has discarded all his or her cards by matching.

11. If players use all the cards in the stacks of sentence cards or punctuation mark cards, they shuffle all but the top card in the discard pile and turn these face down to use as a new stack.

353

Name_____ Section_____

Answer Key for Punctuation Game

1. Martin, principal,
2. no error
3. records, jeans, and beads
4. difficult;
5. "The Road Not Taken"?
6. late: Bill, Mary, Bob, Martin, and Maureen
7. slippery, therefore,
8. going?
9. ; however,
10. Yes,
11. August,
12. thoughtful,
13. Dobbs, M.D.,
14. Darwin, White, and Company, Incorporated
15. Mrs. Waters, Mr. Moore, and Ms. Woodruff
16. license,
17. thunder,
18. "Stop... now," yelled, "or... you."
19. "Out, out ... candle."
20. "May... quote?"
21. Oh,
22. February 23, 1976, Sally
23. Maple Tree Falls, May 9,
24. The Mill on The Floss, a sensitive, Eliot,
25. Seventeen magazine; Time
26. The Readers' Guide to Periodical Literature
27. "He... sails." Larry,
28. "What's... funny?"
29. house,
30. ladies'
31. Carolyn's
32. James's torn, ripped,
33. Smiths'
34. students'
35. children's
36. no errors
37. no errors
38. no errors
39. no errors
40. no errors

NAME⎯⎯⎯⎯⎯⎯⎯⎯⎯⎯⎯⎯⎯⎯⎯⎯⎯⎯⎯⎯⎯⎯ SECTION⎯⎯⎯⎯⎯⎯⎯

Punctuation Proofreading Exercise

INSTRUCTIONS: Add all necessary marks of punctuation.

Painting is a multi-faceted versatile and diverse field. There are many different distinctive types of painting such as naturalistic non-representational geometric biomorphic symbolic and literal etc Good artists always consider the possibilities open to them they carefully decide how to communicate their feelings what colors to use what style technique and manner to employ. Competent serious artists use their medium explore its range and scope and attempt to bring both their medium and their message into harmonious lucid focus. Its the artists job according to many experts to convey the message as expressively as possible. Many of the paintings that we laugh off and label simple silly and childish are really the products of enormous effort tenacious unending hard work and limitless creative decision Don't be like one of my neighbors who said that painting is crooked and any two year old could do better Next time you view a painting give it a fair chance consider its message its purpose its expressiveness Dont just decide on face value whether or not its good.

NAME_____ SECTION_____

Sentence Cards for Usage Game

1. The road is froze.
2. He don't want to stay any longer.
3. Sarah is the nicest of the two.
4. Each of you are expected to listen.
5. She must of went to the store with her brother.
6. I couldn't care less.
7. I don't remember never having seen that film.
8. He did it all herself.
9. There isn't no candy left.
10. Don't let no one see these exam papers.
11. Everyone made their own lunch.
12. Drive very careful.
13. She looked very nicely in her new dress.
14. Us students know a lot about our school.
15. I think that politics are interesting.
16. My scissors is broken.
17. Patience and honesty are fine virtues.
18. Bring them papers over here.
19. Ham and eggs are my favorite meal.
20. Field trips is more better than homework.
21. Mrs. Hayden is more nice than Mr. Gray.
22. The television is broke.
23. There isn't nothing more to say.
24. Them shoes is mine.
25. Buy three dozen of eggs.
26. We has all the time in the world.
27. We had just began when it started to rain.
28. We sung for two hours.
29. Leslie and me washed, dried, and polish the car.

30. Harold is old-fashion and prejudice.
31. When you finish wiped the dishes, you can leave.
32. This is between Mary and I.
33. Her and her brother are my cousins.
34. Alls you got to do is read the directions.
35. She must not of been very happy.
36. You are smarter than her.
37. They has got my folder.
38. She's the beautifullest person I ever meet.
39. I tried to be honest with he.
40. Communications are a new and exciting field.
41. We will run, jump, do some racing, jogging, and exercising.
42. He's more skinnier than me.
43. We swum all afternoon.
44. I was all shoken up by the accident.
45. The child snuck down the stairs quiet.
46. They had a real nice day.
47. We was home by nine o'clock.
48. Yesterday I went ice skating and come home exhausted.
49. The job, although interesting and exciting, weren't exactly what I wanted.
50. To who do you wish to speak?
51. I seen Jill downtown.
52. John one of two hundred boys participating, are winning every event.
53. Mrs. Fine, which is my typing teacher, is retiring.
54. There is two kind of books— dull and interesting.
55. I read where she got sick.

56. Each of the five hundred team members are signed up.
57. Whom may I ask are you?
58. I wish to see Cathy and he.
59. The weatherman forecasted rain for tonight.
60. I was very tired when I finally sit down.
61. This is a occasion to remember.
62. Karen and me is friends.
63. You look very sickly.
64. That music sounds well.
65. Ask whoever you wish.
66. That pair of shoes are beautiful.
67. My pants is torn.
68. There is less apples in that bag.
69. You done everything real good.
70. There isn't any more potatoes.
71. Him and me went to the concert.
72. I am older than she.
73. This is between David and me.
74. This problem is among the two school boards.
75. Either Marty or Jeff are going to go to Yale.
76. Stealing these books are prohibited.
77. There isn't any quick answers.
78. The media are always objective.
79. I got into my car, fastened my seatbelt, checked my mirrors, locked the door, turned on the motor, and starting driving away.
80. They got a nice house.
81. Mary has often spoke of you.
82. Following training, the dog reverted back to his old ways.
83. Lisa sprung her ankle.

84. Annie had took all my cigarettes.
85. Lenny loaned he ten dollars.
86. That was the worstest game I ever seen.
87. The both of us went together.
88. My sister she is very irritating.
89. They did that there art work all by theirselves.
90. Joanne's childrens is real fresh.
91. That there girl is Kevin's sister.
92. We will leave the door opened.
93. By this time next week, we will have already went.
94. She must of gave me the keys.
95. She went with they to the movies.
96. One of my friends and I is going to New York.
97. Ceramics are my favorite hobby.
98. Mr. Mitchell and his wife, two of our best customers, is sick.
99. Neither Kristin nor Juanita are old enough to vote.
100. She came in, sat down, and starts talking.
101. I was suppose to write an essay.
102. I sat down and rest.

NAME_____ SECTION_____

Instructions for Playing The Usage Game

1. Approximately four persons can play this game.

2. Lay the game board on the floor or other flat surface such as a table or a desk.

3. Give the answer key to one person (either a player or someone who wants to watch but not play). This person will consult the answer key when necessary to check an answer, and hence will be referred to as "the Judge." Warn the Judge not to let anyone see the answers.

4. Shuffle and stack all the sentence cards. Place them face down near the game board.

5. Roll dice or draw lots or guess a number to determine who goes first.

6. Place your markers in the space labelled "Start" on the game board.

7. The first player draws a sentence card from the top of the stack. The player reads it and determines whether or not it contains any error(s) in standard English. Sentences may contain no, one, two or three errors.

8. If the player decides there are no usage errors in the sentence, he or she must show it to the other players to see whether they agree. If they don't agree, the Judge checks the answer key. If the Judge upholds the player's opinion, then the player may move ahead two spaces. If the player is wrong, that is, if the sentence does contain one or more usage errors, then he or she loses the next turn.

9. A player who decides that the sentence does contain a usage error must identify each error, correct it, and explain the correction to the other players. If the Judge and other players agree with the correction, the player may move ahead the number of spaces equal to the number of usage errors in the sentence. If the other players do not agree, then the group must discuss the issue until they reach agreement. If they cannot agree, they must consult the Judge. The Judge's answer, based on the key, overrules all other players. The Judge must explain the answer to the other players. If the player's answer is upheld by the Judge, then the player may move ahead as many spaces as there are usage errors in the sentence. If the player is wrong, he or she loses the next turn.

10. The player whose marker reaches the "Finish" space first is the winner.

NAME_____ SECTION _____

Answer Key for Usage Game

1. frozen	(1)	41. run, jump, race, jog, and exercise.	(3)
2. doesn't	(1)	42. He's skinnier than I	(2)
3. nicer	(1)	43. swam	(1)
4. is	(1)	44. shaken up	(1)
5. must have gone	(2)	45. sneaked quietly	(2)
6. no error	(2)	46. really	(1)
7. ever	(1)	47. were	(1)
8. himself	(1)	48. came	(1)
9. any	(1)	49. The job .... wasn't	(2)
10. anyone	(1)	50. whom	(1)
11. his or her (not their)	(1)	51. I saw	(1)
12. carefully	(1)	52. John ... is	(1)
13. nice	(1)	53. who (not which)	(1)
14. We	(1)	54. are ... kinds	(2)
15. politics is	(1)	55. that (not where)	(1)
16. scissors are	(1)	56. Each .... is	(1)
17. no error	(2)	57. Who	(1)
18. those	(1)	58. him	(1)
19. is	(1)	59. forecast	(1)
20. are better	(2)	60. sat	(1)
21. nicer	(1)	61. an	(1)
22. broken	(1)	62. I are	(2)
23. anything	(1)	63. sick	(1)
24. Those ... are	(1)	64. good	(1)
25. dozens	(1)	65. whomever	(1)
26. have	(1)	66. is	(1)
27. begun	(1)	67. are	(1)
28. sang	(1)	68. are fewer	(2)
29. I, polished	(2)	69. did ... really well	(3)
30. old-fashioned, prejudiced	(2)	70. aren't	(1)
31. wiping	(1)	71. He and I	(2)
32. me (not I)	(1)	72. no error	(2)
33. She	(1)	73. no error	(2)
34. All you have	(2)	74. between	(1)
35. have (not of)	(1)	75. Either ... is	(1)
36. she	(1)	76. Stealing ... is	(1)
37. have	(1)	77. aren't	(1)
38. most beautiful person I ever met	(2)	78. no error	(2)
39. him	(1)	79. drove	(1)
40. is (not are)	(1)	80. have	(1)
		81. spoken	(1)

82. reverted (not reverted
    back)   (1)
83. sprained   (1)
84. had taken   (1)
85. lent (not loaned) him   (2)
86. worst . . . saw   (2)
87. Both (not the both)   (1)
88. My sister is   (1)
89. did that (not that
    there), themselves   (2)
90. children are really   (1)
91. That (not that there)   (1)

92. open   (1)
93. gone   (1)
94. must have given   (2)
95. them   (1)
96. are   (1)
97. Ceramics is   (1)
98. are   (1)
99. Neither . . . is   (1)
100. started   (1)
101. supposed   (1)
102. rested   (1)

NAME _____ _____ SECTION _____

"The Grammar Witch"

Once upon a time a long time ago in a green asbestos-shingled cottage by a deep dark lake which they say had monsters in its depths their was a lady who was known as the grammer witch. The number of people who was lost in her grammer ovens were never known for sure but it must have been high based on local gossip about who's family had lost it's third member and who's family had lost it's forth fifth sixth ect.

She was one of those witches also who doesn't care about others misusing grammer as long as they try really try as hard as her. Alot of people don't feel that way, they think your a social outcast who's need for grammer and usage lessons outweighs any good points, which you might have. Either they or she are wrong its obvious in there attitude.

Anyhow this witch used to set herself down by the lake as comfortable as can be, and watch for unwary victims who she could entice into her grammer ovens, their were many a weary traveler she caught on there way past her cottage. Going home from work. She would lay in wait ten hours at a time, thats a long tiring time to set in one place. As a matter of fact ten hours are to long to do any one thing it seems to me. However remember she was a witch and there not like the rest of us.

Well she would lay their and wait and turn over in her mind all the grammer lessons she would teach to whoever she caught. No matter whom they were. Either subjects or objects was her favorite lesson and she would teach it to absolutely anyone, she wasn't particular. A businessman for instance along with alot of employees were her favorite victims. It was them who aroused in her a regular frenzy of teaching, and inspired her to pedagogical extreams that were her's alone.

Be that as it may since the victims she lured in and tried to teach, were seldom fascinated by her efforts she usually ended up in a violent towering rage, and popped them screaming writhing and sobbing into her ovens which always had clouds of smoke pouring from their chimneys.

Now that may sound cruel inhuman and atrocious to you but if so your not thinking enough about how hard all this was on the poor frustrated grammer witch. Think how she must have felt when whomever she was trying to teach just ignored her fine lessons, and acted as if they thought they're lives would be perfectly happy without knowing grammer isn't that disgusting.

One day in her ovens a quite routine day actually their was a businessman who she'd caught on his way home from work a truck driver who's car had stalled near her cottage a high school student who had forgotten to do his homework and three pastry cooks who she felt convinced she could never educate to the joys of grammer. Poor things. There attitude was not good, they were less willing than the high school students although they were to tell the truth somewhat smarter than him. I would not like to be him. Would you? Oh well.

Now if your wondering why this short unhappy story of the grammer witch is indeed short which is seldom the case of stories these days let me remind you dear students that another day another hour you might well have another story to read carefully trying to catch all errors in grammer and that other story will have spelling problems in it so this story — or another one like it — cant be to long, isn't that right. Oh well.

NAME_____ SECTION_____

Avoiding Pretentious Language

INSTRUCTIONS: *Select the word in each pair which is more simple, direct, and precise, and hence, more suitable for use in writing.*

face — countenance

said — uttered

head — cranium

leg — limb

feet — pedal extremities

toes — pedal digits

hair — crowning glory

sky — heavens

building — edifice

car — vehicle

die — pass away

green — verdant

minister — man of the cloth

carried — conveyed

truthfulness — veracity

talkative — verbose

poor — poverty stricken

eye — orb

sun — solar body

star — heavenly body

man — gentleman

ate — consumed

lie — prevaricate

chew — masticate

kiss — osculate

NAME_____ SECTION_____

Avoiding Inappropriate Informal Language

INSTRUCTIONS: *Decide which word in each of the following pairs is the more appropriate for formal, written expression.*

snuck — sneaked

all shook up — all shaken up

I could care less — I could not care less

kid — child

guy — man or boy

phony — false

ripped off — stolen

rap — discuss

they fell out — they quarreled

had a fit — became upset

told her off — criticized her frankly

had a ball — had a good time

irregardless — regardless

fantastic — very satisfactory

fabulous — unbelievably satisfactory

broke up — ended the relationship

he's crazy — he's wrong

took the rap — took the blame

a jerk — someone I don't like

laid it on the line — spoke frankly

pulled the rug out from under someone — removed someone's support

369

NAME_____ SECTION_____

Identifying and Replacing Clichés

INSTRUCTIONS: Locate all trite expressions and clichés in the following paragraphs. Rewrite each paragraph, replacing the overused expressions with fresh and original language.

A. First and foremost, with your permission, I'd like to give you a rundown of facts and figures on George Johnson, our captain. He is a fine figure of a man, towering over most ordinary men at a height of 6'3". He is as strong as a bull and light on his feet as well, with bulging muscles and rugged features. Rough and ready and always spoiling for a fight, he never runs from trouble, but to be perfectly frank about it, runs after it fast and furious. It will come as no surprise to you, then, to learn that trouble is his middle name, or that he often finds himself on the wrong side of the law. Nonetheless he has a gentle side to his nature as well, and is considered far and wide—when all is said and done—to be a pillar of the community.

B. The next member of the team to claim our attention is none other than Bob Jones, the pride and joy of the fans and a mountain of a man with a heart of gold. He is a tiger during games, but off the field is as meek as a lamb, a paragon of manly virtues admired by young and old alike. He is generous to a fault and always ready to lend a helping hand to those less fortunate than himself. A cool customer when the game is up for grabs, he relaxes when it is in the bag and plays as hard off the field as he works on it.

APPENDIX
C

Feedback Form

Your comments about this book will be very helpful to us in planning other books in the *Guidebook for Teaching* Series and in making revisions in *A Guidebook for Teaching Composition*. Please tear out the form that appears on the following page and use it to let us know your reactions to *A Guidebook for Teaching Composition*. The authors promise a personal reply. Mail the form to:

Dr. Gene Stanford and Mrs. Marie Smith
c/o Longwood Division
Allyn and Bacon, Inc.
470 Atlantic Avenue
Boston, Massachusetts 02210

Your school:_____

Address:_____

City and state:_____

Date: _____

Dr. Gene Stanford and
Mrs. Marie Smith
c/o Longwood Division
Allyn and Bacon, Inc.
470 Atlantic Avenue
Boston, Massachusetts 02210

Dear Gene and Marie:

My name is _____ and I wanted to tell
you what I thought of your book *A Guidebook for Teaching Composition.* I liked certain
things about the book, including:

I do, however, feel that the book could be improved in the following ways:

There were some other things I wish the book had included, such as:

Here is something that happened in my class when I used an idea from your book:

Sincerely yours,

_____